SAMUEL JOHNSON
AND POETIC STYLE

William Edinger

SAMUEL JOHNSON

AND POETIC STYLE

The University of Chicago Press

Chicago and London

The University of Chicago Press, Chicago 60637
The University of Chicago Press, Ltd., London

WILLIAM EDINGER, formerly assistant professor of
English at the University of California, Los Angeles,
is an Andrew Mellon Fellow at Harvard University.

Library of Congress Cataloging in Publication Data

Edinger, William.
  Samuel Johnson and poetic style.

  Includes index.
  1. Johnson, Samuel, 1709-1784—Knowledge—Literature.
2. Criticism—History.   3. Poetics—History.
I. Title.
PR3537.L5E3   868'.6'09   77-5137
ISBN 0-226-18446-3

For Sara

[Tacitus] robs us of the true Objects, to leave us
pleasing Idea's in their room.

Charles de St.-Evremond, 1664

The poet represents the mind in the act of defending us against itself.

Wallace Stevens, *Adagia*

Contents

Acknowledgments

This book has been several years in the making, and during this time I have incurred many debts. For their invaluable help with research materials I should like to thank the librarians and staffs of the British Museum; the Henry E. Huntington Memorial Library, San Marino, California; the William Andrews Clark Library and the University Research Library of the University of California, Los Angeles; the Library of the University of Wisconsin, Madison; and the British Council Library and the American Library in Paris.

For their comments, criticisms, and suggestions on earlier versions of this book I am indebted to Professors Madeleine Doran, Mark Eccles, and Ricardo Quintana of the University of Wisconsin, Madison; Earl Miner and Wilbur Samuel Howell of Princeton University; W. B. Carnochan and Wesley Trimpi of Stanford University; Gwin J. Kolb and Edward W. Rosenheim, Jr., of the University of Chicago; and to my friends and colleagues in the English Department at UCLA, Charles Gullans, H. A. Kelly, Paul Sellin, and Paul Sheats.

Like other students of Samuel Johnson and eighteenth-century literary criticism, I have received my education largely at the hands of Paul Alkon, Lionel Basney, Leopold Damrosch, Scott Elledge, Donald Greene, Lawrence Lipking, W. R. Keast, Eric Rothstein, Arieh Sachs, Richard Schwartz, R. D. Stock, Geoffrey Tillotson, Robert Voitle, Howard Weinbrot, René Wellek, W. K. Wimsatt, and other modern masters of the neoclassical period. Three authorities I reserve for special mention: M. H. Abrams, whose *The Mirror and the Lamp* supplies an indispensable foundation for any type of inquiry into eighteenth-century literary theory; Jean Hagstrum, whose

viii

Samuel Johnson's Literary Criticism has long been, and will long remain, the standard work on the subject; and Walter Jackson Bate, whose wisdom, learning, and concern for neoclassical values, as reflected especially in *From Classic to Romantic* and *The Achievement of Samuel Johnson*, inspired me many years ago to undertake the study of eighteenth-century criticism and of Samuel Johnson's in particular.

Students of style and related critical issues in seventeenth-century poetry and prose will recognize the extent of my obligation to the work of Robert Adolph, Morris Croll, K. G. Hamilton, William Bowman Piper, and George Williamson.

For my understanding of the historical method employed in this book I am especially indebted to R. S. Crane and J. V. Cunningham. For my understanding of the particular critical issues to which this method is here applied I am indebted above all to two distinguished scholars of critical and rhetorical theory, Wilbur Samuel Howell and Wesley Trimpi, whose studies have embraced virtually the whole of the western critical tradition from Plato to the eighteenth century and beyond. Without their work, frequently cited in the following pages, I should have been unable either to formulate the questions with which the present study began or to discover and interpret the materials in which the answers to those questions are provided. To Professor Trimpi I should like to acknowledge a more personal and radical obligation, since it was he who first introduced me to the aims and methods of humanistic study and helped me to determine the directions which my scholarship was to take.

To Carmen M. Carlton I owe special thanks for assistance in the final preparation of the manuscript.

I owe my deepest and most gratefully acknowledged debt to my wife, to whom this book is dedicated, and without whose patience and industry, assistance and support as homemaker, bibliographer, critic, editor, typist, and receptive audience of one it would quite simply not have come into existence.

Introduction

This study began as an attempt to recover Samuel Johnson's standards for poetic style. It was conceived in response to a difficulty that I, like other twentieth-century readers, encountered in reading the *Lives of the Poets*, namely, that Johnson's discussions of particular poets and poems often left me with an inadequate sense of the logic informing his critical judgments. Modern scholarship on Johnson has, over the years, done relatively little to eliminate this difficulty, remaining surprisingly indifferent to the challenge implicit in T. S. Eliot's well-known remark that ''we must not reject the criticism of Johnson (a dangerous person to disagree with) without having mastered it, without having assimilated the Johnsonian canons of taste.''[1] Johnson scholars have on the whole preferred to focus on problems concerning Johnson's general theoretical position rather than on questions of his literary taste, no doubt for understandable reasons. Johnson's theoretical statements, though by no means always self-explanatory, are nevertheless more coherent, self-contained, and readily systematized than many of his critical judgments; for the latter are dependent on Johnson's perception of individual literary texts and may involve purely personal elements which the historian cannot explain. Yet taste, as well as theory, has its logic, and I wished to see how far one might go toward reconstructing the premises of some of Johnson's more obscure opinions.

For me the crucial text was the critical portion of the *Life of Cowley*. There Johnson's procedure is to state the facts about metaphysical style as he sees them but to neglect almost entirely to discuss the standards which make the facts significant. We are told that in metaphysical poetry the ''most heterogeneous ideas are yoked by violence together,'' that ''nature and art are ransacked for illustrations, comparisons, and allusions,'' that these poets ''broke every image into fragments,'' and that ''whatever is improper or vicious'' in their works ''is produced by a voluntary deviation from nature in pursuit of something new and strange.''[2] To illustrate these assertions Johnson adduces a large number of critical specimens. These help us to locate the facts to which he wants to call attention, though often enough even this is a problem. But the nature of the ''nature'' from which the metaphysical poets deviated is nowhere defined; the critical norms by which the facts are judged are not given.[3]

Nor are these norms easily recoverable from relevant contexts elsewhere in Johnson. On the infrequent occasions when Johnson commits himself to an explanation of his premises (and the *Preface to Shakespeare* is the only really comprehensive such attempt) the resulting theory is often too abstract to take hold of individual objects of judgment. It is easy to forget how different the logical content of a theory is from its practical and historical significance. The abstract meaning of concepts such as mimesis, ''general nature,'' or the tests of duration and breadth of appeal—to mention the three cornerstones of Johnson's critical theory—is timeless and always pertinent: we may share such principles with Johnson today. But it is much more difficult to share the perceptions which for Johnson they conditioned. Thus, for example, we may be perfectly satisfied with Johnson's observation in the *Preface to Shakespeare* that ''the irregular combinations of fanciful invention may delight a-while, by that novelty of which the common satiety of life sends us all in quest; but the pleasures of sudden wonder are soon exhausted, and the mind can only repose on the stability of truth.''[4] We know that the first part of Johnson's sentence applies to the fashionable ephemera of every historical period, and we may believe that the second part explains the value and longevity of every ''classic.'' But when we discover that the critical portion of the *Life of Cowley* was written to demonstrate how it was that Donne and his followers ended up in the first category rather than the second, we may be startled to discover too how little our understanding of the theoretical bases of Johnson's criticism helps to take us into Johnson's own literary world. The historical—actual—meaning of critical principles is determined in critical practice: Johnson's principles were meaningful to him as they guided his perceptions and his judgment. Thus if we wish to recover the spirit as well as the letter of Johnson's critical thought—to read him with a sense of the esthetic or moral or intellectual expectations he brought to a given work—we must find a way of making the principles and the practice illuminate each other. But the gap between high-level abstractions like ''truth'' and ''general nature'' and Johnson's comments on the poems of Milton or Donne is too wide. There must be a connection through intermediate principles.

Where the short poem is concerned, the intermediate principles are chiefly stylistic. In forms which preclude a fully developed plot, much depends on the principles which the poet elects (consciously or unconsciously) to govern his choice of words, syntax, ornaments, and consecutive structure—the elements of disposition and style, to use the terminology of traditional rhetoric. Correspondingly, much depends on the analogous critical principles which, as expectations, the reader brings to his experience of a work. Johnson's response to Donne is in large part the commentary of his stylistic principles upon those of Donne as realized in his verse. The difficulty is that in the critical record of these confrontations only one side is adequately represented. Most of Johnson's objections to metaphysical poetry are simply descriptions of its stylistic principles as he perceives them. But Johnson's own stylistic principles, the principles which Donne violates and by which he is measured, are left largely out of account. Instead of defining the standards by which Donne is to be judged, Johnson appeals to the discretion of his readers.

This fact suggested the direction which my research initially took. When Johnson appeals to the judgment of his readers he is invoking common principles, shared expectations. To put this another way is to say that he accepts the common meanings of his normative terms. When he describes the metaphysical poets' faults as deviations from nature in pursuit of something new or strange, he is confident that every reader will be able to pick the meaning of the term (to us so maddeningly equivocal) which suits the given case. To recover Johnson's standards for poetic style is in large measure, then, to recover the neoclassical connotations of terms like ''nature.'' These lie in the tradition of their use; more simply, they are that tradition. To examine the tradition informing Johnson's terms is to examine preceding and contemporary usage and to find a body of usage consistent enough to provide a wide range of meaning without self-contradiction. It is to look in particular for more explicit definitions than Johnson offers and for contexts in practical criticism which make the stylistic values behind a term unmistakable. I therefore pursued the terminology of eighteenth-century stylistic criticism—and especially the correlative terms ''nature'' (''natural'') and ''simplicity,'' which summarize so much that is distinctive in that criticism—from Johnson's time back through the discussions of the early eighteenth and later seventeenth centuries, when neoclassical stylistic orthodoxy took form, to the Greek and Roman literary and rhetorical authorities on whom the neoclassical critics so heavily relied.

As the tradition of Johnson's stylistic criticism began to define itself for me, however, I found Johnson himself becoming interesting not merely as an isolated figure, but as a major synthesizer of ancient and modern thinking on certain critical issues of a radical and comprehensive kind. Johnson's achievement is a step—a significant step, but not the ultimate step—in an ongoing effort to clarify the kind of knowledge which literature communicates and the principles of style best suited to such communication. When we look at this effort in its entirety, we find that it produced a gradually unfolding critical logic which began with the work of the ancient rhetoricians and continued through Wordsworth and Coleridge. The study of this logic provides clues to the intellectual and moral values informing the evolution of eighteenth-century taste in poetic style from Dryden to the Romantics and gives to the stylistic theory of the whole period a coherence and continuity which previous scholarship has not, it seems to me, fully disclosed. At the same time, a knowledge of the tradition provides a point of view from which tendencies in Johnson's criticism which have usually been treated in isolation can be reconciled and Johnson's own critical thought—like that of his age—shown to be more coherent and unified than it has seemed before. The task, then, is to make Johnson and his age illuminate each other—to describe a significant portion of Johnson's critical achievement in terms of his success or failure in dealing with the issues bequeathed him by his tradition and to measure his achievement against the potentialities manifested by the tradition as a whole.

The problem of the kind of knowledge communicated by literature is crucial to a distinction which we may draw between the conservative and liberal impulses in the rhetorical and literary theory of both the classical and neoclassical periods. Johnson's deepest affinities lie with the liberal critics of both periods, who are linked by their common refusal to separate the theory of style from the broad cultural and philosophical issues which determine its most general function. In opposition to the conservative critics, who tend to restrict stylistic theory to the study of means rather than ends and to rely upon method and rule, the liberal critics express a distrust of all routine procedures (seeing these as a source of mannerism or other limitation in practice) and insist that the ultimate source of all stylistic virtues is the informed individual intelligence.[5] The history of liberal stylistic theory, then, is the history of the emergence of an individualistic standard for style—individualistic not in the sense of a standard which sets a premium upon eccentricity, but of one which requires the freshness and immediacy of observations which are only available to a mind in direct contact with its experience. The movement toward this individualistic standard can be seen in the shift in emphasis from the conceptual to the perceptual, from the Ramist, didactic, and neo-Platonic tendencies in seventeenth-century criticism, with their faith in abstract moral truth and idealized representation, to the later demand that poetic style embody an authentic and direct perception of the sensory world.

The order I have chosen for my discussion of these issues is one which begins with the broader, more philosophical questions—questions concerning the status of the language arts and the kinds of knowledge these arts make available—and explores the liberal line of thought on these questions from the classical rhetoricians through Johnson. In the ancient rhetorics, the ethical and cognitive values which inform standards for style are most often discussed in the context of the problem of fragmentation—the tendency toward specialization in the liberal disciplines and their excessive reliance upon abstract methodology. In chapter 1, therefore, I describe the most complete classical discussions of fragmentation, chiefly in the mature rhetorical works of Cicero, and trace the reemergence of this issue in the language philosophies of Bacon, Arnauld, and Fénelon. The essential concern of chapter 2 is the eighteenth-century attempt to make a place for the language arts in a world which now includes the Baconian or scientific model for genuine knowledge, as well as the earlier humanistic one. And in chapter 3 we see that Johnson's empirical conception of mimesis establishes a defensible moral and cognitive function for literature within a Baconian framework.

In chapter 4 we find that the philosophical tendencies we have been examining are accompanied by certain changes in standards for poetic style, as the logic of an individualistic standard for style works itself out in criticism from Dryden to Wordsworth. With an awareness of these changes, we can return in chapter 5 to the classical sources of Johnson's critical terms and metaphors and describe the specific nature of Johnson's liberal neoclassicism—a neoclassicism which finds continuing relevance in ancient principles, but which uses these principles to support an understanding of human perception and the imitation of perception which is thoroughly modern.

No one can claim that all of Johnson's criticism can be seen in these terms, and I devote chapter 6 to material which is incompatible with what I see as Johnson's major critical achievement. But, despite the unsystematic nature of Johnson's thinking about style, and the inconsistencies within it, his use of the traditions available to him did produce a synthesis which was the most intelligent, comprehensive, and flexible of its age. And it is on this achievement that the greatest stress should fall.

1

The Problem of Fragmentation

The emergence of a more perceptual standard for style during the seventeenth and eighteenth centuries is most clearly evident in the critical emphasis upon a ''natural'' style, a style that attains the ideal of ''simplicity.'' Critics speak of this ideal sometimes in rhetorical terms, sometimes in mimetic, and with reference to both poetry and prose. In a rhetorical context, where language is seen as an instrument of communication, the primary concern is with the ''utilitarian'' values of intelligibility and persuasive efficacy. Here the distinctive features of a ''natural'' style are perspicuity, connection, and economy: the intellectual ideal (to speak generally of neoclassical views) is the transmission of revised and coherent understanding to the widest possible audience. Under mimetic premises language is seen as an instrument of representation; the primary concern is with fidelity to the object being portrayed. Here the chief virtues of a natural style are flexibility, spontaneity, the absence of apparent art: the style must be a faithful record of the ways men really perceive, think, and speak. It will be noticed that, thus abstractly stated, the two standards, rhetorical and mimetic, overlap to a degree and also conflict. They overlap insofar as the rhetorical ideal of generality and the mimetic ideal of fidelity to the actual processes of thought and speech both prescribe the same qualities of language, i.e., an unspecialized style is in some measure a mimetic style, and vice versa. They conflict to the extent that the rhetorical emphasis on product—on considered judgment and connected understanding—runs counter to the mimetic emphasis on process. Morris Croll has described the representation of the process of thought as a distinctive feature of so-called Baroque style in prose.[1] The neoclassical critics, reacting in part against the incoherence of that style, stressed the rhetorical virtues; but they did not want these at the expense of the liveliness—the conviction of dramatic relevance, so to speak—which the mimetic virtues bring. What they wanted was product with the appearance of process, or process alone, if it was the process of a comprehensive and orderly mind.

Thus broadly defined, the ideal of simplicity applied to all forms of polite writing and to poetry and prose alike. The neoclassical critics were aware that poetry, taken as a whole, differs from polite prose in its several genres in many ways; but on the level of style poetry was thought to have enough in common with prose (and especially with oratorical prose) that the same general formulations of stylistic principles could serve equally well for both.[2] Moreover, since many of these principles, mimetic as well as rhetorical, along with much of the critical vocabulary in which poetic style was discussed, were adapted or borrowed directly from classical rhetorical theory, it is impossible to separate the tradition of ''natural'' style in neoclassical poetic theory from the parallel tradition in the neoclassical treatment of prose; nor can one be adequately understood without consideration of the other. The radical issues informing the premises of simplicity in style were, like the premises themselves, much the same for both traditions and had been best defined by the ancient authorities in connection with prose.

Res and Verba in Classical Rhetoric

Among these authorities it was Cicero who described the broadest context of stylistic issues. For him the problem of style was the problem of the separation of *verba* from *res*, words from things. This, in turn, was an instance of the larger problem of specialization and fragmentation in intellectual culture. Cicero traces the problem of words and things to its source in the Socratic repudiation of rhetoric, which by creating a divorce between rhetoric and moral philosophy led to their establishment as separate and competing disciplines—a crucial error, since these studies are by nature interdependent, or rather,

Cicero argues, they are aspects of a single concern. For philosophy, rightly understood, is the pursuit of practical wisdom for use in public life; rhetoric is the art of applying that wisdom to particular issues in courtrooms and political assemblies. Ideally, rhetoric complements moral philosophy by keeping it in touch with common human experience and restraining its tendency to withdraw into abstract speculation. The pursuit of eloquence itself contributes to this end, for the tact necessary to the public speaker, his responsiveness to his rhetorical situation, helps to keep him clear-sighted about the world to which he must make his appeal. To this extent, the development and practice of a flexible, unspecialized, and persuasive style involves a continuing test of the philosopher's abstractions against the concrete experience from which they must ultimately be derived.

On the other hand, rhetoric without philosophy would lose the dignity of a liberal discipline and become the mere art of expedience which Plato condemned.[3] If rhetoric helps to keep philosophy in touch with concrete reality, philosophy helps to keep rhetoric aware of the moral or political universals implicit in the particular cases with which it deals. Thus in the *De Oratore*, Crassus, Cicero's principal spokesman, argues at length for the importance of training the would-be orator in the moral philosophy of the Peripatetics and Academics, especially the latter, whose tradition of *pro et contra* disputation on general moral and political issues should help him to develop the dialectical resourcefulness necessary for political and forensic debate.[4] Cicero's defense of the philosophical orator attempts to be idealistic and pragmatic at the same time: in the first place, he wishes to defend rhetoric against the Platonic charges, and this can scarcely be done without claiming for rhetoric an immediate concern with moral and political principles. In response to Plato Cicero recreates, in effect, the Isocratean vision of liberal education, in which the unity of all knowledge is reflected and made known in the wholeness of the orator-statesman's moral being. Cicero's ideal orator is the man in whom the life of thought and the life of action are perfectly combined and whose acquaintance with every department of useful knowledge, nourished by experience, gives him a universal competence in the world of affairs.[5] But Cicero also wishes to protect rhetoric from its official representatives, the professional teachers of public speaking, whose "schools of impudence" the real Lucius Crassus, as censor, had once banished from Rome; against them he defends the relevance of philosophy on more practical grounds. If the ideal dignity of rhetoric depends upon the philosophical generality of its deliberations, so does its practical effectiveness as well. For it is not true, Crassus insists, that the content of most speeches consists of more or less specific political or legal information which can be acquired at need. The most eloquent speeches are those which move from the specific point at issue to the general principles which it implicitly embodies, and this requires a philosopher's command of all the abstract lines of argument pertinent to a given case. The chief task of rhetorical invention is to bridge the gap between the particular issue (*causa, controversia, quaestio certa*) and the general question (*consultatio, thesis, quaestio infinita*) in order to explore the universals which define the full significance of the case.[6] This is the source of the orator's copiousness and fecundity.

It is also the source of distinction in style. Cicero repeatedly insists upon the indivisibility of style and subject: it is customary, he says, to discuss embellishment separately from invention and arrangement, yet this is to separate from one another "things that cannot really stand apart" (*De Oratore*, III.v.19). For it is "impossible to achieve an ornate style without first procuring ideas and putting them into shape, and at the same time ... no idea can possess distinction without lucidity of style" (ibid., III.vi.24). Accordingly, it is breadth of implication which gives grandeur to eloquence: "a full supply of facts begets a full supply of words, and if the subjects discussed are of an elevated character this produces a spontaneous brilliance in the language" (ibid., III.xxxi.125). The most "ornate speeches" (*Ornatissimae ... orationes*) are "those which take the widest range and which turn aside from the particular matter in dispute to engage in an explanation of the meaning of the general issue" (ibid., III.xxx.120). Ornateness in Cicero means not verbal decoration, but fluency, scope, and variety of matter.

On these terms Cicero's defense of a philosophical rhetoric has implications for literary theory, and, on the highest level of generality, bears an interesting analogy to Bacon's conception of nominalistic empiricism ("science") as well, as Wesley Trimpi has pointed out.[7] The problem of reciprocal relations between the *thesis* (moral philosophy: abstract generalization: universal truth) and the *causa* (rhetoric: the details of the particular case) exists for poetic theory as the problem of the moral value of literature—the question of how fictional particulars are made to embody general moral truth, or, conversely, how moral truth is made persuasive by being embodied in a fiction. This is the main subject of Sidney's *Defense of Poesy*, where the correlative disciplines in terms of which literature is construed are moral philosophy and history (the latter taking the place of rhetoric); it is likewise the subject of Johnson's defense of the concept of "general nature." For Bacon the difficulty in bridging the gap between a nominalistic reality of discrete particulars and scientific knowledge (i.e., abstract generalization) supplies the chief justification of his empirical method, a method which on at least two occasions he described in terms sufficiently general to be applicable to the literary as well as the scientific side of the problem (see pp. 10–12).

But the terms in which Cicero accounts for the historical decline of rhetoric have an even broader range of application. His defense of the ancient Greek notion of the unity and interdependence of the sciences is the classic Latin statement of the humanist's faith in liberal education, while his description of the decay of Hellenistic culture as a result of the increasingly abstract and useless speculations of philosophers, who had abandoned the sphere of public life, provided a model for "utilitarian" critiques of seventeenth-century learning. As for rhetoric, Cicero shows that, once it had been denied access to the topics of moral philosophy which formed the backbone of its subject matter, there was no way of protecting its liberal status against the rigidities of the pedagogues: it became the study of form without content, a compendium of rules for finding arguments, constructing speeches, and embellishing style—as though these skills could be taught systematically and did not depend primarily upon knowledge, talent, experience, and the imitation of sound models, that is, upon natural gifts improved by a general education (ibid., III.vi.21, xiv.54–xx1.81, xxx.120–21, xxxi.125).

Cicero is unspecific about the practices of the Roman rhetorical schools and about their effect upon style, but his indictment indicates the general conditions which ought to produce decadence and which, in the estimation of later Roman critics, did produce it. When the *De Oratore* was written, the rhetorical schools were scarcely established, and much of the achievement of Roman literature in the so-called Golden Age still lay in the future. But the schools flourished in post-Ciceronian Rome and in the next age were seen as perhaps the most influential cause of the decline of eloquence, and of literary style in general, in the Silver Latin period. The extreme specialization of rhetorical training in the first century A.D. was described and ridiculed by Tacitus and Petronius: students were taught to dispute and declaim on the most lurid and sensational subjects—it is nothing but "pirates standing in chains on the beach, tyrants pen in hand ordering sons to cut off their fathers' heads, oracles in time of pestilence demanding the blood of three virgins or more," Eumolpus says in the *Satyricon*—and thus to cultivate an ingenuity which had no bearing on real issues of politics or law.[8] In this setting style could have no serious persuasive function and so became an instrument of display, entirely given over, as Quintilian complains throughout the *Institutes*, to the cult of novelty and pursuit of applause. The new style (this "modern immigrant from Asia") was sententious and epigrammatic, overloaded with far-fetched metaphors and schemes of sound; in its preoccupation with local felicities at the expense of the coherence of the whole it mirrored the fragmentation of the culture which fostered and received it. Quintilian blamed Seneca for introducing it into other departments of Roman letters, and in his criticism of Seneca for impairing "the solidity of his matter by striving after epigrammatic brevity" (*si rerum pondera minutissimis sententiis non fregisset*) the seventeenth century found a *locus classicus* for its own concern with fragmentation in prose and with the cultural milieu conducive to it.[9]

BACON'S APPROACH TO THE PROBLEM OF FRAGMENTATION

In retrospect, then, the *De Oratore* presented a comprehensive analysis of the conditions which make possible the emergence of what we should call a period or, more exactly, a coterie style. In seventeenth-century England the only comparably inclusive modern treatment of the subject was Bacon's critique of sixteenth-century culture in the *Advancement of Learning*. For Bacon Scholasticism stood in place of Cicero's wrangling Hellenistic sects, while the abuses of Ciceronianism corresponded to those of Roman rhetorical education. Scholastic rationalism illustrated for Bacon what its earlier counterparts had shown Cicero: the incapacity of speculative reason, when cut off from the direct knowledge of things, to arrive at demonstrable fact or even to conserve defensible opinion in a generally useful form. It was the useless subtlety of Scholastic controversy, Bacon explains, as well as the irrelevance of its jargon, which had brought it into contempt among the representatives of a renascent humanism; yet the humanists in their turn had abused their rhetorical discipline—for Bacon an admirable and indispensable practical art, though scarcely the *ne plus ultra* of the *De Oratore*—by hunting ''more after words than matter; and more after the choiceness of the phrase, and the round and clean composition of the sentence, and the sweet falling of the clauses, and the varying and illustration of their works with tropes and figures, than after the weight of matter, worth of subject, soundness of argument, life of invention, or depth of judgment.''[10] The *De Oratore* may well have been present in Bacon's mind when he observed of this ''distemper of learning, when men study words and not matter'' that it was recurrent and that, although he had given an example from recent times, ''yet it hath been and will be *secundum majus et minus* in all time''—a truth brought home by the Latin version of the *Advancement* published in 1623, in which Bacon appended to his critique of Ciceronianism a brief description of the new stylistic vogue which by that time had replaced it. "The labour here," Bacon remarks in part, "is altogether, *That words may be aculeate, sentences concise, and the whole contexture of the speech and discourse, rather rounding into it selfe, than spread and dilated*: So that it comes to passe by this Artifice, that every passage seemes more witty and waighty than indeed it is."[11] The new style emulates the mannerisms of Silver Latin prose: Bacon mentions Seneca, Tacitus, and the younger Pliny as its sources. His description of it hints at faults to which Quintilian had objected and to which critics later in the century would devote considerable attention.

Bacon and Cicero were alike in their disdain for speculative abstruseness and in their belief that the end of knowledge is use rather than amusement or show, and both posited an ideal of unity or interdependence among the sciences. Yet their solutions to the problem of fragmentation were widely different, as Bacon himself on one occasion pointed out. In the *De Interpretatione Naturae* (ca. 1603), Bacon alludes to the *De Oratore*, summarizing Cicero's attack on Socrates for separating rhetoric from philosophy and agreeing with him that the specialist in any art is likely to be hampered by his ignorance of other arts. But his own ideal of the reunification of learning differs, he explains, from Cicero's and from the Greek notion of the circle of the sciences in this respect: the ancient ideals stressed the relatedness of the sciences for the sake of "ornament or help in practice, as the orator hath [use] of knowledge of affections for moving, or as military science may have use of geometry for fortifications"; whereas he, Bacon, envisions the likelihood of direct correspondences, so that known principles in one art may illuminate, or even prove directly transferable to, analogous but hitherto unexplained instances in another. Since, for example, the same "delights of the mind" are to be found in music, rhetoric, and even in "moral philosophy, policy, and other knowledges," it is likely that one of these sciences will afford an "axiom," applicable to the others, which will explain this similarity among them (*Bacon*, 3:228–31).

Bacon's distinction points to larger differences between himself and Cicero which he does not define, but which are quite apparent to the modern reader. These are differences, simply, between a cultural and a scientific ideal. The intellectual world of the *De Oratore* is limited by the general aims of a liberal education and by the rhetorical needs of the politician and lawyer; its principal subject matter is moral and political—the realm of educated opinion rather than of fact, of probable rather than demonstrative argument. The ideal unity of knowledge which Cicero sought might be realized secondarily in the form of an educational program, such as that represented in Quintilian's *Institutes*, for example, or those of humanists such as Elyot and Ascham in the sixteenth century, but primarily it would be realized by the accomplished individual, as a quality of mind. When Bacon speaks of the need to ''abridge the infinity of individual experience,'' his goals are not humanistic but scientific. His ultimate aim is demonstrable knowledge, especially of the material world, ''for the glory of the Creator and the relief of man's estate''; his immediate object is the devising of an experimental method which will supply the deficiencies of unaided observation and provide sound rules of inference for the induction of general laws. In the *Magna Instauratio* he distinguished sharply between these goals and the pursuit of practical wisdom (ibid., 4:17–18, 23–24, 42, 112). Until such time as the study of man and society could be comprehended under experimental methods (and Bacon thought that it could), the traditional realm of the humanities would remain outside the scope of his program, which addressed itself first of all to natural philosophy. There the problem of fragmentation would be circumvented by the inductive process itself, which begins with fragments and particulars and rises toward generalization by analyzing real relationships between them.

These differences between Bacon and Cicero are striking today, for we are familiar with their practical results over a period of three centuries. But in the neoclassical era the so-called conflict between the humanities and science, where it existed at all, usually occupied the traditional moral, rather than epistemological, grounds, as in Milton or the third book of *Gulliver's Travels*. And in any event many of Bacon's criticisms of modern learning contained implications in no way limited by his scientific aims. Bacon himself was extraordinarily aware of this: the awareness is implicit in the analogical habit of mind which guides his rhetoric in the *Advancement of Learning*, enabling him to describe the "deficiencies" or explain the principles of one science in terms or examples borrowed from others—a practical application of his hypothesis that the true "axioms" of arts and sciences are held largely in common. For example, Bacon is primarily concerned with the problem of specialization and fragmentation in learning as it pertains to philosophy, and especially to natural philosophy, where the Scholastic reliance upon Aristotelian logic and upon the method of *pro et contra* disputation had substituted controversy about the meanings of abstractions for the direct investigation of things. Yet his remarks on this subject usually invoke a wider context than the merely scientific. "The strength of all sciences," Bacon observes, "is, as the strength of the old man's faggot, in the bond."

> For the harmony of a science, supporting each part the other, is and ought to be the true and brief confutation and suppression of all the smaller sorts of objections; but on the other side, if you take out every axiom, as the sticks of the faggot, one by one, you may quarrel with them and bend them and break them at your pleasure: so that as was said of Seneca, *Verborum minutiis rerum frangit pondera* [*sic*], so a man may truly say of the schoolmen, *Quaestionum minutiis scientiarum frangunt soliditatem*. For were it not better for a man in a fair room to set up one great light, or branching candlestick of lights, than to go about with a small watch candle into every corner? [Ibid., 3:286]

However different they may be in other respects, the dialectic of Scholastic science and the rhetoric of Seneca's moral philosophy are alike in their failure to preserve the integrity of connected understanding, on which the utility of each depends. In a similar statement, the comparison is between philosophy and history: when, says Bacon, we read in Tacitus of the actions of a Nero or a Claudius, related "with circumstances of times, inducements and occasions," we find them comprehensible (or at least "not so strange"), whereas when we read of the same events in the disjunctive and anecdotal account of Suetonius they seem "more monstrous and incredible": such is the difference, Bacon concludes, between knowing a philosophical system in its entirety and knowing only its tenets in abstraction from the supporting arguments (ibid., 3:365-66). And in a third statement—this one a plea for keeping open the lines of communication between the various sciences so that "the continuance and entireness of knowledge [may] be preserved"—Bacon alludes again to Cicero's attack upon Socrates for separating rhetoric from philosophy, "whereupon rhetoric became an empty and verbal art" (ibid., 3:366-67). The implication of such passages is that order and connection are essential virtues of discourse in general; Bacon's description of the relation between fragmentation in methods of discourse and specialization in the arts and sciences is comprehensive enough to be equally pertinent to the scientist and the literary critic.[12]

In the same way, the significance of Bacon's skepticism concerning speculative reason (expressed everywhere in his works, but illustrated most fully in the *Novum Organum* aphorisms on the Idols of the Mind) transcends the immediate context of his scientific program. Although Bacon specifically intended his analysis of the Idols to clear the way for the establishment of his new scientific logic, much of what he says about the enchanted glass of unaided intellect speaks quite directly to humanist concerns. This is especially true of his Idols of the Theater, which represent the tendency of rationalistic philosophers to invent fictions of the universe instead of examining its material contents—fictions which, like those of the poets, are usually "more compact and elegant, and more as one would wish them to be than true stories out of history." Here what is for Bacon an impediment to science is for the Christian humanist a major form of intellectual pride, and thus one finds writers as far removed from Bacon's intellectual position as the French Jesuit critic René Rapin objecting to the system builders in terms which recall Bacon's. Rapin attacks Copernicus, for example (an unfortunate choice, as it turned out) for having the temerity to set up his "Private Judgment as a Common Law to Mankind, and to oblige the whole World to believe, that Nature is mov'd and govern'd in concert with" his "Imagination." Rapin's comments recall the query of Swift's hack writer in the *Tale of a Tub*: "For, what Man in the natural State, or Course of Thinking, did ever conceive it in his Power, to reduce the Notions of all Mankind, exactly to the same Length, and Breadth, and Height of his own?"[13]

Yet other parts of the Idols run counter to widespread humanist assumptions. Bacon's account of the Idols of the Marketplace ("the most troublesome of all," he thought) is profoundly incompatible with that naive faith in the all-sufficiency of "good sense" which one encounters so frequently in neoclassical critical writing. "Good sense" (often bolstered by the authority of Aristotle) was Rapin's alternative to speculative uncertainty; but Bacon saw in the tenacity of "vulgar understanding" the most serious threat to the conduct of science. The best that Bacon can say for the "light of common notions" is that, although it is "faint and superficial" it is "yet in a manner universal, and has reference to many things," and so is preferable to the dogmas of what he calls the Empirical school, whose followers leap to hasty generalization from the "narrowness and darkness of a few experiments." But ideally the Baconian scientist will begin his inquiries in a state of perfect unbelief, unprejudiced by received ideas of any kind (*Bacon*, 3:388; 4:65).

Despite this divergence, however, even Bacon's positive program for the pursuit of scientific knowledge could be made to serve humanistic purposes, though at the expense of a blurring of distinctions between a genuinely scientific process of inquiry, including the strict application of experimental methods, and the loose "empiricism" of skeptical common sense. In his *History of the Royal Society* (1667), Bacon's disciple Thomas Sprat was able to present Baconian science to the skeptical courtiers of Charles II as, in effect, a kind of urbane good sense reduced to method. Sprat, like Bacon, understood the difference between the rigor of scientific induction and the haphazardness and partiality of our ordinary attempts to elicit general truths from the data of personal experience. But it was in his rhetorical interest to depict the new science as the opposite of everything abstract, academic, narrow, and useless, and he did this in part by representing it as a practical application of intellectual principles which were in their general nature Ciceronian.

Sprat's critical account of philosophy before Bacon can be described as humanistic or Baconian with equal justice. In the days of the Greeks, he tells us, "Philosophy was made too subtile, for the *common*, and *gross* conceptions of men of business. It had ... in a measure been banish'd, by the Philosophers themselves, out of the World; and shut up in the shades of their walks. And by this means, it was first look'd upon, as most *useless*; and so fit, soonest to be *neglected*."[14] The new "*Art* of *Experiments*," by contrast, "consists not in *Topicks* of reas'ning, but of working": it is indeed "full of doubting and inquiry, and will scarce be brought to settle its assent: But it is such a doubting as proceeds on *Trials*, and not on *Arguments*"; nor does it "practice nor cherish this humor of disputing, which Breaks the force of things by the subtily of words; as *Seneca* was said to do by his style" (*History*, p. 332). The precedent of Sprat's *History* made it possible for later writers to praise Bacon on strictly humanistic grounds, if they so chose, not as the inventor of new principles but as the recoverer of old ones. So in the following assessment of Bacon's contribution to learning, published in 1706, the union of modern scientific and ancient rhetorical tradition is complete:

[Bacon] *first disdain'd the Old Method* of breaking the weight of things with the nicety and minuteness of Questions, *and, according to his own Comparison, instead of* going up and down with a small Watch-candle into every Corner of *Knowledge, set* up one great Branch of lights, by which all *might* be seen at once. *He seems to have govern'd himself by the same Maxim in his Philosophical, that Quintilian propos'd in his Oratorical Institutions*; I would have the Person whom I instruct, to be rather a Wiseman of *Rome* than of *Greece*: One that is not so much vers'd in Notional Debates, as in real Experiments and Effects, not so much a Subtle Disputer, as a

Man of Conversation and Business. *His admirable Works, that especially which is so worthily entituled* of the Advancement of Learning, *establish'd the first Marriage Articles between the Rational and the Experimental Philosophy, from which Alliance has sprung all the fair Offspring of Modern Discoveries.*[15]

Bacon's epistemology had important implications for rhetoric and poetic, but Bacon himself did not pursue these implications very far. He had argued that all inquiry must be inductive, that the syllogistic logic of Aristotle is merely a technique of specifying the implications of general principles by their application to particulars and not a means of discovery, and that its usefulness depended entirely upon the validity of the principles employed, whereas in most sciences these had been neither accurately derived from the careful study of particulars nor exactly defined. He had attacked the excessive preoccupation with stylistic ornament in modern rhetorical training and in modern eloquence; and he had stressed the importance of subordinating all types of discourse, technical and popular alike, to utilitarian ends. These considerations contained the potential to revolutionize the established logic and rhetoric of Aristotle and Ramus, as the subsequent history of these studies in the seventeenth and eighteenth centuries shows.[16] Yet apart from throwing out Aristotelian logic as a tool of inquiry, Bacon made no other radical modification in these disciplines when he reviewed them in the *Advancement of Learning* and again in the *De Augmentis*. He demurred from Ramist logical doctrine on a number of points, notably in regard to Method, where his utilitarian approach to discourse is most apparent; but he left intact the central fabric of traditional logic, taking for granted the utility of its inventional machinery and its emphasis on syllogism, to the theory of which he added an enlarged conception of sophism illustrated by an early version of the Idols of the Mind.[17] Rhetoric he pronounced to be "a science excellent, and excellently well laboured," and although his conception of it is far more liberal and inclusive than that of the Ramists, who defined it simply as the art of speaking ornately and restricted it to the study of style (i.e., ornament) and delivery, still he has little new to say about the practical side of the art and contents himself with giving a general description of its function and defending it against the Platonic objections. His brief and well-known discussion of poetry affords, again, a general theory of its nature and function, without descending to considerations of structure or style.[18]

FRAGMENTATION AND STYLE IN SEVENTEENTH-CENTURY RHETORIC (1): ARNAULD ON RAMISM

While Bacon's concern for a simple and direct style was preserved and enlarged upon in the rhetorical theory of such English disciples as Wilkins, Glanvill, Boyle, and Sprat, it is in the logic and rhetoric of two Frenchmen, Antoine Arnauld and Salignac de la Mothe Fénelon, that the full pattern of concerns defined in the *De Oratore* reemerges as the background of a distinctively modern theory of communication, a theory which drew its inspiration not from Bacon but from classical tradition, Augustine, and Descartes.[19] In Arnauld's *Logique, ou L'Art de Penser* (1662)—better known in England, where it was extremely popular, as the Port-Royal Logic—the Cartesian influence is predominant. Arnauld's leading principles are utility and the individualistic rationalism celebrated and given a program in the *Discourse on Method*; his antagonists are Scholastic logic in general and more particularly the logic and rhetoric of the Ramists. His attitude toward Ramism closely resembles Cicero's toward the Roman rhetorical schools: for Arnauld Ramist theory is of little use, not merely because it relies on an inadequate (i.e., Aristotelian) logic, but because its very conception of the arts of logic and rhetoric is pedantic and narrow. There is a historical irony in this, since Ramus's own reform of Aristotelian logic and rhetoric was undertaken in the name of utility.[20] The point at issue between Arnauld and Ramus was really the Scholastic conception of an art or science in itself. ''An Art,'' in the definition of the English Ramist Abraham Fraunce, ''is a Methodicall disposition of true and coherent preceptes, for the more easie perceiving and better remembring of the same.''[21] An art, so conceived, was not primarily either a practical skill, such as we would understand today by the art of painting or of poetry, nor was it a means of inquiry. Rather, it comprised the systematic exposition of a particular body of knowledge, which could be contemplated in and for itself, or applied to practical uses, or analyzed according to the methods of Scholastic disputation. Ramus's ideal of utility, then, chiefly concerned economy of presentation, and also logical exactness, as a prerequisite for meaningful debate; least of all was it concerned with practice. Hence the importance of his ''law of justice,'' which specified, for the sake of avoiding ambiguity and redundancy, that the description of a given art must include no proposition peculiar to any other art: thus the art of logic should include no proposition pertaining to grammar, the art of rhetoric no proposition pertaining to logic, and so on with the rest of the arts.

Informing this conception of the arts was the characteristic Scholastic assumption that the human mind ''naturally'' thinks in accordance with the rules of Aristotelian logic and will therefore be best instructed by a method which adheres to those rules as closely as possible. Ramus's preferred method of systematizing and teaching the various arts—he called it the ''natural'' method—was, accordingly, rigorously deductive; it began with the most general axiom belonging to a given art and derived all subordinate propositions in strict logical fashion, usually by a process of dichotomy. A typical Ramist rhetoric, for example, would begin: rhetoric is an art of speaking ornately; it has two parts, style and delivery; style is divided into the tropes and figures; there are two types of figure, figures of words and figures of thought—and so on, down through the description and illustration of particular figures contained within each class. Now this faith in the all-sufficiency of deductive logic was no longer possible for Bacon, as we have seen; yet Bacon confined his quarrel with Ramism chiefly to the issue of Method. In contrast, Arnauld, who in the preface to the Port-Royal Logic acknowledges an indebtedness to Descartes and Pascal, questions the Scholastic presuppositions of Ramism at every level. The Ramist ''law of justice,'' he implies, works against utility, not for it. Ramus himself had defended logic as the *scientia scientiarum*, the tool by which all the other sciences could be put in good order. But how can the practical relevance of logic to other disciplines be convincingly displayed if one is forbidden, when explaining its contents, to draw upon matter of other arts? The *lex justitiae*, designed to make the arts easier to teach and to learn, actually impoverishes them by cutting them off from one another. Logic and rhetoric themselves, Arnauld implies, are in reality closely related aspects of the single study of effective communication; yet the law of justice, by giving invention, judgment, and method into the exclusive possession of logic, leaves rhetoric with nothing but the cataloguing and illustration of the ornaments of style (together with a few precepts for oral delivery). This in turn encourages a distorted view of eloquence, which actually depends very little on a knowledge of the tropes and figures.[22]

In short, the Ramist law of justice supports—indeed, insists upon—the separation of the sciences; and Arnauld's objections to this form of fragmentation are much the same as Cicero's. But the paucity of Ramist rhetoric was not owing entirely to the application of the *lex justitiae*; the concept of art which Ramus had inherited from Scholasticism was itself inadequate to utilitarian needs. With his faith in the systematic presentation of information, Ramus had restricted the scope of rhetorical theory to materials which lent themselves readily to definition, formula, and rule—hence the almost exclusive emphasis on the tropes and figures. The problem of how this information was to be employed in the writing of speeches, letters, or poems was glossed over with a few simple precepts; Abraham Fraunce, for example, deals with the relation between Ramist stylistic theory and practice in a single sentence: ''Thus much of Eloquution in tropes and figures: in al which observe this one lesson, the more the better: yet with discretion, and without affectate curiositie.''[23] No doubt the individual instructor would teach his students ''discretion,'' and how to avoid ''affectate curiositie,'' in the course of classroom exercise; these were matters of his own prerogative and beyond the reach of abstract doctrine. But on the other hand, how intelligently could these subjects be discussed without the guidance provided by a general theory?

The burden of Arnauld's remarks on rhetoric (incidental though they are in a book which is after all devoted mainly to logic, and not simply the argumentative logic on which rhetoric depends, but the new logic of inquiry which Arnauld is developing out of Descartes)—the burden of Arnauld's remarks on rhetoric is clearly that a genuinely useful rhetorical theory must concern itself with every aspect of the process of verbal persuasion: with style and logic, yes, but with these as they may be understood in a broad context of psychological considerations.

Arnauld is like Bacon in his awareness of the psychological sophisms which corrupt eloquence by distorting an author's understanding of his subject, his task, and ultimately, it may be, himself. Here Arnauld identifies the ''internal sophisms'' of self-love, interest, and passion in a discussion particularly notable for its unforgiving attack upon the libertinism and egotism of Montaigne, whom Arnauld uses to illustrate the ''evil custom of some Persons, who never talk but of themselves, and are always quoting themselves, when there is no question concerning their Sentiments.'' Montaigne affects to ''entertain his Readers with nothing else but his own humors, his own Inclinations, his own Fancys, his own distempers, vertues and vices: all which arises as well from a defect of Judgment as from a violent love of himself.'' And Arnauld cites a rule, which he attributes to Pascal, that ''every wise man ought to abstain from so much as naming himself, or making use of the words *I*, or *Me*,'' whenever possible. Here too Arnauld discusses the fallacies arising from a vain love of style, commenting on the danger of subordinating matter to the search for syntactic elegance (for this is seldom done ''without wresting and screwing the Truth, to make it conformable to [the] Figure'') and ridiculing Bembo and the sixteenth-century Ciceronians. Arnauld's discussion of sophism culminates in the statement of a principle which was to become widely popular among neoclassical critics: ''Such false Reasonings as these which we meet with frequently in the writings of such Authors as affect Eloquence,'' Arnauld concludes, make it appear how much it concerns those persons that speak or write, to keep close to that excellent Rule, that there is nothing *lovely but what is true*; which would prune off an infinite number of false thoughts, and vain Embellishments from their Writings. True it is that this exactness renders the stile less Pompous, and more Barren; but it renders it more lively, more serious, more clear, and more becoming a candid Ingenuity: It makes a deeper Impression, and more durable. Whereas that which arises from Periods adjusted, is so superficial, that it vanishes almost as soon as the Periods are heard.[24]

A truly practical rhetorical theory, Arnauld implies, will consist mainly of cautionary principles of this sort. As for the traditional rhetoric (or logic and rhetoric, in Ramist terms), Arnauld dismisses it out of hand: "we considered," he writes in the prefatory "Second Discourse" of the *Logic*, "that there is little advantage to be drawn from that Art, for the finding out of thoughts, expressions, and embellishments. Our wit furnishes us with thoughts; Use affords us Expression, and for figures and ornaments they are many times superfluous; so that all the Benefit from thence consists in avoiding certain evil habits of writing and speaking, especially an Artificial and Rhetorical style compos'd of false Imaginations, Hyperboles, and forc'd Figures, the most unpardonable of all Vices in an Oratour" (*Logic*, p. 27). The Ramist logic and rhetoric is not merely useless but a positive source of vices both of matter and style. The vain love of ornament endemic among modern orators is, Arnauld implies, directly connected to the Ramist preoccupation with the tropes and figures, while the inventional machinery of traditional logic is not merely unnecessary (since "our wit furnishes us with thoughts") but encourages an excessive study of *copia* and an uncritical use of received opinion and traditional lore. It would be more to the purpose, Arnauld observes in dismissing the doctrine of the commonplaces, "to teach men to hold their tongues than to talk, and how to retrench low, common and false Notions, then [*sic*] how to produce as they do, a confus'd *oglio* of good and bad Arguments, with which they fill their discourses" (ibid., 2d pt., pp. 81–82).

The premises of Arnauld's attack upon Ramism can properly be called modern. Among his characteristic assumptions concerning the arts of discourse, as Wilbur Samuel Howell has shown, are several which serve to distinguish the post-Cartesian era in general from the world of the Middle Ages and much of the Renaissance. Implicit in Arnauld's rejection of the doctrine of commonplaces, for example, is a rejection of the authoritarianism which supported the accumulation of that vast body of traditional argument and opinion within which the intellectual life of the earlier periods found its community. Arnauld is asking that that inheritance be submitted to the examination of a skeptical, critical, and self-consciously independent—in short, ''modern''—intelligence. Again, in rejecting the Ramist doctrines of the law of justice and the ''natural'' method, Arnauld is implicitly attacking the traditional conception of dialectic and rhetoric as separate and opposed modes of communication, the one adapted to a popular audience and, as Bacon says, handling reason ''as it is planted in popular opinions and manners,'' the other adapted to a learned audience and handling reason ''exact and in truth,'' transmitting the dry light in a dry style. Upon this Scholastic distinction depended in great part the separation of the learned and public worlds of the Middle Ages and Renaissance, a separation which it was in the interest of Arnauld's utilitarianism to abolish. The Port-Royal Logic itself, Arnauld declares in the ''Second Discourse,'' employs a method which is truly ''natural'': adapted to amateur and specialist at once, it presents its subject fully and without misrepresentation while at the same time demonstrating its practical importance and making it easier to learn by drawing upon a broad range of illustrative material from other sciences. Such a conception of discourse was the theoretical prerequisite to the development of Enlightenment learned style—the style of Voltaire and Berkeley and Hume—in which abstract inquiry is approximated to the world of ordinary experience through the agency of a flexible, unspecialized, and unobstrusively elegant vernacular prose.

Finally, Arnauld is modern in his recognition that the arts of discourse differ from the other abstract sciences in that they include the development of practical skills which lie beyond the reach of precept and of systematic knowledge. Here Arnauld's quarrel with Ramist and Scholastic tradition turns ultimately upon Pascal's distinction between the spirit of geometry and the spirit of finesse (though Arnauld does not state it in these terms). For the Ramists logic and rhetoric comprised a species of abstract knowledge which could be transmitted in the form of information and rules. For Arnauld the primary object of communication theory is understanding rather than knowledge. Understanding can be achieved but not taught: it proceeds by the discovery of principles, rather than by the application of methods and rules, and by the cultivation of a largely intuitive grasp of the relevance of general principles to particular problems, rather than by the mastery of fact. In the case of communication theory the principles are the fruit of a general inquiry into the ends which communication serves and the means available to it. The remainder of the art is practice, which in its dependence upon the aptitude of the individual student and his exposure to sound models is equally outside the scope of traditional rhetorical doctrine. It was owing to the widespread acceptance during the neoclassical period of premises such as these that the Ramist rhetorical tradition declined and eventually died, though, admirably suited as it was to the most routine instincts of the pedagogue, it clung to life for longer than might have been expected.[25]

FRAGMENTATION AND STYLE IN SEVENTEENTH-CENTURY RHETORIC (2): FÉNELON ON CONCEIT

It is historically accurate to describe the principles outlined above as modern, yet the extent to which they coincide with the liberal premises of the *De Oratore* will already be apparent. With Arnauld the coincidence may or may not indicate a direct indebtedness to the ancients; the clearest influence upon the Port-Royal Logic is that of René Descartes. But it is important to remember that other critics of eloquence whose views closely resemble those of Arnauld claimed to have derived them from classical rhetorical tradition. René Rapin is one such; Fénelon, whose *Dialogues on Eloquence* represent probably the most comprehensive and intelligent examination of stylistic principles to be found in the neoclassical period, is another. The question of influence is not in itself of any great moment, but the question of context is. If we unduly restrict our awareness of the historical sources of a given body of doctrine, such as the neoclassical doctrine of style, by focusing our attention upon one or two strains of influence to the exclusion of others, we shall almost inevitably distort the meaning of that doctrine. And this has happened in the study of seventeenth-century poetry and prose, where the movement of stylistic reform has been on the whole narrowly construed in terms of modern influences, those of empirical science and of Cartesian rationalism in particular. It is true that the more naive misunderstandings resulting from an uncritical assimilation of literary to philosophical and scientific norms of discourse have recently been cleared away, mainly by scholars who have found the evidence against such an assimilation in the modern works themselves. But our notion of the values and assumptions implicit in neoclassical standards for style in both poetry and prose will remain incomplete until we place these standards against a sufficiently detailed background of classical criticism and rhetorical theory. When this is done, we shall rediscover the justification of the term "neoclassical" itself and be able to give it an important and definite content.[26]

Hence the significance of Fénelon's *Dialogues*, in which a detailed knowledge of ancient criticism is applied to modern occasions in the most liberal spirit of neoclassicism. In order to define what he sees as the widespread decadence of modern pulpit oratory, Fénelon constructs a single classical tradition of right rhetoric, which includes Quintilian and Longinus, but whose principal authorities are Plato, Cicero, and Augustine, and an opposing tradition of sophistic or epideictic speaking (for in his view these terms are virtual synonyms) originating with Gorgias and Isocrates, reappearing after the classical period of Rome, and descending without interruption to the present.

Like Bacon, Fénelon is aware that the vices of style and the motives behind them are fundamentally the same in every age and recur "*secundum maius et minus* in all time." The current taste in pulpit eloquence for striking ornament, novel and ingenious methods of disposition, and moralistic portraiture in the manner of La Rochefoucauld reflects, in his view, the conception of eloquence typical of Isocratean tradition, in which the principal aim of speaking is to give pleasure (rather than to instruct or to move) and in which style is cultivated for the sake of its own intrinsic beauty. More specifically, modern style is modeled upon the sophistic rhetoric of the patristic period: "We are descended," says Fénelon's chief spokeman in the *Dialogues*, from "the barbarians who over-ran the Roman Empire" and who "tended everywhere to show ignorance and bad taste"; and although literature "may have begun to revive during the fifteenth century, its recovery has been slow."[27] The hallmark of this style is the conceit, defined simply as any thought which does not immediately conduce to instruction, moving the emotions, or vividness of circumstantial detail. The function of the conceit is to be pleasing in itself, apart from the context to which it belongs, and—more important—to call attention to the cleverness of its author. It therefore tends to appear in analytic kinds of discourse, such as eulogy or the moralistic anatomizing currently in vogue, where the speaker talks about his subject instead of presenting it to his listeners directly through narrative or visual description. Here, although the ostensible subject is the man being praised or criticized, in a sense the real subject is always the speaker himself, kept constantly before the attention of his auditors by the ingenuity of his style (*Dialogues*, pp. 77–78, 91–95).

True eloquence is something quite different. It is the product, in Fénelon's view, of principles to which Plato, Cicero, and Augustine subscribed in common. Fénelon's desire to create the impression of a unified classical tradition leads him to overlook the theoretical differences which exist between these writers and to simplify some of their views. Although he refers to Plato as his highest authority, for example, his most basic assumptions are more Ciceronian than Platonic. He is not interested in the dispute between Cicero and Plato concerning the status of dialectic and the possibility of demonstrable proof in moral inquiries, nor does he respect the differences between Plato's ideal rhetoric of rational communication and Cicero's ideal rhetoric of emotional manipulation. It is enough for him that Plato and Cicero agree that the ideal orator is first of all a philosopher, although the philosopher whom Fénelon proceeds to depict is really the model humanist of the *De Oratore*, given, of course, a Christian as well as a classical education.

In what Fénelon sees as the central classical tradition, rhetoric is conceived of, not as an art of verbal display, but as a branch of moral philosophy dealing with the rectification of the individual human soul. The object of eloquence is the communication of wisdom in such a way that it will be not only known but loved and followed; and rhetoric is the study of the means to this end (ibid., pp. 82-84, 89-90). For since simple logical conviction "is not capable of winning men and putting goodness in their hearts," everything in eloquence consists in "adding to solid proof the means of interesting the listener, and of using his passions for the purpose which one has in mind. One inspires him to anger at ingratitude, to horror of cruelty, to pity for misery, to love for virtue, and so on" (ibid., p. 90). Fénelon is not troubled by Platonic qualms about appealing to the emotions, since, first of all, he accepts an Aristotelian or Thomist psychology in terms of which eloquence is justified as a means of bringing emotion into harmony with rational understanding, and, second, he accepts the Augustinian view that emotional appeals are justified by the eloquence of Holy Scripture (ibid., pp. 101-2, 123-33). The aims of his right rhetoric have, then, nothing in common with those of scientific or philosophic discourse beyond a mutual concern for factual and logical truth; although Fénelon's concern that style be used to convey intellectual substance rather than to display verbal ingenuity is harmonious with the ideals of a scientific program, his aims go beyond the scientific purpose of accurate presentation of fact. His main ambition is to restore to pulpit oratory its rightful power over the emotions, and his main objection to the modern epideictic style is to its frigidity. His preferred model is the impassioned rationality of Demosthenes (ibid., pp. 63, 125-41).

Fénelon gives much attention to the arguments of the third book of the *De Oratore*. "Solid proof" is the backbone of eloquence, but such proof is not the result of a formal logical method: the knowledge out of which the orator speaks is personal and inward, a part of his intelligence and moral character, and the product of long study, reflection, experience, and a native aptitude for clear thinking. What the Christian orator needs more than any formal training is an initimate knowledge of Scripture, the Fathers, and the doctrines of the Church. When eloquence is pursued apart from the aims of general education, the results are inevitably such as Cicero has described in attacking the separation of eloquence from philosophy in ancient times. In the last century, for example, "there were, on the one hand, the literary scholars, who sought only purity of language and works elegantly written. These, with their elegance and erudition, and without a sound basis in principle, were for the most part freethinkers. On the other hand, you found the dry and thorny Scholastics, who set forth the truth in so disagreeable and so insensitive a way that they repelled everybody" (ibid., pp. 82-85, 89-90, 126). Fénelon's view of fragmentation in sixteenth-century culture thus corresponds in general to Bacon's, but Fénelon is more strictly Ciceronian than Bacon in the exclusiveness of his concern with healing the split between eloquence and moral philosophy and in his indifference to the shortcomings of Scholastic science.

When Fénelon comes to the shortcomings of Scholastic rhetoric, he extends and amplifies the objections of Arnauld. The procedures of Scholastic inventional theory, he implies, are useful only to those who betray a want of inward touch: if you have spent years, Fénelon's spokesman remarks, in getting abundant resources, the immediate preparation of a speech costs little.

> But if you have only applied yourself to the preparation of particular subjects, you are reduced to paying off in the currency of aphorisms and antitheses; you treat only the commonplaces; you utter nothing

> but incoherencies; you sew up rags not made for each other; you
> do not show the real principles of things; you are restricted to
> superficial and often false arguments; you are incapable of showing
> the full extent of truth, because all general truths have necessary
> interconnections, and it is obligatory to know almost all of them
> in order to handle adequately a particular one. [Ibid., p. 85]

Here the term "commonplaces" has its modern pejorative connotation: the commonplaces are the source of the trite and ready-made, whereas true understanding, as Fénelon explains elsewhere, is coherent and organic, growing in discourse as a single process from beginning to end.

So too with style. Howell, in noting that the *Dialogues* contain no mention of the tropes and figures, implies that the omission is as telling as any direct attack upon them could have been.[28] If the tropes and figures are of no special importance, what then are the sources of an effective style? Fénelon's answer is given in a discussion not of style but of delivery:

> The entire art of the good orator consists only in observing what
> nature does when she is not hampered. Do not do what bad
> speakers do in striving always to declaim and never to talk to their
> listeners. On the contrary, each one of your listeners must suppose
> that you are speaking particularly to him. There you have what
> produces natural, familiar, and suggestive tones. . . . To succeed in
> painting the passions, one must study the movements which they
> produce. For example, observe what the eyes do, what the hands
> do, what the whole body does, and what its posture is. . . . There
> you have nature revealing herself to you. You have only to follow
> her. If you use art, conceal it so well by imitation that one will take
> it for nature herself. [Ibid., p. 104]

"Follow nature." Scarcely a novel suggestion—but one which, in the context of the *Dialogues* as a whole, and given a background of Ramist and Scholastic rhetoric, is instinct with the differences between a liberal rhetoric and a rhetoric of methods and rules. By classifying extraordinary linguistic configurations and presenting them for the most part without a context, the Ramist rhetoric of tropes and figures contributed to the impression (whether intentionally or not) that eloquence is more or less synonymous with ornament and requires the avoidance of the language and structure of ordinary speech.[29]

Fénelon's concern is to show that good style consists precisely in a selection and purification of the ordinary. The source of a "natural" style is "nature"—"nature" as opposed to "art." And "nature" is the way men speak when they are intent upon their meaning rather than upon eloquence. The "art" of speaking "naturally," then, consists in the ability to locate the norms of common speech and appropriate them as a standard. And the artistic product of these norms will differ from ordinary utterance less in ornament than in economy: the two will coincide in their essential form, but the one will be sharper, clearer, more efficient. Because the sources of effective speaking, as described above, lie outside the province of "art" in the Scholastic sense, "nature" becomes in Fénelon—and in neoclassical stylistic criticism generally—the slogan of artistic individualism. To discover the norms of style one must rely upon his native powers of observation, just as he must rely upon his own intelligence and fund of wisdom in discovering what to say. Careful observation is, nevertheless, a source of principles, especially when it is employed in the study of models, and Fénelon describes several principles which have an important bearing on neoclassical taste.

The most general of these is the cautionary precept, perhaps borrowed from Arnauld, that in speaking there is nothing beautiful but what is true (*Dialogues*, p. 60). The full meaning of "true" in the context of Fénelon's stylistic theory is revealed during a discussion of what Fénelon calls "portraiture," a technique of vivid description or narration similar to the *enargeia* or *visiones* of classical rhetorical doctrine.[30] "Portraiture" is for Fénelon the most important legitimate source of emotional appeal. Somewhat illogically, it is introduced at first as an end of eloquence. According to the classical doctrine of the three levels or characters of style, the function of the middle style is to give delight. Fénelon, however, rules out pleasure as an end of oratory: to treat pleasure as an end rather than a means would in his view be to sanction a conceited style and the epideictic tradition of Isocrates in general. Thus in the *Dialogues* the ends assigned to eloquence become teaching, moving, and "portraying" (*Dialogues*, pp. 92-93). Yet as

Fénelon proceeds to describe it, portraiture is really a means of arousing emotion, not an end in itself. As a technique, it contrasts sharply with the moralistic character drawing which Fénelon disparages in modern oratory, and the contrast discloses a special application of Arnauld's rule (or Pascal's) that the speaker should avoid calling attention to himself as far as possible (see pp. 18–19). Where the moralistic portraiture which Fénelon condemns is seen as an excuse for the display of style and obtrudes the speaker himself as a manipulative presence, Fénelon's own ideal of portraiture is an act of sympathetic imagination, of ''negative capability,'' by which the speaker disappears into the experience of his subject (a saint's life, for example) and dramatizes that experience instead of merely telling about it. The method is justified, Fénelon explains, by man's inability to attend to the abstract. We have been ''entirely enmeshed in palpable things'' since the time of original sin, and we must have ''images to beguile [us].'' It is therefore necessary to give a ''physical body to all the instructions which one wishes to inject into [man's] soul.'' The technique itself is best learned not from orators but from poets; the secret of its power lies in a vivid particularity of realization: ''To portray is not only to describe things but to represent their surrounding features in so lively and so concrete a way that the listener imagines himself almost seeing them.'' It is verbal painting, says Fénelon—*ut pictura poesis*:

> For example, a dispassionate historian who tells of the death of Dido will content himself with saying that she was so overcome with grief after the departure of Aeneas that she could not bear to live; and that she went upstairs in her palace, threw herself upon a pyre, and killed herself. In listening to these words, you take in the happening, but you do not see it. Listen to Virgil, and he will put it before your eyes. Is it not true that, when he assembles all the surrounding features of her despair, when he shows you the savage Dido, the lineaments of death already etched upon her face, when he makes her speak with her eyes upon Aeneas' portrait and upon his sword, your imagination transports you to Carthage, you believe that you see the Trojan fleet receding from the beach and the queen whom nothing can console. You enter into all the feelings which the actual spectators had as they looked. It is no longer Virgil whom you

listen to—you are too attentive to the last words of the unhappy
Dido to think of him. The poet disappears. You see nothing but
that which he makes visible; you hear nothing but those whom
he makes speak. There one sees the power of imitation and of
portraiture! [Ibid., pp. 92–94]

It is plain that the ''truth'' which eloquence embraces is more
than a truth of fact or of logic. It includes a truth of experience
which can only be rendered by dramatic—that is to say,
mimetic—means. Behind Fénelon's theory of portraiture lies
the recognition that the abstract truths of dogma or moral
precept which the preacher wishes to inculcate can become
persuasive only when they are embedded in the concrete texture
of individual lives and actions and so made available to the
sympathy and imaginative participation of the hearer. It is
plain, too, that the style through which this end is to be
accomplished requires one virtue above all others—verisimilitude. If the preacher has occasion to imitate the speech of
others, as the poet does with Dido, his style must be capable of
duplicating the flexibility and freedom of spontaneous utterance; in circumstantial narration or description it must be an
absolutely transparent medium through which one sees only
the things and actions themselves.

A conceited style, in Fénelon's sense of conceited, would be
incapable of these functions, for the effect of obtrusive ornament is to draw attention from matter to manner, either to the
style itself, as a repertory of distinctive linguistic gestures, or
(perhaps at best) to the style as reflective of a distinct—i.e.,
unique—personality or sensibility. And to be aware of manner
is to be aware, however marginally, of the distorting influence
of an agency intermediate between the experience itself and the
hearer at whom its representation is directed. For the original
data are either submitted to the tyranny of the figures, as
Arnauld pointed out in condemning the sixteenth-century
Ciceronians, or they are translated into the more subtle but
more subjective structures imposed by an avid and perhaps
eccentric sensibility. Fénelon, on the other hand, is seeking a
style which will seem to give direct access to the events themselves
and in which the events will seem to disclose an inherent

meaning. Such a style will preserve the illusion of providing an immediate encounter with reality; yet, again, this is in no accurate sense a scientific style, nor is it conceived upon a scientific model, as we have already seen from Fénelon's appeal to the poets. It is a moral style, animated by a moral presence— it could scarcely be otherwise, since vivid and focused description or narration always betrays a moral perceiver, who selects and responds out of some human concern. Yet the "natural" style does not call attention to its author as an individual because he has no unique sensibility to exhibit (or indulge): for it is not that his responses confer importance upon his subject, but rather that the subject itself compels an appropriate response. The author is effaced, in short, owing to the very centrality of his moral intelligence. He is the ideal, and therefore representative, human observer, whose ability to render events with a fully circumstantial plausibility is at once a certain proof of the accuracy of his perceptions and the basis of his moral authority, for it is the completeness of his contact with a concrete and objective reality which validates the general truths which he is attempting to explain.

Such a style is, then, "objective" in the accuracy with which it portrays external reality and yet it is fully human at the same time. The humanity is of the kind which Fénelon celebrates in praising Demosthenes: "His is an argument tight and urgent, his the liberal feelings of a soul which conceives nothing but the great, his a discourse which grows and supports itself at each word by new proofs, his a chain of bold and striking figures. You do not know how to read him without seeing that he carries the republic in the depth of his heart. It is nature herself who speaks in his ecstasy—the art is so perfect that it does not appear anywhere—nothing ever equalled his rapidity and vehemence" (ibid., p. 63). It is humanity in this sense which ultimately makes possible the generality which the neoclassical period sought in style—a generality not of averages, as some scholars have thought, not of the colorless or abstract or vague, but of inclusiveness and moral community. This was what the "natural" style, in its freedom from mannerism, from period or coterie limitation of any kind, was designed to conserve.[31]

2

Empiricism and Literary Realism

We have seen that Cicero, Quintilian, Arnauld, and Fénelon are linked by their unwillingness to discuss style apart from the requirements of persuasion on the one hand and fruitful inquiry on the other. All of these critics regard style as a means rather than an end—as an instrument whose nature must be inferred from a consideration of the functions which it serves. Thus they seek in various ways to effect a rapprochement between rhetoric (the theory of communication, especially popular communication) and dialectic (the theory of inquiry, especially moral inquiry), seeing in the latter a necessary foundation for a noble rhetoric which would reconcile the demands of truthfulness and persuasive efficacy. In Arnauld rhetoric is tied to a Cartesian dialectic; Fénelon's inventional theory reflects the eclecticism and commonsense empiricism of Ciceronian tradition. The most advanced rhetoric and literary theory of the eighteenth century is similarly responsive to broader epistemological issues. Now, however, and especially in Britain, the theory of inquiry which the language arts must accommodate is no longer either Aristotelian, Ramist, or Cartesian; it consists instead in the empiricist principles laid down by Bacon and Locke and increasingly regarded as defining the only valid approach to knowledge.

W. S. Howell has shown in detail how writers such as Campbell, Priestley, and Adam Smith, in what he calls the tradition of "new rhetoric" in the eighteenth century, accommodated rhetorical theory to the empiricism of Bacon and Locke.[1] In the following pages I shall say relatively little about rhetorical theory itself; instead I wish to examine some of the criteria which not only rhetoric but all forms of imaginative literature must satisfy if they wish to be considered legitimate sources of moral knowledge from an empiricist point of view. These criteria supply one justification for the artistic tradition which we now call literary realism. It is important to understand that Johnson's strongest affinities are with this tradition, as opposed to the neo-Platonic strain of neoclassicism with which he is often associated. For Johnson's theoretical achievement is an appreciation of realism which grows out of a rigorous and sharply defined empiricism, yet which preserves the full range of cognitive and moral concerns to be found in liberal classical and neoclassical tradition.

THE CONFLICT BETWEEN LIBERAL AND EXPERIMENTAL INQUIRY IN THE NEOCLASSICAL PERIOD

To the extent that rhetoric and imaginative literature were juxtaposed at all to the principles of Baconian or Cartesian science during the seventeenth century, the language arts were portrayed by some of the great modern theorists of knowledge as conflicting with science. Thus Malebranche condemns imaginative writing (i.e., figurative style) as a threat to the clear and distinct ideas on which Cartesian inquiry depends, and Locke dismisses rhetoric, in the *Essay concerning Human Understanding*, on the traditional Platonic grounds. If we would speak of things as they are, he says,

> we must allow that all the art of rhetoric, besides order and
> clearness; all the artificial and figurative application of words
> eloquence hath invented, are for nothing else but to insinuate
> wrong ideas, move the passions, and thereby mislead the judgment;
> and so indeed are perfect cheats: and therefore, however laudable or
> allowable oratory may render them in harangues and popular
> addresses, they are certainly, in all discourses that pretend to inform
> or instruct, wholly to be avoided; and where truth and knowledge
> are concerned, cannot but be thought a great fault, either of the
> language or person that makes use of them.[2]

Although a defender of rhetoric and even in certain respects a pioneer of the psychological approach which was to characterize the most advanced rhetorical theory of the eighteenth century, Bacon too tended to perpetuate the grounds of the ancient dispute between dialectic and rhetoric by claiming as much as possible for his scientific method. Bacon agreed with Cicero that the Platonic opposition between dialectic (here meaning specifically moral inquiry) and rhetoric was false: the Stoics, for example, were wrong to couch their moral disquistions in a sharp and thorny style, for "it is a thing not hastily to be condemned, to clothe and adorn the obscurity of philosophy itself with sensible and plausible elocution." But in a larger context Bacon undermined the status of rhetoric and imaginative writing by presenting his experimental method as the only way of arriving at certain knowledge not only in natural but in moral philosophy—at least to the extent that moral knowledge is the same as, or derivable from, psychology, the study of human nature.[3] And the distance between his method and those of the humanities seemed all the greater inasmuch as Bacon conceived of experimental science as a collaborative enterprise involving as many researchers as possible and guided by a procedure "such as leaves little to the acuteness and strength of wits, but places all wits and understandings nearly on a level."[4] So poetry, which "doth truly refer to the imagination," was to be regarded as the opposite of philosophy or science, its object being, not the representation of things as they are, but rather the display of "a more ample greatness, a more exact goodness, and a more absolute variety, than can be found in the nature of things." Poetry "doth raise and erect the mind, by submitting the shews of things to the desires of the mind; whereas reason doth buckle and bow the mind unto the nature of things." Elsewhere Bacon admits that poetry sometimes does represent things as they are and may be a valuable source of information about human passions and appetites. But "it is not good to stay too long in the theatre," and we must approach and view philosophy with more reverence and attention.[5]

Recent scholarship has portrayed the dispute between dialectic and rhetoric in the seventeenth century as being strangely one-sided, in the sense that the poets and literary critics did not often respond to the antirhetorical charges. Dominique Bouhours presents a striking instance. In his *Manière de bien penser dans les Ouvrages d'Esprit* (1687), wishing to defend the truth value of imaginative writing, he adopts Arnauld's maxim that there is nothing lovely but what is true. In his preface Bouhours describes himself as writing a kind of logic and rhetoric for the belles lettres, but he advises that his logic is not to be confused with logic in the strict sense, which handles truth with philosophical exactness (*avec toute l'exactitude que demande la raison*).[6] But if this distinction is allowed, what does it mean to say that in the belles lettres there is nothing lovely but what is true? Bouhours raises this question briefly in the first of his four dialogues. A thought, says his spokesman Eudoxus, is a mental picture of ''any Object spiritual or sensible,'' and it is true ''when it represents things faithfully: and it is false, when it makes them appear otherwise than they are in themselves.''[7] The definition is much too general to serve its purpose. Taken at face value, it fails to distinguish eloquence or imaginative writing from either straightforward dialectic or the factual reporting of a Baconian scientist; and although it might have been made to serve if it had been supported by a careful explanation of what the ''things'' are which polite writing represents, the point is that Bouhours gives no clear explanation.[8] We can say that Bouhours is simply a bad theorist, or we can suppose that the problem did not seem to him important. In any event he comes nearer to confronting it than most other critics of his time. For several other writers whom one would have expected to discuss it the problem seems not to have existed. Both Hobbes and Sprat attack rhetorical abuses and insist upon a severe standard of plainness in philosophical writing; both are at the same time literary critics who discuss poetry with no apparent sense that their strictures upon eloquence might seem to raise questions with which a poetic theorist would have to deal. And it was Dryden, after all, who gave the antirhetorical point of view its most memorable seventeenth-century expression: ''A Man is to be cheated into Passion, but to be reason'd into Truth.''[9]

It has been plausibly maintained that, paradoxical as it may seem, it was the very sharpness of the distinction between dialectic and rhetoric which assured rhetoric and poetry a protected position of their own, by relieving them of the burden of competition with dialectic. Dialectic—so this argument would run—is both a mode of inquiry and a mode of expression; rhetoric and poetry are modes of expression only. Their subject matter is furnished from other sources—from philosophy, Scripture, experience—and their function is to make that subject matter entertaining or persuasive by "clothing" it in fables, images, ornaments of language. Their defense is thus pragmatic: at the least, poetry and eloquence are, or ought to be, innocent amusements; at most they are powerful instruments of persuasion whose use is made necessary by the fact of man's fallen will. The position of Sprat and Hobbes is comprehensible in these terms. For they attacked rhetorical abuses but not the idea of eloquence itself, and they did not attack poetry. Their rhetorical criticisms are directed against what they took to be the decadence of contemporary eloquence, its vain love of ornament at the expense of matter and persuasion. Beyond this, their criticism may be seen as propaedeutic to the establishment of true philosophy: like Bacon before them, they had to set limits to a once-voracious rhetorical humanism in order to clear the way for new discoveries. But since poetry had never exceeded its limits in the way that Renaissance rhetoric had done, no general caveat against the poetic imagination was required, and their criticisms were limited to matters of esthetics and taste.[10]

This defense of eloquence and poetry was coherent, but from a Ciceronian—or a modern—point of view not very satisfactory. In conceding to dialectic (in either its traditional or modern forms) everything that Plato had claimed for it, rhetoric and poetry weaken their title to being considered liberal disciplines in the full sense of the term. If both the discovery of truth and its most faithful expression belong to dialectic alone, then rhetoric, which represents "*Truth*, cloth'd with Bodies" (Sprat) and "as it is planted in popular opinions and manners" (Bacon), is not merely a subordinate and instrumental art but in some degree a technique of distortion and deception, and the claim that it is a political or social or moral necessity does not alter the fact.[11] Moreover, the separation of matter from manner implicit in the pragmatic view of rhetoric and poetry has undesirable consequences for the theory of persuasion and style, as we shall see later in some detail.[12]

If we restrict ourselves to major figures, we can say that by the middle of the eighteenth century the conflict between dialectic and rhetoric had ceased to be a significant issue for either literary critics or philosophers. Exactly how and why this happened is hard to say. I know of no body of argument which can be said to provide a transition from the terms of the seventeenth-century dispute to the new terms of the eighteenth-century rapprochement. The history of the question thus seems oddly discontinuous. If one considers the chief representatives of British philosophy, one moves from Locke, for whom rhetoric was a perfect cheat, to Berkeley, Hume, Kames, Priestley, Adam Smith, George Campbell, and others for whom the value and dignity of eloquence could be taken, it seems, almost for granted. And the few literary critics, such as Dubos and Joseph Warton, who refer to the antirhetorical position do so in passing, without serious discussion.[13] As with the literary critics of Dryden's time, the problem is not a problem and the absence of discussion makes it hard to recover the terms of the new rapprochement. Nevertheless, in a remarkable essay R. S. Crane has reconstructed a number of assumptions which enabled eighteenth-century writers to view the arts and sciences as being complementary to one another rather than in competition and thus to posit a new version of the Ciceronian ideal of cultural unity.[14] One of these assumptions has a bearing on the present question and (though Crane does not make this point) may be cited as illustrating one of the ways in which the rhetorical positions of Arnauld and Fénelon anticipated eighteenth-century developments.[15]

The premise in question holds, in effect, that the several genres of discourse to which the names oratory, poetry, and dialectic have been given are not, as it were, ontologically distinct but instead are continuous with one another, so that distinctions between them cannot be turned into oppositions. This view was facilitated by the exchange of Scholastic for utilitarian assumptions which characterized the development of eighteenth-century rhetorical theory as a whole. When classified in Scholastic terms the arts of language can be made to seem quite independent. For Ramus, as we have seen, the definition of an art revealed its essence, and its other properties were more or less logically derived from the definition: the thing itself was thus taken to be as distinct as the categories that could be applied to it. But when this approach is discarded in favor of a utilitarian emphasis upon the adaptation of means to ends, the differences between the genres may suddenly appear less important than their similarities. If oratory, poetry, and even philosophical exposition may all be said to share in one or more of the ends of teaching, moving, and delighting, then they will share as well in the artistic techniques by which these ends are achieved. Thus, in Fénelon's *Dialogues* the principal speaker is asked whether there is no difference between eloquence and poetry and replies: "Poetry differs from simple eloquence only in this: that she paints with ecstasy and with bolder strokes" (*Dialogues*, p. 93).[16]

The abandonment of Scholastic for utilitarian premises is not discussed as such by eighteenth-century critics, but the symptoms of the change are manifold. Perhaps the most decisive is the gradual diappearance during the course of the century of *artes poeticae* on the early neoclassical model of Vida, Boileau, and Gildon, in which each poetic genre is described separately in terms of its own rules. The tendency of later criticism is to discuss techniques and effects, rather than genres, and to speak of more than one genre at a time when they share artistic features in common. Hugh Blair's *Lectures on Rhetoric and Belles-Lettres* (published 1782, begun about 1760) provides at least a partial model of the new approach, which can be seen to even better advantage in the criticism of Lord Kames, Priestley, Campbell, and Adam Smith.[17] As Howell has noted, the appearance and widespread adoption during the first half of the century of the term *belles lettres* is itself another symptom of the change, the collective term indicating the importance of the common features of the ''polite'' genres.[18] Finally, one finds in the period a blurring or expansion of definitions: Campbell abandons any notion of essential differences between the genres in defining eloquence simply as ''that art or talent by which the discourse is adapted to its end''; Blair observes that it is ''hardly possible to determine the exact limit where Eloquence ends, and Poetry begins,'' adding that there is no occasion ''for being very precise about the boundaries, as long as the nature of each is understood''; and Johnson remarks in the *Life of Pope* that ''to circumscribe poetry by a definition will only shew the narrowness of the definer.''[19] Obviously, to critics for whom the premise of continuity between the genres was fundamental, the conflict between dialectic and rhetoric as portrayed in the seventeenth century would have seemed simply misconceived and, to that extent, a false problem.[20]

Yet the premise of continuity just described does not represent a solution to the dispute between dialectic and rhetoric in all respects, for it portrays the various genres as complementary modes of communication, rather than as complementary modes of inquiry, and so avoids the question of their inventional status. But this question is primary: if rhetoric and poetry are not to be relegated to the subordinate and pragmatic role described above in connection with Sprat and Hobbes, they must claim to be valid modes of discovery as well as of transmission. Ideally, they ought to be able to show that the principles of individual and liberal inquiry which they represent are entitled to full dignity in intellectual culture and are not to be regarded as inferior substitutes for the supposedly more exact methods of philosophy or science. Now it is still, I think, widely supposed that eighteenth-century critics lacked the resources to make this case. K. G. Hamilton asserts, for example, that in the time of Pope (and presumably later) the concept of imitation ''was unable to provide poetry with any new directions in the face of the rise of science. The neo-classic period could see poetry as utilitarian in the sense of providing delight or moral instruction, but it was difficult for it to be convincing beyond this level.''[21] But perhaps the question here is: convincing to whom? It may be true that no eighteenth-century critic offers a strong defense of poetry and the humanities against the claims of experimental science, but if no defense of the kind was felt necessary at the time, its absence proves very little; and it would be idle to remark that eighteenth-century criticism failed to do what it never attempted. Crane's essay on the harmony of eighteenth-century culture goes very far toward explaining why the kind of defense for which Hamilton is looking is absent from eighteenth-century criticism. But something more can be said on this question. For the premises required for seeing experimental and liberal inquiry as complementary rather than competitive were available in the eighteenth century; they were accepted by Johnson and by other important spokesmen for liberal inquiry during his time; and they enable us to consider Johnson's literary theory—and in particular his concept of mimesis—as representing a cogent solution to the quarrel between dialectic and rhetoric, and, more generally, as a way of overcoming the divorce between words and things.

THE GROUNDS OF A SOLUTION

The premises required for seeing experimental and liberal inquiry as complementary were available in Locke, as an obvious inference from his doctrine of nominal essences. Locke belongs, of course, to the story of the issues mentioned in this essay in many ways. His *Essay concerning Human Understanding*, appearing toward the close of the seventeenth century, stands as a final and exceptionally thorough summary of the objections to Scholastic learning developed earlier by Bacon, Descartes, and Arnauld. Locke repeats the arguments of these writers against the authoritarianism of Scholastic tradition, its disputatiousness, and its habit of beginning at the wrong end of the process of inquiry by arguing deductively from axioms or ''maxims'' of doubtful strength; and his attack on the art of syllogism, as being useless for inquiry and unnecessary for exposition, was regarded by Johnson, and doubtless by many others, as conclusive.[22] The whole of Book III of the *Essay*, ''Of Words,'' is devoted to the most subtle and comprehensive analysis of the relations between words and things (or, in Locke, words and ideas) that had yet appeared, and in the long concluding sections on the imperfection and abuse of words, Locke interprets the history of fragmentation in philosophy in terms of the failure of previous philosophers to recognize and respect the nature and limitations of language.[23] But it is the doctrine of nominal essences which specifically concerns us, because it provided an alternative to the sharp Baconian distinction between scientific method and the methods proper to the belles lettres.

The doctrine has to do with our knowledge of substances, by which Locke means primarily material objects. Scholastic philosophy, which for him is synonymous with some form of realism, pretends that what it calls essences are substantial forms which stamp the individual with the character of its species and which govern our knowledge, our "naming," of the thing as well. But in fact, Locke argues, such essences are merely nominal, merely words—terms for ideas abstracted from our sensory experience of the objects which they designate, and given an altogether spurious prestige as determining properties. The determining properties of things are unknown: all we can do is describe appearances, and appearances give little knowledge of things in themselves. Our knowledge of the "primary qualities" of matter is limited to solidity, extension, figure, and mobility; everything else is "secondary" or phenomenal: we know modifications of consciousness rather than real properties (*Essay*, II.viii.7–26; III.vi.1–9). And Locke concludes from this that the true function of substantive definition is utilitarian rather than scientific: since an object can be described in a variety of ways, and since the description involves its appearance rather than its essence, the purpose of the definition is simply to mark off the object as belonging to this class rather than that so as to avoid ambiguity in communication. By this standard, Locke observes, Aristotle's definition of man as a rational animal may well be considered inferior to Plato's definition of him as "a two-legged animal with broad nails, and without feathers,'' since the defining properties chosen by Plato serve to identify the class and are less ambiguous than Aristotle's ''reason'' (*Essay*, III.x.17, xi.20).

But we can better appreciate how little definition has to do with natural philosophy by analyzing the concept of species itself. Scholastic philosophy imagines that the ranks and classes of which it speaks exist in nature; in fact they are inventions of the mind. The individual objects which comprise a given species may really exist, and so of course may their properties, as ''primary'' or ''secondary'' qualities; but individuals are sorted into classes for our convenience in thinking and talking about them, and the classes exist merely as names. Thus ''a silent and a striking watch are but one species to those who have but one name for them; but he that has the name *watch* for one and *clock* for the other, and distinct complex ideas to which those names belong, to *him* they are different species.'' One can, if he chooses, make any number of species of clocks or watches, each distinguished by some feature of construction or appearance. It is merely a question of interest or need (*Essay*, III.vi.7,13,26,35–39).

The premises of Locke's nominalism eliminate the basis of Scholastic natural science, at least as Locke represents it, but they also place the experimental method in a rather different light from that in which it appeared to Bacon or Sprat. Bacon had said that poetry submits the shows of things to the desires of the mind, while reason buckles and bows the mind unto the nature of things, but Locke's epistemology makes it plain that, however painstakingly the mind buckles and bows itself unto the nature of things, it will be dealing merely with their shows—with the mental phenomena which, apart from the few primary qualities of matter, are all that it can know. Moreover, such phenomena are likely, in Locke's opinion, to remain impenetrably contingent: the real essences of objects lie (he supposes) hidden in the microcosms of their corpuscular structure, unavailable to our senses now and likely to remain so. In its present state, experimental natural philosophy can describe appearances but not explain them: cause—and therefore necessity—remain beyond its grasp. Finally, Locke points out that induction is incapable of reaching demonstrably universal conclusions, since it cannot be shown that what is true of certain individuals of a given class must be true of all, or even, for that matter, where the boundaries of the class lie. Since for Locke science implies the discovery of propositions which are self-evident, necessary, and universal, he concludes that experimental inquiry is not scientific: inductive generalizations are hypothetical, and a hypothesis "amounts only to opinion, and has not that certainty which is requisite to knowledge" (*Essay*, IV.vi.13). Locke is evidently concerned to distinguish sharply between scientific and empirical inquiry because he distrusts the pretensions of modern natural philosophy: we must beware, he remarks at one point in the *Essay*, "that the name of *principles* deceive us not, nor impose on us, by making us receive that for an unquestionable truth, which is really at best but a very doubtful conjecture; such as are most (I had almost said all) of the hypotheses in natural philosophy" (*Essay*, IV. xii. 13).

Considered, then, from Locke's point of view, the physical scientist, as we call him, has no essential advantage over the empirical moralist such as Cicero or Montaigne. True, the object of the latter's study—human nature—may be inherently more complicated than the material substances investigated by the natural philosopher, or apprehensible under a more bewildering variety of relations, or more difficult to observe. But these are practical, not theoretical, differences; and if one were to accept Locke's conservative and even pessimistic estimate of the achievements of modern "science," even these differences would be easy to exaggerate. What is important—and this became something of a commonplace among eighteenth-century writers who accepted empiricist principles—is, not that the investigation of one subject matter may yield firmer conclusions than the investigation of another, but that both investigations be conducted in a way calculated to yield the best possible results. In short, Locke's analysis of induction removes any basis for making a sharp distinction between the experimental philosopher and the empirical moralist on methodological grounds; or, to put the matter positively, provides a way of seeing both as engaged upon the same kind of enterprise and limited by the same theoretical considerations.

Now Locke himself, as it happens, did not see natural and moral philosophy as allied in this way. He is sufficiently doubtful about the possibilities and importance of natural philosophy to conclude, with Socrates, that *"morality is the proper science and business of mankind in general,"* but he means *science* here in its technical sense; that is, he believed that ethical inquiry is, at least in principle, capable of demonstration (*Essay*, IV.xii.11). He grounded this belief on his analysis of the nature of ethical abstractions, or as he calls them, "mixed modes." Mixed modes are complex notions of relation, such as *drunkenness, murder, government, justice*. These differ from our complex ideas of substances chiefly in being mental fictions with no corresponding existence in empirical reality. That is, although the ideas of the actions, parties, intentions, etc., comprehended in our notion of *murder*, for example, may have direct reference to experience (as they do whenever murders are committed), the mixed mode itself is merely an arbitrary composition of abstractions united by the term *murder*. Such notions, Locke explains, are made by the mind, usually in response to social or moral needs, and obtain a kind of general existence through the currency, in a particular culture or language, of the terms which represent them. Both their arbitrariness and their cultural origin are seen in the fact that such words are frequently untranslatable from one language to another.[24] Since the existence of a mixed mode is purely ideal, its definition is its real essence; this means that all valid propositions about a mixed mode will be universally valid (*Essay*, III.v.1–15). But these, Locke observes, are precisely the conditions which make demonstration possible in geometry: it is because a triangle is a mental fiction whose essence is its definition that its subsequently discoverable properties are intuited as necessary rather than contingent and universal rather than particular. If, then, Locke argues, we can arrive at clear and distinct ("determined" or "determinate") ideas of mixed modes—such as *justice*, *right*, *virtue*, etc.—we should be able, by analyzing in geometrical fashion the agreements and disagreements between such ideas, to arrive at demonstrable conclusions (*Essay*, III.xi.15-18; IV.ii.2-10, iii.18, iv.5-9, xii. 7-8). Thus, "'where there is no property there is no injustice,' is a proposition as certain as any demonstration in Euclid: for the idea of property being a right to anything, and the idea to which the name 'injustice' is given being the invasion or violation of that right, it is evident that these ideas, being thus established, and these names annexed to them, I can as certainly know this proposition to be true, as that a triangle has three angles equal to two right ones."[25]

In Books III and IV of the *Essay* Locke refers repeatedly to this geometrical conception of ethics, but is unwilling to pursue any of the questions which it inevitably raises. He is, however, aware of how difficult it is to reduce many moral abstractions to clear and distinct "determined" or "determinate" ideas. He insists again and again upon the importance of supplying the mixed modes with exact and complete definitions and of using them unequivocally in discourse, both because these procedures are required by his notion of moral science, and, more generally, because they seem to him to represent the only hope of escape from the fragmentation of moral philosophy, in which the contention among the various sects reveals, in his view, little more than the "abuse of words." Yet his exhaustive analysis of the difficulties involved in fixing the meaning of the mixed modes, and especially in communicating them with precision, may easily convince an unbiased reader that his faith in the possibilities of definition must be in large part misplaced. Thus he observes, for example, that the connotations of many mixed modes embrace extraordinarily complicated combinations of ideas, which are seldom ascertained in their full extent even by those who seek to use moral terms with care.[26] Again, since the mixed modes are mental fictions, they "want standards in nature whereby men may rectify and adjust their significations": the individual is at liberty either to define them as best he can for himself, out of the resources of his education and experience, or to accept the lowest common denominator of meaning attached to moral terms through common usage, or, indeed, to use such terms for their emotive value without attaching any ideas to them at all. And Locke realistically suggests that the two latter alternatives are by far the most common: as children we are, as Pope said, "first slave[s] to words," and as adults we do not always take the trouble to free ourselves. But however scrupulous men may be in their use of moral terms, and however devoted to the virtues of definition, it is clear from the nature of the mixed modes themselves that many of them will vary almost as widely as individual experience, reflecting a diversity of attitudes and values which Locke's abstract definitions can neither express nor overcome (*Essay*, III.ix.6–10, x.1–13, 22, xi.9, 17–18, 22, 24, 26; IV.iii.18–20, 30, v.3–4).

Of all philosophers after Bacon, Locke is the one who presents most clearly the contrast between the realm of abstractions, whose terms are ambiguous as generally used, and the world of specific perceptions from which all genuine knowledge is drawn. Instead of attempting to avoid the difficulties inherent in a system of abstractions, as Locke did himself in proposing a scientific ethics, most writers influenced by Locke preferred to emphasize those Lockean arguments which are critical of abstract reasoning. Eighteenth-century moral theorists were on the whole more inclined to stress the limitations of reason in moral inquiry (as well as in the making of specific moral choices) than to seek ways of strengthening its authority.[27]

EMPIRICIST MORAL THEORY AS THE INTERPRETATION OF PARTICULAR MORAL SITUATIONS

The eighteenth century abounded with intuitionist and sentimentalist moral theories, some naively anti-intellectual, some not. It could be agreed that, in the best of possible worlds, moral judgment would not be a matter of intricate deliberation, as Gulliver discovered that among the Houyhnhnms, "*Reason*" is not a "Point problematical as with us, where Men can argue with Plausibility on both Sides of a Question; but strikes you

with immediate Conviction,'' so that ''Controversies, Wranglings, Disputes, and Positiveness in false or dubious Propositions, are Evils unknown.''[28] Out of hatred for such wranglings
and disputes, Shaftesbury allowed himself to think that on
moral matters ''men's first thoughts ... are generally better
than their second: their natural notions better than those
refined by study or consultation with casuists''; and Pope tells
his readers more than once to ''Take Nature's path, and mad
Opinion's leave / All states can reach it, and all heads
conceive.''[29]
But Pope also managed to define the problem more perceptively:

> Our depths who fathoms, or our shallows finds,
> Quick whirls, and shifting eddies, of our minds?
> Life's stream for Observation will not stay,
> It hurries all too fast to mark their way,
> In vain sedate reflections we would make,
> When half our knowledge we must snatch, not take.
> On human actions reason tho' you can,
> It may be reason, but it is not man:
> His Principle of action once explore,
> That instant 'tis his Principle no more.
> Like following life thro' creatures you dissect,
> You lose it in the moment you detect.[30]

To any but the most rigid moralist, questions concerning the
source or nature of moral principles are likely to be less pressing
in daily experience than questions concerning the tactful application of such principles; and to the empirical moralist, who
seeks to elicit his principles as directly as possible from the
observation of human nature, questions of tact and of specific
moral interpretation are everything. To this extent the problem
defined above by Pope is primary, and the nature of one's moral
theory as a whole is likely to be in large part determined by the
means chosen to deal with it. The problem was primary for
Pascal, who concluded that the kind of intelligence required for
moral interpretation is quite distinct from linear or geometrical
reason. The principles of the latter, says Pascal, ''*sont palpables,
mais éloignés de l'usage commun; de sorte qu'on a peine à
tourner la tête de ce côté-là, manque d'habitude: mais pour peu*

*qu'on l'y tourne, on voit les principes à plein; et il faudrait
avoir tout à fait l'esprit faux pour mal raisonner sur des
principes si gros qu'il est presque impossible qu'ils échap-
pent.''* But with *''l'esprit de finesse,''* or the moral intellect,
*''les principes sont dans l'usage commun et devant les yeux de
tout le monde. On n'a que faire de tourner la tête, ni de se faire
violence; il n'est question que d'avoir bonne vue, mais il faut
l'avoir bonne: car les principes sont si déliés et en si grand
nombre, qu'il est presque impossible qu'il n'en échappe. Or,
l'ommission d'un principe mène à l'erreur; ainsi, il faut avoir
la vue bien nette pour voir tous les principes, et ensuite l'esprit
juste pour ne pas raisonner faussement sur des principes
connus.''*

Concerning the perception of the principles involved in moral
judgment Pascal goes on to say:

> on les voit à peine, on les sent plutôt qu'on ne les voit; on a des
> peines infinies à les faire sentir à ceux qui ne les sentent pas d'eux-
> mêmes: ce sont choses tellement délicates et si nombreuses, qu'il
> faut un sens bien délicat et bien net pour les sentir, et juger droit et
> juste selon ce sentiment, sans pouvoir le plus souvent les démontrer
> par ordre comme en géométrie, parce qu'on n'en possède pas ainsi
> les principes, et que ce serait une chose infinie de l'entreprendre. *Il
> faut tout d'un coup voir la chose d'un seul regard*, et non pas par
> progrès de raisonnement, au moins jusqu'à un certain degré.[31]

Pascal's position is thus the reverse of Locke's: the comparison
of moral and geometrical reason discloses essential differences,
and the two kinds define each other by contrast. Gibbon,
Burke, and Johnson repeat the comparison in favor of Pascal,
sometimes employing the technical language of Locke's *Essay* in
implicit refutation of the latter. So Gibbon observes, speaking
of Bishop Hurd's literary criticism—a type of study which he
considers analogous to moral inquiry—that ''these inquiries are
delicate; sometimes we think we are reasoning upon things,
when in fact we are only cavilling about words. It is more
especially so with regard to those ideas which do not represent
substances, but only modes of thinking, and moral combinations. There we can be guided only by practice and experience.
They are out of the province of reason.''[32] Johnson agreed with

Locke that "we are entirely ignorant of the principles of [material] things." Nor do we know that "spiritual substances" such as reason or mind have ever been "properly defined."[33] But, like Gibbon, he extended this skepticism to the moral realm. "Life," he says in the conclusion of *Adventurer* 107, "is not the object of science: we see a little, very little; and what is beyond we can only conjecture." Locke would reduce morality to definitions; but "definition," Johnson remarks in *Rambler* 125, "is, indeed, not the province of man; every thing is set above or below our faculties. The works and operations of nature are too great in their extent, or too much diffused in their relations, and the performances of art too inconstant and uncertain, to be reduced to any determinate idea." In *Rasselas* the Princess Nekayah points out the difference between moral and mathematical reasoning in explaining to the Prince why no one can choose between marriage and celibacy on rational grounds:

> Where we see or conceive the whole at once, we readily note the discriminations, and decide the preference: but of two systems, of which neither can be surveyed by any human being in its full compass of magnitude and multiplicity of complication, where is the wonder that judging of the whole by parts, I am alternately affected by one and the other as either presses on my memory or fancy? We differ from ourselves just as we differ from each other, when we see only part of the question, as in the multifarious relations of politicks and morality; but when we perceive the whole at once, as in numerical computations, all agree in one judgment, and none ever varies his opinion. [*Works*, 3: 377]

But it is Edmund Burke who, in refuting the concept of human rights proposed by the political rationalists of the 1790s, provides the most complete critique of Locke's approach to ethics. For Burke the meaning of relational terms such as "justice" or "human rights" is not a matter of fixed definition, but varies with their application to concrete moral or political situations. Rationalist theories, which treat "human actions, and human concerns, on a simple view of the object, as it stands stripped of every relation, in all the nakedness and solitude of metaphysical abstraction," are "in proportion as they are metaphysically true, ... morally and politically false.''[34] For it is the circumstances of the particular case which ''give in reality to every political principle its distinguishing color and discriminating effect. The circumstances are what render every civil and political scheme beneficial or noxious to mankind'' (*Reflections*, p. 8). Human rights lie, therefore, ''in a sort of *middle*, incapable of definition, but not impossible to be discerned'' (ibid., p. 71). Their meaning in the given case can be discovered by minds capable of attaining to what Burke calls, in contrast to the ''simplicity' of metaphysical views, an excellence in ''composition,'' uniting ''into a consistent whole the various anomalies and contending principles that are found in the minds and affairs of men'' (ibid., p. 198). Political reason is thus a ''computing principle: adding, subtracting, multiplying, and dividing, morally and not metaphysically, or mathematically, true moral denominations,'' and as such it is guided by intuitions which are themselves largely incapable of analysis (ibid., p. 71). Sound political judgment is often ''the result of profound reflection, or rather the happy effect of following nature, which is wisdom without reflection, and above it.'' ''All our sophisters,'' Burke tells the rationalists, ''cannot produce anything better adapted to preserve a rational and manly freedom than the course that we have pursued, who have chosen our nature rather than our speculations, our breasts rather than our inventions, for the great conservatories and magazines of our rights and privileges.''[35]

Like Pascal, Burke proposes, in place of ethical science, a more modest art of moral understanding—more modest and more prudent, but truer as well, since the art may hope to do greater justice than the science to objects too complicated and variable to be framed in language. But if, as Burke thought, the moral intelligence is too subtle to be rationalized, how is it to be expressed? Today it is often said that this is the function of fiction or mimesis: what cannot be told can be shown, and if the ''circumstances'' of moral situations are as decisive as Burke believed, it is fiction, with the variety of dramatic techniques at its disposal, which is best adapted to give them their full due.

This may seem a modern answer—it is true, at least, that the full realization of the implications of this position, the epistemological defense of the art of fiction as a mode of inquiry, is not explicitly present in eighteenth-century criticism.[36] Nonetheless, in eighteenth-century formulations of mimetic standards—not just for poetry and fiction, but for history, biography, and all the more circumstantial genres of the belles lettres—one can find a considerable though varying awareness of the relationship between those genres and the pursuit and transmission of moral knowledge.

David Hume states that ''all polite letters are nothing but pictures of human life in various attitudes and situations, and inspire us with different sentiments of praise or blame, admiration or ridicule, according to the qualities of the object which they set before us.'' And for Hume, as for many modern literary apologists, it is the mimetic character of these genres which guarantees their value. The object of belletristic moral philosophers, such as Cicero and La Bruyère, is to paint virtue ''in the most amiable colours, borrowing all helps from poetry and eloquence, and treating their subject in an easy and obvious manner, and such as is best fitted to please the imagination, and engage the affections. They select the most striking observations and instances from common life, place opposite characters in a proper contrast, and, alluring us into the paths of virtue by the views of glory and happiness, direct our steps in these paths by the soundest precepts and most illustrious examples.'' They deal, it is true, with ''the obvious and outward appearances of life and manners'' and purpose ''only to represent the common sense of mankind in more beautiful and more engaging colours''; but these ends, limited though they may seem, are at least capable of attainment, and they have made ''easy philosophy'' more certain and more useful, as well as more agreeable, than any speculative morality that has so far appeared. ''It is easy,'' Hume explains, ''for a profound philosopher to commit a mistake in his subtle reasonings; and one mistake is the necessary parent of another''; but the easy philosopher, ''if by accident he falls into error, goes no farther;

but renewing his appeal to common sense, and the natural sentiments of the mind, returns into the right path, and secures himself from any dangerous illusions. The fame of Cicero flourishes at present; but that of Aristotle is utterly decayed. La Bruyère passes the seas and still maintains his reputation; but the glory of Malebranche is confined to his own nation and to his own age. And Addison, perhaps, will be read with pleasure when Locke shall be utterly forgotten."[37] For Hume, as for Pope, the value of easy philosophy, and by implication of the belles lettres generally, is that they give us back the image of our minds, not through precept and argument alone, but through mimetic representations which appeal to the reader's intuitive knowledge of human nature.

Yet Hume's description of the belles lettres suggests that they are to be viewed more as modes of illustration than as modes of inquiry. To speak of precepts and illustrious examples, of painting virtue in amiable colors and of representing the common sense of mankind, is to use the standard formulas of the pragmatic tradition: Hume does not treat mimetic particulars in the way in which Burke treats the "circumstances" of actual moral and political situations, namely, as being cognitively prior and primary—the source of a moral significance which is immanent in and inseparable from them—but implies instead that the belletristic writer's "pictures of human life" are vehicles for moral truths which have their own independent existence. Although Hume played an important role in ushering in the view of particularity which we are seeking, the persistence in his thought of the formulas of the pragmatic tradition points to a fact about eighteenth-century criticism which we shall have to discuss later—that many critics of Johnson's time, including Johnson himself, continued to subscribe to the pragmatic view of rhetoric and poetry and to use its traditional terminology, when the characteristic tendencies of their critical thought reflected the influence of very different premises. It is the persistence of the older view, at a time when actual literary taste was reflecting the partly hidden growth of new assumptions, which makes it so difficult to know exactly how conscious the critics of the middle part of the century were of their departures from the literary theory of their predecessors.

FICTION AS A SOURCE OF MORAL KNOWLEDGE (1): NEO-PLATONIC AND HORATIAN TENDENCIES

The difficulties inherent in such a mélange of competing critical principles are no doubt responsible for the conflicting views of Johnson presented in modern criticism, and in particular for the recurrent placement of Johnson within the neo-Platonic tradition of neoclassicism. Yet it is important to distinguish Johnson from the members of this tradition. Far from representing a "massive summary of the neo-Platonic drive in literary theory," as W. K. Wimsatt has argued, Johnson's criticism in fact affords the most comprehensive alternative to that tradition produced in the eighteenth century, and an alternative unique in this respect, that it constitutes a fundamental reinterpretation of traditional neoclassical values rather than a substitution—as with so many of the associationist and sentimentalist critics—of newer values in their place.[38]

Johnson agreed with the spokesmen for neoclassical neo-Platonism that the purpose of literature is preeminently to instruct rather than to please or move and also that its instructional value resides ultimately in its power of generalization: at their best, both the discursive and the mimetic forms of the belles lettres provide a knowledge which is conceptual, though they may—and in Johnson's opinion should—begin with the observation of particulars. But Johnson differed fundamentally from the neo-Platonic critics, first, in his understanding of the nature and source of the concepts proper to literature—especially mimetic literature—and, as a consequence, in his notion of the literary forms best suited to their expression. The neo-Platonic critics of the seventeenth and eighteenth centuries normally regarded the conceptual character of fiction as an essence which differentiated it from all other forms of discourse. Aristotle had distinguished poetry from history on the ground that poetic statements "are of the nature rather of universals, whereas those of history are singulars,'' a universal statement being ''one as to what such or such a kind of man will probably or necessarily say or do''; and Renaissance and later interpreters of the *Poetics*, variously influenced by Scholastic, Stoic, and neo-Platonic assumptions, had tended to portray the poet as intuiting or creating a conceptual universe which stood in rather stark contrast to the disorderly world of concrete fact and appearance with which the historian was obliged to deal.[39] Neo-Platonism proper involved the belief that the poet could discover the universal (ideal) forms of human character, as well as of natural objects, by an act of introspection which is independent of his knowledge of empirical reality—that, in the words of Sidney, the poet, ''freely ranging only within the zodiac of his own wit,'' brings into being ''another nature, in making things either better than nature bringeth forth, or, quite anew, forms such as never were in nature,'' and in so doing borrows ''nothing of what is, hath been, or shall be.''[40] John Dennis uses neo-Platonic language in advising the poet ''not to draw after particular Men, who are but Copies and Imperfect Copies of the great universal Pattern; but to consult that innate Original, and that universal Ideal, which the Creator has fix'd in the minds of ev'ry reasonable Creature.''[41] More often, however, the metaphysics of what I am calling neo-Platonic criticism involved a vague compromise between neo-Platonism and Aristotle. According to Bellori (1664), beauty resides in the ideal form of each species of natural object, which God joined with matter in creating actual individuals. Because of ''the inequality of matter,'' the objects which comprise sublunary nature are subject to disproportion and change and so are all imperfect. Nevertheless, it is through the empirical study of such individuals, and not by an act of introspection, that the painter is to arrive at the knowledge of ideal forms; for knowledge begins in sensory experience, and the human imagination must be regulated and corrected by an objective and external standard. Ideal nature is thus held to be implicit in actual nature and is known as an abstract idea formed out of the most perfect features of imperfect individuals. This, with certain minor modifications, is the view which Reynolds repeated a century later in his *Idler* essays on beauty and in the third *Discourse*.[42]

Reynolds himself, however, is unwilling to give the metaphysics implicit in his esthetics a literal value: the artist's idea of the perfect species "has acquired . . . and *seems* to have a right to the epithet *divine* . . . *appearing* to be possessed of the will and intention of the Creator, as far as they regard the external form of living beings."[43] He does not claim, in short, that the Idea is a subsistent reality; and, as Jean Hagstrum has noted, Reynolds's reticence on this point is like that of Dryden in dealing with similar notions out of DuFresnoy.[44] In an age and country increasingly dominated by the empiricism of Bacon and Locke, the language of neo-Platonism would necessarily seem anachronistic. Yet it was perfectly suited to express the conceptual nature of fiction and the fine arts as the neo-Platonic critics conceived it, and so the language of Peripatetic and neo-Platonic tradition appears again and again in definitions of the kind of beauty which the plastic arts afford and the kind of truth which guarantees the value of poetry: Davenant associates poetry with the "contracted *Essences*" and "utmost strength" of Nature; for Dennis the order and harmony of human reason reflects the "Order and Rule, and Harmony in the visible World," which the poetic Rules are designed to preserve in Poetic imitations; and Charles Gildon speaks of "the Particles and Seeds of Light in the Primocal Chaos" struggling in vain "to exert their true Lustre, till Matter was by *Art Divine* brought into order, and this *noble Poem* of the *Universe* compleated in *Number* and *Figures*."[45]

Now it should be noted that since, according to the esthetics of Bellori and Reynolds, the process of artistic creation is an empirical one, the process alone cannot always be taken to distinguish esthetic neo-Platonism from empirical theories of artistic invention, excepting only for that extreme naturalism which requires the artist to duplicate exactly the appearance of the object imitated—to make what Coleridge calls a "copy" rather than an "imitation." In other words, to the extent that an art work is held to consist of a *selection* of observed details, it necessarily departs from actual nature in the direction of some form of *la belle nature*. This fact may help to explain the persistence of neo-Platonic terminology in critics such as Hume and Hurd, whom one is tempted to label ''transitional'' in view of their significant differences from earlier neo-Platonic tradition. These critics have dropped all pretense of supporting their esthetics with metaphysical claims; they retain the ideal of *la belle nature*, but for them *la belle nature* has become nature enlivened by the fancy of the artist—and fancy here is a highly individual faculty, not a means of insight into the general or ideal. Hurd's view, for example, of the artist's relation to nature is quite the reverse of Dennis's and Gildon's: there is nothing, he remarks, ''in the nature of things to fix *the order and connection of single parts*. And here, it will be owned, is great room for *invention* to shew itself. The materials of poetry may be put together in so many different manners, consistently with the *form* which governs each species, that nothing but the power of *imitation* [i.e., literary imitation: the authority of poetic models] can reasonably be thought to produce *a close and perpetual similarity*'' between works.[46] The principle that nature is merely an indeterminate source of raw material for the artist fits nicely with Hurd's well-known demand that the poet be freed from the constraint of verisimilitude and encouraged to ''*outstrip* nature,'' addressing himself ''to our wildest fancy, rather than to our judgment and cooler sense'' (ibid., 2:8–9). This is the ''pre-Romantic'' Hurd of the *Letters on Chivalry and Romance*; yet in his commentary on the *Ars Poetica* the same critic can explain in neo-Platonic language that the artist may err by following nature too closely in two ways: ''For, 1. the artist, when he would give a copy of nature, may confine himself too scrupulously to the exhibition of *particulars*, and so fail of representing the general idea of the *kind*. Or, 2. in applying himself to give the *general* idea, he may collect it from an enlarged view of *real* life, whereas it were still better taken from the nobler conception of it as subsisting only in the *mind*. The last is the kind of censure we pass upon the *Flemish* school of painting, which takes its model from real nature, and not, as the *Italian*, from the contemplative idea of beauty.''[47]

To make matters still more confusing, Hurd belongs, again with Hume, to that large number of midcentury critics who emphasize the esthetic value of vivid particulars in a way foreign to seventeenth-century neo-Platonism. Hurd praises Shakespeare for ''preferring the *specific* idea to the *general* in the *subjects* of his metaphors, and the *circumstances* of his description'' and explains elsewhere that *ut pictura poesis* implies a process ''by which not only the general nature of things are [*sic*] described, and their more obvious appearances shadowed forth; but every single *property* marked, and the poet's own image set in distinct *relief* before the view of his reader.''[48] The point to be noticed is not that Hurd is guilty of any theoretical inconsistency in combining neo-Platonic esthetic principles with a taste for circumstantiality and ''Gothic'' supernaturalism, but something almost the reverse: that the neo-Platonic account of the artistic process can be used to rationalize almost any kind of taste. If *la belle nature* implies nothing more than a principle of selection by which the artist makes his work in some way more lively, beautiful, or entertaining than natural objects themselves, then it can serve just as well to describe a landscape by Constable as one by Claude or Poussin—or a novel by Austen as well as a tragedy of Racine. Yet Constable and Poussin, Austen and Racine, worked in very different artistic traditions. The presence in a given critic of neo-Platonic language does not, then, in itself entitle the literary historian to classify that critic as a neo-Platonist. If the term ''esthetic neo-Platonism'' is to be given a precise historical meaning, it should be restricted to those critics for whom the ideal and universal is opposed to the actual and individual as perfection to imperfection, and for whom these terms have an ontological, and not merely a psychological, significance. In this view Dryden and Reynolds can be placed within neo-Platonic esthetic tradition in a limited way, while Hume would be excluded, and Hurd might be called a neo-Platonist in his commentary on the *Ars Poetica*, but not in his emphasis upon the psychological effects to be produced by the unrestrained imagination.[49]

Having said this, we may return to the issue of the conceptual nature of fiction—the issue on which Johnson differs most radically from neo-Platonic tradition properly so called. To the extent that neo-Platonic critics took literally the notion that the poet is to represent the Idea or species or universal as opposed to the factual and individual, they were logically obliged to hold what to modern readers seems a rather simple view of the conceptual character of fiction. For the more sharply the universal and the individual are opposed, the more rigidly categorical the former must become. In part at least, it was by taking a simple and categorical view of the universals inherent in human nature that the neo-Platonic critics came to apply such a restrictive standard of decorum to fictional characterization, limiting the poet, in effect, to moral exemplars— Sidney's "notable images" of virtue or vice—or to representative types, governed by such broad categories as age, sex, profession, social position, etc., in the tradition of Theophrastus. So—to cite familiar instances—Shakespeare violated Dennis's notion of the general nature of Roman senators by making Menenius a "buffoon" and Rymer's notion of the typical soldier ("open-hearted, frank, plain-dealing, ... a character constantly worn by them for some thousands of years in the World") by making Iago a busy and insinuating rogue.[50] Moreover, the same simple view of the conceptual element in fiction is ultimately responsible for two other major limitations of neo-Platonic poetic theory: its inadequate concept of fictional action (i.e., plot or "fable") and of the function of stylistic ornament.

This will become clearer if we consider the logic of the alliance which obtained during the neoclassic period between neo-Platonic esthetics and the pragmatic view according to which poetry is in effect a species of rhetoric. In the degree to which the moral ideas said to be embodied in fictional characters are regarded as absolute and categorical, they become capable of expression in the precepts and definitions of moral philosophy; and it is for this reason that Sidney and, after him, so many other neo-Platonic critics, can move without effort from strictly neo-Platonic premises to the view that poetry is a synthesis of moral philosophy and history, teaching and delighting by coupling "the general notion with the particular example" (Sidney, *Defense*, p. 14). But to describe poetry in this way is to treat its conceptual content not only as capable of abstraction from fictional particulars—as, for example, the interpreter or explicator of a fictional work may be inclined to do—*but as preceding any fictional embodiment in a form proper to itself*. This, it will be noted, is to establish with respect to fiction the same sharp distinction between dialectic (moral philosophy) and rhetoric by which the latter was restricted, as in Ramism, to a merely pragmatic role. So too the role of fiction becomes pragmatic when—to repeat—the moral concept is considered in the light of a firm category, so that, logically speaking, the only relationship that can obtain between it and its fictional embodiment is that of universal to instance or precept to example. When this is the case, the embodiment is—and appears—optional; it has no organic relation to the conceptual matter which it serves to communicate. Thus it can only be justified as a source of useful emotional or imaginative effects *considered as independent of cognition*. Fiction adorns, surprises, moves, entertains. As René Rapin put it, "morality, which undertakes to regulate the motions of the heart by its precepts, ought to make itself delightful that it may be listened to, which can by no means be so happily effected as by poetry."[51] We need not wonder that Horace's disjunctive formulas for the ends of poetry—*aut prodesse, aut delectare*, and *miscuit utile dulci*—became so popular in the neoclassical period in view of the way in which both the neo-Platonic and pragmatic conceptions of poetry contrived to give their disjunctiveness full theoretical support.

Needless to say, the same logic holds for Ramist rhetoric, enforcing in a quite literal way the notion that rhetorical ornaments are the "dress" of thought. If moral truth is by nature abstract, then it belongs properly to dialectic, and rhetoric (i.e., figurative style) is, like fiction, an optional mode of communication. The willingness, then, of neo-Platonic critics to adhere to the logic of didacticism as just described had chiefly these consequences for the theory of literary form. First, critics such as Le Bossu, Blackmore, Gildon, and Dennis think of epic and sometimes of tragedy as formally indistinguishable from allegory and apologue, John Dennis, for example, knowing of "no difference ... between one of *Aesop*'s Fables, and the Fable of an Epick Poem."[52] Allegory and apologue are, of course, the forms most exactly representative of the precept-plus-example theory of fiction, forms in which concepts exercise the fullest measure of control over fictional particulars. Second, the normal vocabulary for discussing the functions of poetic ornament is a pragmatic one: descriptions, episodes, the tropes and figures are said to move, astonish, surprise, or, more generally, to refresh the attention and give delight through novelty and variety—effects which imply the essential independence of ornament and matter.[53]

The formal difficulties to which the neo-Platonic and pragmatic theories described above may lead when applied to literary practice are many and varied, and include, as we shall see in a later chapter, the general problem of stylistic mannerism—a problem perceived by the neoclassical critics, though not always seen as proceeding from the causes given here. At the moment, however, it is enough to mention just one type of formal difficulty—admittedly a simple and extreme one—in order to indicate the value of empiricist epistemology in affording an alternative to the sharp opposition between the conceptual and perceptual fostered by the neo-Platonic and pragmatic traditions. Every reader is familiar with the logical and psychological problems which arise from the attempt to make a more or less realistic fiction serve a simple didactic end; they are apparent in works as different in other respects as the *de casibus* tragedies of the *Mirror for Magistrates* and those neoclassical tragedies which adhere to the convention of poetic justice in an effort to "teach" the reality of Divine Providence. Structurally and morally, such works are weakened by an antagonism between the fiction itself and the moral formula which it is intended to exemplify. Whereas the animal fables of Aesop or La Fontaine may be simply entertaining, and whereas the fictions of the *Faerie Queene* may be sufficiently "romantic" (i.e., lacking in verisimilitude) to be wholly subservient to their conceptual function, fictions which, in Johnson's phrase, "make some approach to the condition of real life" inevitably suggest the inadequacy of the universals they are meant to specify. When realistic particulars are wholly mastered by a simple conceptual scheme they appear "contrived"; for to the extent that they do seem realistic they assert their autonomous right to the reader's attention, demanding in effect to be considered as the ground of a moral significance which arises from them inductively, and thus denying their exemplary function. The conflict, in short, is between the inductive logic of probability and the deductive logic of exemplification; and when the probability of the fiction is sufficiently compelling, the conflict appears to the reader in the light of an inductive fallacy: the fictional "example" does not (and of course cannot) "prove" the truth of the formula, which is then seen as an inadequate summary of the fiction.

FICTION AS A SOURCE OF MORAL KNOWLEDGE (2): EMPIRICIST TENDENCIES

All this goes to say what Bacon put more simply in discussing the importance of history and biography to political and moral inquiry. Moral and political wisdom, he remarks, can be expressed in parable or aphorism or fable; but fables are inferior substitutes for historical instances:

> [N]ow that the times abound with history, the aim is better when the mark is alive. And therefore the form of writing which of all others is fittest for this variable argument of negotiation and occasions is that which Machiavel chose wisely and aptly for government; namely, *discourse upon histories or examples*. For knowledge drawn freshly and in our view out of particulars, knoweth the way best to particulars again. And it hath much greater life for practice when the discourse attendeth upon the example, than when the example attendeth upon the discourse. For this is no point of order, as it seemeth at first, but of substance. For when the example is the ground, being set down in an history at large, it is set down with all circumstances, which may sometimes control the discourse thereupon made and sometimes supply it, as a very pattern for action;

whereas the examples alleged for the discourse's sake are cited succinctly and without particularity, and carry a servile aspect toward the discourse which they are brought in to make good.[54]

Knowledge drawn freshly and in our view out of particulars, knoweth the way best to particulars again. Empiricism posits an organic relationship between the general and the particular comparable to the one implicit in Aristotle's notion of fictional probability, for here the conceptual constitutes an *interpretation* of particular circumstances, which is to say that it is immanent in them. Bacon implies: (1) that the most valuable kind of moral or political knowledge is that which has "life for practice," and that such knowledge is not abstract and theoretical, categorical and absolute, but is limited instead to situations like the one which originally gave rise to it (it is a "variable argument of negotiation and occasions"); (2) that the circumstances of historical situations ought to be allowed, as far as may be, to speak for themselves, controlling the discourse made upon them and supplying a pattern for action in place of abstract moralizing.

Bacon's emphasis upon the priority of circumstances over discourse may be seen as a reflection of his general belief that "the subtlety of nature is greater many times over than the subtlety of the senses and understanding": in moral writing the circumstances must be kept in as full view as possible because they are the test as well as the source of the writer's concepts, whose adequacy can only be measured against the reader's independent view of the facts. In deductive writing, where the examples are "alleged for the discourse's sake," no such test can be applied. The meaning of the particulars is predetermined, and the question, What guarantees the validity of the author's governing concepts? cannot be answered by the work itself.

Immediately after the passage quoted above, Bacon goes on to observe that as history ("history of Times") is the best source of political knowledge, so biography ("histories of Lives") is the most proper ground for "discourse of business, as more conversant in private actions"; then he adds that discourse upon letters, such as those of Cicero to Atticus, may be an even more valuable source of prudential knowledge than biography, since letters have a "more particular representation of business than either Chronicles or Lives."[55] Johnson's respect for empirical fact inclined him toward a similar view: his favorite literary genre was biography. Even so, Johnson was far from concluding that the factual genres of the belles lettres are necessarily superior to fiction as empirical sources of moral knowledge, and the example of his literary criticism may serve to remind us that fiction may reflect as great a respect for the authority of fact and empirical observation as any shown by the biographer or historian. It does so by becoming realistic—by treating particular details with a verisimilitude so complete that the reader accepts them as proof of accurate observation and so as an adequate basis for inductive moral discoveries. Given this foundation, the freedom to invent and select which the fiction writer enjoys may serve moral inquiry in ways which the historian and biographer cannot always duplicate, for those particulars which contribute to vividness and emotional force are not always interesting or even available to the historian, whose search for "fact" tends to exclude the minutiae of individual behavior. This, it will be remembered, was the case with Fénelon's "dispassionate historian," who relates the death of Dido in relatively colorless and abstract language, while the poet's technique of vivid "portraying" takes the reader further into the moral reality of the situation.

We can summarize the matter in this way: a work of fiction meets the one essential condition of empirical moral inquiry when its particulars appear to be as autonomous—as free from conceptual determination or distortion—as objective historical facts. One is tempted to say that this principle is implicit in Fénelon's doctrine of "portraiture." But perhaps it would be more accurate to say that the principle makes the contrasts which Fénelon draws between the conceited style of modern poetry and preaching and the "natural" style of the ancient orators and poets somewhat more intelligible than Fénelon makes them himself. We have seen in the previous chapter that Fénelon's basic objection to witty preaching is, if not precisely to the conceptual overdetermination of mimetic particulars which results from their subservience to an exemplary function, then to the analogous fault of disregarding the empirical value of such particulars out of a misplaced devotion to what may be called the formal universals of style—that is, to one's favorite tropes and figures. Etymologically, the term "conceit" itself— It. *concetto*, Sp. *concepto*—implies the activity of Wordworth's "meddling intellect" either in the discovery of occult resemblances in things apparently unlike—that is, when heterogeneous ideas are yoked by violence together—or, as the term may apply to those *pensées ingénieuses* of which Fénelon's critical adversaries, the French moderns, were so fond, in the expression of moral insights as aphoristic universals in the manner of La Rochefoucauld. Either way, the conceited writer is tempted to regard his "matter" (so Fénelon implies) not as providing an opportunity for accurate moral perception but as the occasion for the exercise of cultivated habits of thought and expression.

Thus in his *Letter to the French Academy* (1714) Fénelon characterizes the typical modern poet as one who "sets a value on all the fruits of his invention; and labours hard to crowd various thoughts into the narrow compass of a verse; .... He endeavours to dazzle and surprise his readers, to convince them that he has more wit than they," and in all this "self-love makes him over-shoot the mark."[56] For, as we have already seen from the *Dialogues*, poetry "succeeds only when it objectifies things with all their surrounding detail." A "natural" poet such as Homer or Virgil "stakes his reputation upon not appearing at all, in order to engage you in the things which he paints, as a painter aspires to put before your eyes forests, mountains, rivers, distances, buildings, men, their adventures, their actions, their various passions, without your being able to take notice of the strokes of his brush."[57] Such a poet, as Fénelon explains in the *Letter*, respects the autonomy of fictional particulars by preserving "an exact likeness" to the objects represented, without exaggeration or "too bright colouring," and by leaving the reader "alone in full liberty" to contemplate the scene which he sets forth (pp. 44–47).

Fénelon calls for a poetic style which will preserve the integrity of observable detail in the same way that Bacon's empirical historian will respect the integrity of historical circumstances. In the same way, but not, finally, for the same reason: for if we are to appreciate the force and significance of Johnson's most important contribution to the empiricist critical theory of his day, the fact to be noted here is that Fénelon's defense of a strict or naturalistic standard of verisimilitude takes place within a pragmatic rather than an epistemological context. Fénelon's principal reason for rejecting conceit is that conceit is not persuasive: the abstract and witty moralizing in vogue among the preachers of the 1670s ''is only a beautiful image that passes before your eyes. You listen to speeches as you read a satire; you regard the speaker as a man who acts well in a kind of comedy; you believe more in what he does than in what he says'' (*Dialogues*, p. 78). By the same token, the only explicit justification offered for the doctrine of mimetic portraiture is the fact that men ''cannot for long be attentive to that which is abstract'' (ibid., p. 94). The ultimate strength of Fénelon's rhetorical theory is undoubtedly that, in the context of the *Dialogues* as a whole, he does not imply a distinction between the cognitive and emotional value of mimetic detail but suggests instead that a talent for vivid portraiture would be a proof of moral understanding. Nevertheless, it is the emotional or suasory value of portraiture which receives the most comment, and this continues to be true for those later critics, such as Hume, Gerard, and Kames, who did the most to give the doctrine of literary particularity a comprehensive psychological and even ethical justification.

Eighteenth-Century Approaches to Particularity: Esthetic, Sentimental, Cognitive

Johnson's approach to the value of literary particulars is specifically cognitive: vivid detail moves or delights us by informing us or (more commonly) by refreshing and clarifying our awareness of what we already know, and is the ground of our understanding of the representation as a whole. It is the cognitive emphasis which most sharply distinguishes Johnson from his contemporaries in empiricist literary theory. The latter used the principles of Bacon and Locke to develop esthetic or sentimentalist theories which led away from the traditional neoclassical concern with the moral value of literature. Johnson used the same principles to achieve a distinctively empiricist conception of the relation between particular representation and general moral truth.[58] Johnson's conception of this relationship is subtle and nowhere fully explained; it must be inferred from a variety of contexts in which it implicitly directs his disposition of specific critical problems. We may best appreciate the uniqueness of Johnson's theoretical accomplishment, however, by looking first at some of the common views of particularity in eighteenth-century empiricist criticism from which Johnson's view is a significant departure.

Except for the *Lives of the Poets*, almost all of Johnson's published criticism appeared between 1745 and 1765, and it was during this same period that the characteristic tendencies of British empiricist literary theory fully declared themselves. The more philosophical and systematic of the empiricist critics, such as Hume, Burke, Gerard, Lord Kames, and Joseph Priestley, shared the common aim of explaining the nature and origins of the esthetic and emotional effects of belletristic writing in general and of poetry and fiction in particular—an aim which also strongly colored the interests of less systematic critics such as Blair, Beattie, Young, Hurd, Joseph Warton, and Adam Smith. According to Alexander Gerard, the critic's proper task is to teach correctness of taste (''justness of thinking'') ''by explaining the kind and degree of every excellence and blemish, by teaching us what are the qualities in things to which we owe our pleasure or disgust, and what the principles of human nature by which they are produced.''[59] From this somewhat exclusive preoccupation with the ''affective'' dimension of literary art emerged three characteristic tendencies in empiricist theory presently of concern to us: (1) insofar as the empiricist critics accepted the traditional neoclassical distinction between judgment and fancy, and placed the source of esthetic pleasure in the latter faculty as opposed to the former, they continued to endorse the pragmatic or ornamental view of literary particulars typical of earlier didactic theory; (2) insofar as they placed the essence of poetry in its power to afford specific esthetic pleasures (such as the sublime and the pathetic), their poetic theory became increasingly hedonistic in outlook, and the question of the moral significance of fiction tended to be left out of account; (3) insofar as their literary criticism drew upon the premises of sentimentalist ethical theory, the empiricists tended either to identify the moral and esthetic effects of fiction, or to regard the former as an incidental and rather automatic consequence of the exercise of critical judgment. It will be noticed that in each instance literary particulars are valued more as stimuli to (almost mechanical) imaginative or emotional responses than as objects of cognition.

Joseph Addison, who perhaps may share with a Frenchman, the Abbé Dubos, the title of founder of British empiricist esthetics, will illustrate the first of these generalizations. In his famous *Spectator* series Addison seeks to isolate esthetic from other kinds of pleasure on the basis of a simple faculty psychology: the ''pleasures of the imagination'' are, he says, ''not so gross as those of sense, nor so refined as those of the understanding.'' And he adds that ''the last are, indeed, *more preferable*, because they are founded on some new knowledge or improvement in the mind of man; yet it must be confest, that those of the imagination are as great and as transporting as the other.''[60] In other words, esthetic pleasures *per se*, and by implication the kinds of perception which give rise to them, have no cognitive value. Thus when in *Spectator* 421 Addison comes to speak of the function of the imagination in belletristic composition he is logically obliged to take a pragmatic view of ornament, and accordingly he explains that writers on such abstract subjects as morality or criticism can provide the pleasures of the imagination by drawing similitudes, metaphors, and allegories from ''the visible parts of nature. By these allusions a truth in the understanding is as it were reflected by the imagination; we are able to see something like colour and shape in a notion, and to discover a scheme of thoughts traced out upon matter. And here the mind receives a great deal of satisfaction, and has two of its faculties gratified at the same time, while the fancy is busy in copying after the understanding, and transcribing ideas out of the intellectual world into the material.'' Ornaments of this kind thus constitute ''an embellishment to good sense.'' And Addison makes at least a gesture toward verisimilitude: in literary comparisons the ''likeness ought to be very exact, or very agreeable, as we love to see a picture where the resemblance is just, or the posture and air graceful.'' Yet throughout his critical writing Addison repeatedly endorses Bacon's view that poetry submits the shows of things to the desires of the mind in opposition to the function of reason, and for Addison the highest merit of the imagination is seen in its power to make ''new worlds of its own'' and to ''fill the mind with more glorious shows and apparitions, than can be found in any part of [nature]'' (*Spectators* 419, 421). Here the distinction between the faculties of understanding and imagination ultimately supports both a pragmatic theory and an empiricist version of *la belle nature*.

In contrast to Addison, the Abbé Dubos avoids the pragmatic view by disregarding the teaching function of poetry altogether.[61] And he rejects the ideal of *la belle nature* on the ground that realism is an essential condition of poetic pleasure. Both positions follow logically from premises which are not merely empiricist but positivist: for Dubos the only valid critical principles are factual generalizations about the experience of qualified readers, or immediate inferences from such generalizations, and the critic's first question must be, not, What ought poetry to be? or even, What is poetry? but, Why do people read poems? Dubos's answer—offered as an empirical observation—is that in reading a poem we are actuated by a ''quite contrary motive . . . from what we are in perusing any other book.''

> In reading a history, for example, we look upon its style, as only an accessory part. The matter of importance is its truth and the singularity of those facts, with which it acquaints us. In perusing a poem, we do not consider the instructions we may chance to receive from

> thence as the principal part. 'Tis the style that is of greatest impor-
> tance, for the pleasure and amusement of the reader arise from
> thence. Had the poetic style of the romance of Telemachus been
> flat and insipid, very few readers would be at the trouble of reading
> the whole work thro', were it even to abound with the same useful
> instructions.[62]

Dubos explains that the typical reader's experience of a poetic text is serial and sensational rather than reflective: the poems he likes best are those which hold his attention and give him the most pleasure from moment to moment. These, therefore, are the best poems.[63] The pleasure in question proceeds, Dubos explains, from the exercise of sympathetic imagination, and Dubos's analysis of the causes of the reader's sympathetic participation in works of fiction leads him to argue for the importance of maintaining an exact standard of verisimilitude—for, in effect, the basic conventions of literary realism. "The power of truth is such, that imitations and fictions never have greater success, than when they swerve from it least." When the poet's subject matter is historical, for example, he ought never to deviate from accepted historical fact, since to do so would be to weaken the effect of his work by reminding the reader that it is only fiction. There is no essential difference between poetry and history, though the poet ought to make his chosen historical subject as interesting and moving as possible by dramatizing it in a realistic manner. Again, since the mind "is but slightly touched with the picture of a passion whose symptoms it is a stranger to" and has "but an imperfect knowledge of passions which the heart has never felt"; since, moreover, when it is shown what is strange to it, "it is afraid even of being the dupe of an unfaithful imitation," we are naturally "prejudiced in favor of imitations, wherein we discern ourselves represented in others; that is, wherein we behold personages abandoned to such passions, as we either at present feel, or have formerly been swayed by." And Dubos concludes that the poet earns his reputation, not primarily as an inventor or designer, but through his skill in "giving the action treated of, a capacity of moving the passions; which is effected by

forming a right judgment of the sentiments suitable to personages, as supposed in a particular situation; and in drawing from
one's own fund, such strokes as are properest for expressing
justly these sentiments.''[64]

As the immediate instrument of such effects, style is to be
considered the most important of the formal elements of
poetry—the importance attached by Aristotelian critics to the
design of the work as a whole is, like that attached to the moral
content of poetry by didactic critics, in Dubos's opinion quite
unwarranted, since neither of these features has a major influence upon the taste of most readers. The principal virtues of
style are, as one would expect, those most closely connected
with realism: simplicity and descriptive vividness. Simplicity
pertains chiefly to the imitation of emotion as expressed in
spontaneous language—for ''where affectation discovers itself,
there is an end of the language of the heart.'' But in all
instances where fidelity to the actual process of thought and
speech does not exclude ornament, ''the poetic style ought to
be filled with figures so perfectly descriptive of its objects, *as to
render it impossible for us to hear them, without having our
imaginations filled with a continued succession of images*, in
proportion as the periods of the discourse follow one another.''[65]

In Dubos, then, the doctrine of realistic particularity is fully
developed as early as 1719: later critics such as Kames, Blair, or
Priestley merely make it somewhat more explicit by appealing to
the nominalist psychology of Hartley or Hume. Priestley's
statement is representative:

Now in nature, and real life, we see nothing but *particulars*, and to
these ideas alone are the strongest sensations and emotions annexed. General and abstract names are only substitutes for the particular, and are therefore farther removed from their connection
with real objects; insomuch, that when general and abstract terms
are used, the imagination must be employed to reduce them to particulars, before any real scene can be imagined, or any passion
raised. Now since general terms do not, without an effort of the
imagination, suggest those determinate ideas which alone have the
power of exciting the passions . . . it is proper that the writer, who
would thoroughly affect and interest his reader, should, as much as

possible, make that effort unneccessary, by avoiding general and abstract terms, and introducing the proper names of persons and things, which have a more immediate connection with scenes of real life.[66]

Again it is notable that Priestley's context is affective or pragmatic: in poetry as in eloquence, the concrete and verisimilar, and the kind of truth or probability which they represent, are regarded as means rather than ends.

By midcentury the critical hedonism of Dubos was widely accepted. For Hume, Gerard, Kames, Blair, Hurd, Adam Smith, Joseph Warton, James Beattie, and Thomas Twining, the principal end of poetry is to amuse or please. Occasionally, Johnson's formula, that "the end of poetry is to instruct by pleasing," is reversed: Beattie explains that while historians and philosophers "please, that they may instruct," poets "instruct, that they may the more effectually please."[67] Many of these critics continued to affirm the moral value of poetry, regarding pleasure (as Aristotle may have done) not as an exclusive end, but as a logically necessary final cause justifying the formal properties (e.g., fiction, verse) by which poetry differed from the other genres of belles lettres. Yet some critics were led to describe the sources of poetic pleasure in ways which suggested that such pleasure may be independent of, and in certain cases even opposed to, the kinds of truth associated with poetry in earlier neoclassical tradition. In his well-known dedication to *An Essay on the Genius and Writings of Pope* (1756), Joseph Warton wrote that "the most solid observations on human life, expressed with the utmost elegance and brevity, are MORAL-ITY, and not POETRY," and that the "Sublime and the Pathetic are the two chief nerves of all genuine poesy"—a standard which pointedly excluded most of Pope. According to Alexander Gerard, "genius for the arts does not exclude that kind of judgment which perceives truth: it demands not, however, an eminent degree of it. But another kind of judgment, that which pronounces concerning *beauty*, and is ordinarily called *taste*, is essential to such genius." Hurd in part defends the poet's use of the tropes and figures on the ground that "the truth of representation [is] of less account in this way of composition, than the liveliness of it"; and Twining, in defense of Aristotle, goes even further:

> [In the *Poetics* Aristotle] never loses sight of the *end* of Poetry, which, in conformity to common sense, he held to be *pleasure*. He is ready to excuse, not only impossibilities, but even absurdities, where that *end* appears to be better answered with them, than it would have been without them. In a word, he asserts the privileges of Poetry, and gives her free range to employ her *whole* power, and to do all she *can* do—that is, to impose upon the imagination, by whatever means, as far as imagination, for the sake of its own pleasure, will consent to be imposed upon. Poetry can do no more than this, and, from its very nature and end, ought not to be required to do less. If it is our interest to be cheated, it is her duty to cheat us.[68]

Critical hedonism was not, of course, an eighteenth-century invention: in the Renaissance Castelvetro, for one, had made pleasure the end of poetry to the virtual exclusion of instruction, and in seventeenth-century England Cowley, Temple, St.-Evremond, and occasionally Dryden were hedonists in poetic theory.[69] Of the most influential critics in France and England between Arnauld and Dubos, however, the majority were moralistic theorists, and the prestige of that group in particular which espoused the Port-Royal maxim that beauty depends on truth—Arnauld, Lamy, Boileau, Bouhours, and Fénelon—was then great. Inasmuch as the estheticism of critics like Hurd, Warton, and Twining reflected a willingness to separate truth and beauty, it represented a new development, and led directly to the unalloyed hedonism of Archibald Alison and many nineteenth-century critics.

Hume, Blair, Kames, Beattie, and occasionally Gerard continued to emphasize the moral value of poetry. They did, so, however, not by discarding the precept-plus-example formulas of traditional didacticism, but by supplementing them with a more moderate version of Shaftesbury's view that the refinement of taste in the fine arts contributes to the refinement of one's moral sensibility, and with a newly detailed explanation of the moral effects of sympathetic imagination. Of these three

approaches, the last, which incorporated the premises of sentimentalist ethics, did the most to advance the cause of literary
realism. To explain the emotional effects of poetry by the new
associationist theories of sympathy developed by Hume and
others was to imply, with Dubos, that the emotional power of a
work would in general depend upon its success in creating an
illusion of reality. Verisimilitude in the overall treatment of
character and action is not necessarily sufficient; what is needed
is a local texture of realistic and vivid detail. For it is "certain,"
as Hume remarked, "that the imagination is more affected by
what is particular, than by what is general; and that the
sentiments are always moved with difficulty, where their objects
are in any degree loose and undetermined." Moreover, "belief
is almost absolutely requisite to the exciting our passions"—
poets themselves, Hume went on, "though liars by profession,
always endeavour to give an air of truth to their fictions; and
where that is totally neglected, their performances, however
ingenious, will never be able to afford much pleasure." Not
surprisingly, Hume shared Fénelon's conception of the formal
differences between poetry and the other genres of belles lettres.
These are differences not of essence or kind, but merely of
degree: poetry differs from history, for example, as Hume notes
in the *Inquiry concerning Human Understanding*, only in its
greater particularity and in a somewhat stricter unity made
possible by the poet's freedom from the historical sequence of
facts. "All poetry being a species of painting, approaches us
nearer to the objects than any other species of narration, throws
a stronger light upon them, and delineates more distinctly those
minute circumstances, which, though to the historian they seem
superfluous, serve mightily to enliven the imagery and gratify
the fancy."[70]

The theory of sentimentalism enchanced the status of a
specifically realistic *enargeia* in poetic imitation and also made
possible, for perhaps the first time in the history of criticism, an
explanation of the persuasive effects of fiction which did not
take for granted the necessity or even the desirability of overt
didactic commentary on character and action.[71] Whereas in

earlier didactic theory the moral content of a poem had often been conceived as a collection of embodied ''morals'' to be apprehended by reason in abstraction from the fiction itself—a process which could be facilitated by the presence in the text of explicit moral generalization—the sentimentalist critic could defend poetry as providing valuable exercise for a ''moral sense'' which operates quite independently of the processes of reflection and abstraction. According to sentimentalist psychology, the moral sense precedes the operations of ethical reason as the original source of all moral distinctions and judgments of good and bad, which it derives in an intuitive and even unconscious manner from the range of emotions aroused by sympathy. The value of reflection upon one's moral experience is not denied, but is seen as complementary to this more fundamental process of sentimental education.[72] On these grounds, the power inherent in poetry to evoke strong and immediate sympathetic emotions could be considered as of potential moral value in itself, regardless of whether it included an explicit appeal to ''reason.''

In short, sentimentalism opened the way for theories of the esthetic and moral significance of fictional particulars which did not require their logical subservience to a conceptual scheme; and, as Walter Jackson Bate has shown, later critics—especially Romantic critics—drew upon sentimentalist premises in developing theoretical alternatives to the didacticism of the eighteenth century.[73] But because the psychology of sentimentalism was a largely mechanical one—a theory of ''conditioned responses''—it lent itself most readily to critical uses as a tool of pragmatic or rhetorically oriented criticism. In Gerard's *Essay on Taste*, for example, the moral sense theory is used to characterize the poet's audience, specifying a set of expectations which must be gratified if a poem is to produce its proper esthetic pleasure. The moral sense, says Gerard, ''renders morality the chief requisite'' of literary works; ''and where this is in any degree violated, no other qualities can atone for the transgression. Particular beauties may be approved, but the work is, on the whole, condemned.''[74] In Kames's *Elements of*

Criticism (1762), the moral sense theory is offered as an explanation of the persuasive power and moral effect of fiction, and it appears in an extreme form. In apparent rebuttal to Hume, who in the *Treatise* had indicated his agreement with Bacon and Johnson that fact is inherently more persuasive than fiction, Kames gave the classical rhetorical doctrine of *enargeia* or *visiones* a new name (''ideal presence,'' or the ''waking dream'') and a sentimentalist interpretation. ''The reader's passions are never sensibly moved,'' Kames argues, ''till he be thrown into a kind of reverie; in which state, forgetting himself, and forgetting that he is reading, he conceives every incident as passing in his presence, precisely as if he were an eye-witness.'' The power to induce ''ideal presence'' depends ''entirely on the raising [of] lively and distinct images,'' which fictional language can do as effectively as factual language: the pictures of human life afforded by Homer and Shakespeare, ''when we are sufficiently engaged, give an impression of reality not less distinct than that given by Tacitus describing the death of Otho: we never once reflect whether the story be true or feigned; reflection comes afterward, when we have the scene no longer before our eyes.'' According to Kames, the moral value of fiction is generally greater than that of history because the former abounds more with characters exemplary of virtue and vice, whose actions and feelings, when portrayed in a way which produces ''ideal presence,'' excite in the reader a ''sympathetic emotion of virtue.'' This, becoming ''stronger by exercise,'' tends to make him ''virtuous by habit as well as by principle.''[75]

Kames's theory of ''ideal presence'' represents a return to the sensationalism of Dubos. Under the spell of the ''waking dream'' reading becomes a purely serial experience, and the ''impression of reality'' which the literary work conveys is perhaps more delusive than illusive: ''reflection comes afterward, when we have the scene no longer before our eyes.'' It was to guard against precisely this reduction of esthetic experience to simple sensationalism, the consequences of which appeared so clearly in the extreme critical relativism of Dubos, that Hume, Burke, Gerard, and others stressed the importance of what they called "judgment," defined by Gerard as "the faculty which distinguishes things different, separates truth from falsehood, and compares together objects and their qualities." Judgment discovers the formal merits of a literary work—the harmony of its parts, unity of the whole, propriety, and elegance of language—as well as its excellence in relation to other works of its class. It also, as Gerard explained, "compares characters with nature; and pronounces them either real or monstrous. It compares them with other characters; and finds them good or bad in the kind, properly or improperly marked.... Truth and justness is the foundation of every beauty in sentiment; it imparts to it that solidity, without which it may dazzle a vulgar eye, but can never please one who looks beyond the first appearance: and to ascertain truth, to unmask falsehood, however artfully disguised, is the peculiar prerogative of judgment" (*Essay on Taste*, pp. 83–87). It was in discussions of "judgment" that the empiricist critics of the midcentury returned, however briefly, to an earlier and more rational standard of propriety, stepping for a moment outside the pragmatic context ·imposed by their mechanical psychology to consider fictional particulars not merely as stimuli but as objects of comparative analysis, and as more or less true. In doing so, they were appealing to principles which were central to Johnson's critical thought, and continually rather than occasionally operative in his critical practice.

Yet there is an important difference between Johnson's conception of judgment, in its relation to sympathy, and that common among the sentimentalist critics of his time. The psychology of sentimentalism encouraged many critics to separate the emotional and imaginative from the judgmental aspects of esthetic experience: it was as though, given an effective poem, without serious flaws, the pleasures of sympathy and imagination would arise automatically and without volition; "judgment" would declare itself later, weighing, measuring, in effect deciding whether the compelled response had been appropriate to standards of good taste.[76] But for Johnson—who argues in the *Preface to Shakespeare* that the spectators at a drama "are always in their senses" and that literary imitations "produce pain or pleasure, not because they are mistaken for realities, but because they bring realities to mind"—sympathy and judgment were aspects of a single mental activity. Johnson's estimate of the moral and esthetic value of sympathetic imagination was perhaps as high as that of most of his contemporaries, though he admittedly talks about it less than many sentimental theorists. "All joy or sorrow for the happiness or calamities of others," he declares at the beginning of *Rambler* 60, "is produced by an act of the imagination, that realizes the event, however fictitious, or approximates it however remote, by placing us, for a time, in the condition of him whose fortune we contemplate; so that we feel, while the deception lasts, whatever emotions would be excited by the same good or evil happening to ourselves."[77] His next sentence reveals his view that sympathy is made possible, and continually sustained, by a reflex act of judgment: "Our passions are therefore more strongly moved, in proportion as we can more readily adopt the pains or pleasure proposed to our minds, by recognizing them as once our own, or considering them as naturally incident to our state of life. It is not easy for the most artful writer to give us an interest in happiness or misery, which we think ourselves never likely to feel, and with which we have never yet been made acquainted" (*Works*, 4:381). This is what may be termed an intellectualist rather than a sentimentalist view of sympathy, and it provides an important clue to the reasons for Johnson's typical concern with the cognitive, as opposed to the esthetic, value of fictional particulars.[78] For the judgmental process described above, which makes possible the reader's sympathetic response to a work of fiction, is the same as that on which Johnson bases his conception of moral inquiry.

The pains or pleasure which fictional representations propose to our minds have a subjective appeal when they seem to mirror our own experience. For Dubos this kind of appeal was sufficient; Johnson, however, habitually seeks to assess the objective authority which fictional particulars possess by virtue of being representative of general human experience: his reader does not merely ''identify'' with fictional characters and events, but estimates their real moral importance. This estimation of importance is based on the reader's sense of probability: what he himself is ''likely to feel,'' likely to experience—or what he can imagine himself feeling or experiencing in a given situation. The reader thus responds to the particular by relating it to the general, but to the general as constituted by his own experience. General nature thus constituted is the fruit of empirical observation and the result of an act of judgment. This inductive process of judgment, which is enacted first by the writer in selecting from his own observations the materials for a fiction, is very much the same process demanded by Bacon: it is important that ''the discourse [attend] upon the example,'' rather than vice versa, for ''knowledge drawn freshly and in our view out of particulars, knoweth the way best to particulars again.'' For Johnson, as for Bacon, the particulars of history or fiction serve as a field for inductive moral interpretation.[79]

3

Literary Realism and Johnson's ''General Nature''

FACT AND ''FICTION''

To understand Johnson's conception of the empirical value of fictional particulars, we must consider the implications of his general preference for the factual genres of the belles lettres, considered as sources of moral knowledge. Like Bacon's, this preference is rooted in a respect for the authority of concrete fact and immediate observation. Although the remarks cited above on the nature of sympathetic imagination embrace the reader's response to fiction as well as to fact, it is significant that the *Rambler* essay in which they occur is devoted to a defense of biography as a species of writing than which ''none can be more delightful or more useful.'' In *Rambler* 60 Johnson argues that biography is more instructive than history because it touches more directly upon the experience of most readers and gives a more detailed account of human character. In *Idler* 84 he argues that autobiography is of still greater value than biography because it is more likely to be true. The biographer, lacking a full and immediate knowledge of his subject, will be the more tempted to rely upon fictional conventions to give it shape and significance: ''he that recounts the life of another, commonly dwells most upon conspicuous events, lessens the familiarity of his tale to increase its dignity, shews his favourite at a distance, decorated and magnified like the ancient actors in their tragick dress, and endeavours to hide the man that he may produce a hero.'' In these essays the moral value of literary forms is determined by a rigorously empirical standard: biographical narratives are more instructive than the ''general and rapid'' narratives of the historian not only because of the biographer's more complete knowledge of everyday

78

affairs, but because the conventions of biography permit the author to "display the minute details of daily life" and to note the "many invisible circumstances which, whether we read as inquirers after natural or moral knowledge, whether we intend to enlarge our science, or increase our virtue, are more important than publick occurrences" (*Works*, 4:384). In *Idler* 84 Johnson is less impressed by the motives which might tempt the autobiographer into misrepresentation than by his opportunity to know the full truth: "Certainty of knowledge not only excludes mistakes, but fortifies veracity. What we collect by conjecture, and by conjecture only can one man judge of another's motives or sentiments, is easily modified by fancy or desire; as objects imperfectly discerned take forms from the hope or fear of the beholder. But that which is fully known cannot be falsified but with reluctance of understanding, and alarm of conscience." The excellence of both biographical genres is to be found in their devotion to concrete fact; the superiority of autobiography lies in the immediacy of the knowledge it conveys. Of all writers, Johnson implies, the autobiographer is he who will be least likely to mingle fiction with truth: he will be least liable to that surreptitious and sometimes wholly unconscious influence of imagination upon perception which Bacon analyzed in his aphorisms on the Idols of the Theater.

The implications of these views for the status of fiction receive their most uncompromising statement in *Rambler* 151, in which Johnson describes what he calls "the climactericks of the mind"—the ages of intellectual man.

> If we consider the exercises of the mind, it will be found that in each part of life some particular faculty is more eminently employed. When the treasures of knowledge are first opened before us, while novelty blooms alike on either hand, and every thing equally unknown and unexamined seems of equal value, the power of the soul is principally exerted in a vivacious and desultory curiosity. She applies by turns to every object, enjoys it for a short time, and flies with equal ardour to another. She delights to catch up loose and unconnected ideas, but starts away from systems and complications which would obstruct the rapidity of her transitions, and detain her long in the same pursuit.
>
> When a number of distinct images are collected by these erratick

and hasty surveys, the fancy is busied in arranging them; and combines them into pleasing pictures with more resemblance to the realities of life as experience advances, and new observations rectify the former. While the judgment is yet uninformed and unable to compare the draughts of fiction with their originals, we are delighted with improbable adventures, impracticable virtues, and inimitable characters: But in proportion as we have more opportunities of acquainting ourselves with living nature, we are sooner disgusted with copies in which there appears no resemblance. We first discard absurdity and impossibility, then exact greater and greater degrees of probability, but at last become cold and insensible to the charms of falsehood, however specious, and from the imitations of truth, which are never perfect, transfer our affection to truth itself.

Now commences the reign of judgment or reason; we begin to find little pleasure but in comparing arguments, stating propositions, disentangling perplexities, clearing ambiguities, and deducing consequences. The painted vales of imagination are deserted, and our intellectual activity is exercised in winding through the labyrinths of fallacy, and toiling with firm and cautious steps up the narrow tracks of demonstration.

The sharp opposition here between truth and fiction—between "truth itself" and "imitations of truth" which are really "falsehood, however specious"—occurs from time to time in Johnson's literary criticism. In *Adventurer* 92 Johnson suggests that the excellence of the first and tenth of Virgil's pastorals, which were "produced by events that really happened," may "be of use to prove, that we can always feel more than we can imagine, and that the most artful fiction must give way to truth." It is an excellence of Pope's *Eloisa to Abelard* that the story is founded on fact, yet so novel and arresting that it "supersedes invention, and imagination ranges at full liberty without straggling into scenes of fable." And of the mythological account of Shakespeare given in Gray's ode *The Progess of Poetry* Johnson remarks: "Where truth is sufficient to fill the mind, fiction is worse than useless; the counterfeit debases the genuine."[1]

On the basis of these and similar comments in Johnson's critical writing, René Wellek has concluded that Johnson is "one of the first great critics who has almost ceased to understand the nature of art, and who, in central passages, treats art as life." Moreover, Wellek finds an "undeniable contradiction" between Johnson's empiricism and the standard of "general nature" which he brings to the judgment of fiction: "There is a contradiction between [Johnson's] constant recommendations of the abstract, the generalized and universal, and his actual practical love of life, of its concrete particularity. The abstract neoclassicism clashes with the new realism; but the former, while deplorable in its desiccated abstractness, did something for Johnson: it gave him a hold on art, some view of the nature and function of art which would not simply identify it with a slice of life, selected and judged by moral standards."[2]

It can be shown, I think, that if there is a major inconsistency in Johnson's critical thought it is to be found in the incompatibility of his apparent rejection of fiction in *Rambler* 151 with his defense of fiction in other contexts; it is not to be found in his simultaneous praise of realism or particularity and his allegiance to a standard of general nature. Given the premise that all "imitations of truth" are "falsehood, however specious," no epistemological defense of fiction, it would seem, is possible. But Johnson's characteristic view of fiction cannot be reduced to these terms. His view of the relationship between particular and general nature, on the other hand, is coherent and comprehensible on the terms which he himself provided for it, though it is true that some of his best-known statements about general nature are imprecise and therefore liable to be misunderstood.

Before we take up the question of general nature, however, there is something to be said in extenuation of Johnson's habit of opposing "fiction" and "truth" in incidental comments of the kind which I have just cited from his literary criticism. In most such comments Johnson appears to take the word "fiction" in a rather special sense—a sense similar to that in which it is commonly used by two critics whom he recommended in his preface to Dodsley's *Preceptor*: Joseph Trapp and Dominique Bouhours.[3] In these critics the terms "fiction" and "fable" are nearly identified with the elements of classical mythology: as George Granville puts it in his paraphrase of Bouhours, "the Poetic World is nothing but Fiction; Pernassus, Pegasus, and the Muses, pure imagination and Chimaera." In Bouhours the opposite of fiction is "truth," defined according to the representationalist standard alluded to in the preceding chapter.[4] A thought is an image—a mental picture—of a thing, and is true when it "represents things faithfully." Bouhours, explaining that fiction need not lie, defends the poetical use of mythology as (in Granville's words) "a system universally agreed on," so that "all that shall be contriv'd or invented upon this Foundation according to Nature shall be reputed as truth."[5] Trapp, who borrows freely from Bouhours in his *Praelectiones Poeticae* (1711), is less tolerant: the wit of epigrams and other small poems "must be built upon something that has an Existence in Nature, and . . . it is absurd to make Fiction the Basis, and the Superstructure too; as they do, more especially, who from the Heathen Mythology supply us with Fable in great abundance. The antiquated Stories of the Heathen Gods ought to afford Matter only for Comparison and Allusion."[6] Johnson (like St.-Evremond before him) rejects mythological fiction categorically: "He that courts his mistress with Roman imagery," as he says of the love elegies of Hammond, "deserves to lose her." To Johnson the mythological conventions of poetry, whether they provide matter for plot (as in Edmund Smith's tragedy of *Phaedra*) or for ornament (as in *Lycidas*), are simply clichés—substitutes for thought, for individual perception.[7]

And this is the objection which Johnson normally intends to convey by the derogatory use of "fiction" and "fictitious." In his criticism these terms express what is now understood by the pejorative sense of "conventional": they refer not only to hackneyed ornament—to "traditional imagery and hereditary similes" of the mythological or other types—but to all established artistic conventions, principles of form, whose use in a given work does not seem justified by the quality of the perceptions which they are supposed to make intelligible. In their broadest signification, the terms "fiction" and "fictitious" can include any and all conceptual orderings of experience which strike the reader as "unearned"—as imposed upon the experience from without, rather than seeming to arise by an intellectual necessity from the accurate contemplation of particular details.

These terms, in short, betray Johnson's concern with what I

have rather inelegantly called the problem of conceptual over-determination—a problem which Johnson, empiricist that he is, traces to a failure in perception. When Johnson says in praise of Addison's poem on Marlborough, *The Campaign*, that "the rejection and contempt of fiction is rational and manly," he means fiction in the special sense just described. The provenance of the remark is suggested by Sir Walter Scott's comment on the poem: "Addison," says Scott, "was the first poet who ventured to celebrate a victorious general for skill and conduct, instead of such feats as are appropriated to Guy of Warwick, or Bevis of Hampton."[8] Johnson's parallel comment is that Addison's poem "is the work of a man not blinded by the dust of learning: his images are not borrowed merely from books." Addison's *Cato*, by contrast, "affords a splendid exhibition of artificial and *fictitious* manners": we see in the play "nothing that acquaints us with human sentiments or human action." And Johnson's other comments recall the issues to which Fenelon responded with his ideal of authorial effacement; *Cato* "delivers just and noble sentiments, in diction easy, elevated and harmonious," and deserves to be placed "with the fairest and the noblest progeny which judgment propagates by conjunction with learning." But Addison's conceptual style robs the play of mimetic vitality, making it merely a vehicle for its author: "the composition refers us only to the writer; we pronounce the name of *Cato*, but we think on Addison" (*Preface*, p. 84, my emphasis).

JOHNSON'S CONCRETE UNIVERSAL

Othello, to which *Cato* is unfavorably compared in the passage from which the above remarks are taken, is the "vigorous and vivacious offspring of observation impregnated by genius." As such, it is not in Johnson's special sense a fiction at all, but something else, for which Johnson has no single term. It is a just representation of nature—"a just representation of things really existing and actions really performed."[9] And it is here, in his descriptions of imaginative works which do not, in his view, involve the conceptual distortion of perceptual material, that Johnson's critical methods become a source of confusion for the modern reader. The "contradictions" which Wellek finds in Johnson can be traced to Johnson's misleading habit of treating the issues of particularity and generality in isolation from one another, as though the general and the particular were distinct opposites, whereas in Johnson's total view these qualities are, as we shall see, synthetically related. The apparent opposition results from a dialectical procedure best illustrated by the *Preface to Shakespeare*. There Shakespeare is praised for being—seemingly by turns—the poet both of particular and of general nature. On the one hand, he is an original writer in the primary sense of that term for Johnson: one of those who "take their sentiments and descriptions immediately from knowledge"—that is, from their own observation and experience. Shakespeare "caught his ideas from the living world, and exhibited only what he saw before him." He was "an exact surveyor of the inanimate world," whose descriptions "have always some peculiarities, gathered by contemplating things as they really exist." He "shews plainly, that he has seen with his own eyes; he gives the image which he receives." The details of Shakespeare's fictions are in the first instance, then, faithful representations of particular nature—of individuals as disclosed to attentive observation. Johnson's standard is Baconian, scientific, reportorial. Such details are not, in themselves, fictitious; Johnson comments that Shakespeare's comic dialogue, for example, is "pursued with so much ease and simplicity, that it seems scarcely to claim the merit of fiction, but to have been gleaned by diligent selection out of common conversation, and common occurrences." Shakespeare's method is here that of the realistic novelist, whom Johnson describes in *Rambler* 4 as being "at liberty, *though not to invent, yet to select* objects, and to cull from the mass of mankind, those individuals [i.e., characters] upon which the attention ought most to be employed."[10]

If fidelity to particular fact were Johnson's only standard of truth in fiction, Wellek would of course be right in describing Johnson's literary theory as naive, "slice-of-life" realism. Such a standard would not allow Johnson to distinguish fiction from nonfiction, or art from life, except insofar as art would represent a selection from the real objects given in the artist's experience. Yet Johnson frequently insists that "the highest praise of genius is original invention"; and he remarks in the *Preface* that "it would not be easy to find any authour, except Homer, who invented so much as Shakespeare" (*Lives*, 1:194; *Preface*, p. 90). Moreover, Shakespeare is great, finally, because he depicted general, not particular, nature, a distinction which seems to imply that his art involves something more than the representation of selected individuals, Shakespeare's characters

> are not modified by the customs of particular places, unpractised by the rest of the world; by the peculiarities of studies or professions, which can operate but upon small numbers; or by the accidents of transient fashions or temporary opinions: they are the genuine progeny of common humanity, such as the world will always supply, and observation will always find. His persons act and speak by the influence of those general passions and principles by which all minds are agitated, and the whole system of life is continued in motion. In the writings of other poets a character is too often an individual; in those of Shakespeare it is commonly a species. [*Preface*, p. 62]

So the questions arise: if Shakespeare merely "copied the manners of the world then passing before him," as Johnson says in his *Proposals* for an edition of Shakespeare, how can his characters not be "modified by the customs of particular places" or by "the accidents of transient fashions or temporary opinions"? Did Shakespeare select, or invent? How does the species differ from the individual?

The species differs from the individual not in its abstractness, but in the quality of the "manners" through which it is represented. In the *Life of Butler* Johnson distinguishes between manners "founded on opinions" and manners founded on "Nature," that is, "general nature." The Puritans of *Hudibras* exemplify manners of the former sort—manners generated by religious and social opinions which were perverse, local, and temporary, having long since, Johnson tells us, passed away. Butler's characters thus represent a type of particular nature. This is an esthetic disadvantage with a cognitive basis: "much

... of that humour which transported the last century with merriment is lost to us'' because Butler's characters ''become every day less intelligible and less striking.'' We do not know ''the sour solemnity, the sullen superstition, the gloomy moroseness, and the stubborn scruples of the ancient Puritans,'' says Johnson; ''or, if we know them, derive our information only from books or from tradition, have never had them before our eyes, and cannot but by recollection and study understand the lines in which they are satirised. Our grandfathers knew the picture from the life; we judge of the life by contemplating the picture.'' The disadvantage of ''particular nature'' in Butler is not that it is concrete, specific, ''minute,'' but that it is unknown. Butler's Puritans will strike most readers as radically novel, and the radically novel in art can only produce the pleasures of surprise or ''sudden wonder''—pleasures which are ''soon exhausted.'' All other esthetic pleasures are responses to the intelligible, for ''imitations produce pain or pleasure ... because they bring realities to mind.'' In Johnson's view of mimesis the ''natural'' is above all the known.[11]

But what is it, precisely, that is known? In the *Life of Butler* Johnson speaks of ''natural'' manners as depending upon ''standing relations and general passions'' and as being thus ''co-extended with the race of man.'' Such manners are therefore comprehensible to everyone. Here it seems implied that ''natural'' manners are as permanent and universal as the ''standing relations'' and ''general passions'' which they express; but in *Adventurer* 95 Johnson stresses their mutability. Human nature, considered in the abstract, is changeless and uniform: ''the anatomy of the mind, as that of the body, must perpetually exhibit the same appearances.'' The ''general passions'' in which, for Johnson, human nature principally consists—love and hatred, resentment and ambition, avarice and indolence—remain ''nearly the same in every human breast'' and will often ''discover themselves by the same symptoms in minds distant a thousand years from one another.'' Yet they also discover themselves through changing social forms. ''Thus love is uniform, but courtship is perpetually varying.... Avarice has worn a different form, as she actuated the usurer of *Rome*, and the stockjobber of *England*; and idleness itself, how little soever inclined to the trouble of invention, has been forced from time to time to change its amusements, and contrive different methods of wearing out the day." And in the mutability of manners Johnson finds an answer to the familiar neoclassical complaint that the ancients have preempted all moral topics. Johnson's argument deserves to be quoted in full:

> It has been discovered by Sir *Isaac Newton*, that the distinct and primogenial colours are only seven; but every eye can witness, that from various mixtures, in various proportions, infinite diversification of tints may be produced. In like manner, the passions of the mind, which put the world in motion, and produce all the bustle and eagerness of the busy crowds that swarm upon the earth; the passions, from whence arise all the pleasures and pains that we see and hear of, if we analyse the mind of man, are very few; but those few agitated and combined, as external causes shall happen to operate, and modified by prevailing opinions and accidental caprices, make such frequent alterations on the surface of life, that the show, while we are busied in delineating it, vanishes from the view, and a new set of objects succeed, doomed to the same shortness of duration with the former: thus curiosity may always find employment, and the busy part of mankind will furnish the contemplative with the materials of speculation to the end of time.
>
> The complaint, therefore, that all topicks are preoccupied is nothing more than the murmur of ignorance or idleness, by which some discourage others and some themselves; the mutability of mankind will always furnish writers with new images, and the luxuriance of fancy may always embellish them with new decorations.

Two points in this argument deserve our notice. First, Johnson makes clear that the universals in which human nature consists are known as such only by a process of "analysis," that is, of abstraction from our experience of particular persons— elsewhere in the same essay Johnson speaks of "conceptions [of human nature] in which all men will agree, though each derives them from his own observation." This view is consistent with

Johnson's empiricism. Second, the object of mimetic representation is not the author's conceptual knowledge of man as it exists in abstraction from particulars, but rather the particulars themselves from which that knowledge is derived—the particulars in which the universals are implicit. It is "the surface of life" that writers are to imitate, "that they may gratify evey generation with a picture of themselves." This is the source of "an inexhaustible variety of images and allusions."

Such advice is consistent with the standard of particularity enunciated in Johnson's periodical essays on biography. The common fault of biography, Johnson observes in *Rambler* 60, is either that it is not detailed enough, or that the details are poorly selected. Most biographers describe the public characters of public men; Johnson wants a rounded portrait of the private individual, a display (as we have seen) of "the minute details of daily life," of the "many invisible circumstances [which are] more important than publick occurrences." Such an art requires the perspicacity which we associate today with the realistic novelist: acknowledging the difficulty of the portraiture he values, Johnson remarks "how few can pourtray a living acquaintance, except by his most prominent and observable particularities, and the grosser features of his mind"; and he praises Sallust—"the great master of nature"—for not forgetting, "in his account of Catiline, to remark that *his walk was now quick, and again slow*, as an indication of a mind revolving something with violent commotion." Biography as Johnson conceives it is essentially a mimetic, not a discursive, art, designed less to communicate the abstract product of an author's understanding than to provide "those parallel circumstances and kindred images, to which we readily conform our minds"—to exhibit an intelligible structure of details. *Rambler* 60 fully justifies Boswell's belief that the *Life of Johnson* represents the application of Johnson's biographical principles. And we may recall that Boswell described the result as a "Flemish picture" of his friend (*Life*, 3:191).

The advice given in *Adventurer* 95 is also compatible with Johnson's taste in fiction. In particular we should remember

Johnson's preference of Richardson over Fielding, the difference between them being as great as the difference between "a man who knew how a watch was made, and a man who could tell the hour by looking on the dial-plate." "This," says Boswell, "was a short and figurative state[ment] of his distinction between drawing characters of nature and characters only of manners" (*Life*, 2:49).[12] Richardson's Clarissa is, I suppose, the most minutely realized character in eighteenth-century English fiction outside of Sterne; Johnson's preference shows how little his standard of general nature has to do with abstraction. If Johnson's principles had been neo-Platonic, and his taste in harmony with his principles, he ought to have admired those genres in which the priority of the conceptual over the perceptual is evident, either the ancient genres which seventeenth- and eighteenth-century neo-Platonists held up as models, or those neoclassical genres which seem compatible with the principles of neo-Platonic esthetics—Greek tragedy, French classical tragedy, the heroic plays of Dryden, the character types of Roman and of neoclassical comedy and satire come to mind. Johnson's taste, in short, ought to have been like Rymer's or Voltaire's. Yet his dislike of most of the above-mentioned genres is notorious. He made an exception of Roman satire, no doubt on account of its realism. As for the theater, when it is not Shakespeare's it is "peopled by such characters as were never seen, conversing in a language which was never heard, upon topicks which will never arise in the commerce of mankind." In Johnson's view of the history of drama, Shakespeare alone succeeded consistently in exhibiting "only what he saw before him" (*Preface*, pp. 63–64).

The foregoing considerations should help us to see that a literary character who represents a "species" is not for Johnson an abstraction, but a fully intelligible individual. Johnson's apprehension of the species in the individual can best be described in terms which John Herman Randall has applied to Aristotle. The process of discovery which Aristotle calls *epagoge* ("induction"), says Randall, the Schoolmen called "abstraction." "This," Randall continues, "was unfortunate,"

for the process Aristotle has in mind has nothing to do with the
process of logical abstraction, or stripping away the particulars from
the universal. It means seeing more than the mere thats, not seeing
less; it is not a process of denuding, but the discovery of additional
meaning. It means seeing not only the particular instances, but
seeing also the intelligible structure of the particulars that is implicit
in the various thats. It is very much like what Hegel called the ''concrete'' universal: Hegel was very consciously trying to get back to
Aristotle in emphasizing the concrete as opposed to the abstract
universal.[13]

Perhaps we can summarize Johnson's view of the relationship
between the general and the particular in literary characterization in this way. What we know is the species, the universals
constituting the ''general nature'' of man. Such knowledge
(Johnson frequently implies) is not so much the product of
conscious reflection as the latent matter which reflection seeks to
put into words. It is not to be confused with opinion, dogma,
belief, or any structure of abstractions. These lie upon the
surface of the mind, oversimplify knowledge, and may often
contradict it; they are often, in one of Johnson's favorite words,
''cant.'' The knowledge with which mimetic literature has to do
is the latent product of one's concrete experience, recoverable—
made available to conscious reflection—through the stimulus of
a just representation of general nature. *What* we know is the
species; *that* we know it we learn afresh each time we read a
successful work of literature, through the contemplation of
intelligible particulars.[14]
The more such particulars a given character affords, the
better, as we learn from Johnson's praise of Richardson and of
the ''ample and general'' characters of Shakespeare. The
universal can scarcely be too concrete, so long as it remains
universal. Johnson's view of general nature is not, therefore, the
view of general nature expressed by J. V. Cunningham. ''To
what extent,'' Cunningham asks in an aphorism from *The
Journal of John Cardan*, ''does scandal reside in the dissemi-
nation of specific circumstances, of realistic detail, which invite
the hearer to re-enact the scene and at the same time offer to
his attention those items of commonness and vulgarity which

qualify the generalities of passion, evil, or social mischance that were the basis of scandal?"

> In these latter some dignity is to be found, at least in the generality of application to others, and in private surmise to the hearer's self. But realistic detail impedes this effect, localizes the general in the particular places, times, and persons concerned, and makes it difficult for one to conceive that this could happen to him who is not those persons nor was in those times and places. So the foundation for sympathy is displaced and there is left chiefly the malice of discomfort at this disturbance of one's social security; the threat to oneself, being suppressed, grows malignant, and the arrogance of spiritual superiority is given full scope.[15]

Cunningham's view surely has its application to eighteenth-century writing. The "generalities of passion, evil, or social mischance," defined without "minuteness" of any kind, achieve their full "dignity" and "generality of application" in the bare and monumental style which Pope created for his *Essay on Man*, a style which Johnson used in *The Vanity of Human Wishes* and which finds a kind of prose equivalent in many moralizing passages of *Rasselas*. It is in many ways the essential style of the age. Yet, for all that, the insight which informs Johnson's conception of general nature almost directly contradicts, I believe, Cunningham's reservations about specific circumstances. For it is implied in the view of particularity given in the *Rambler* essays on biography and in *Adventurer* 95 that the more accurately and completely the individual (whether fictional or actual) is understood by its interpreter or creator, the more clearly will the properties of the species emerge from within its fully rendered individuality. Since there is such a thing as our common humanity, it must appear when an author probes his biographical subject or his fictional creation intelligently and deeply enough. The literary "individual" who remains merely an individual has not been adequately comprehended.[16] The concept of "general nature" exists, then, to distinguish the kind of universality-through-particularity that we acknowledge in such triumphs of realism as Emma Bovary, Gabriel Conroy, and Leopold Bloom, characters which reflect no limitation of moral intelligence—no striving for effect, no personal investment, no ulterior motive—on the part of their authors, but whose humanity emerges with their autonomy, their freedom to be so fully and concretely what they are. Johnson found these qualities in the characters of his favorite authors Homer, Shakespeare, and Richardson, whose "invisibility"—the sign of negative capability and of undistorted perception—compares with that of Flaubert and Joyce.

Since for Johnson the universal is understood in and through its concrete manifestations, we can also say that the concept of general nature enables Johnson to distinguish between meaningful and meaningless (or less meaningful) detail. The concrete universal will remain universal only when its concreteness is of a certain type, that is, when the "manners" of which it is composed point beyond themselves to essential traits. Thus the merely verisimilar, used for the sake of plenitude, novelty, or local color, is deficient. In the *Preface* (p. 70) Johnson compares "the adventitious peculiarities of personal habits" to "superficial dies, bright and pleasing for a little while, yet soon fading to a dim tinct" because they lack meaning. Hence too the distinction between natural manners and manners based on opinions; the latter have meaning—they are not mere surface—but the generalities they point to are still more superficial than not: socially fashionable attitudes, affectations, or opinions which are doubtless really signs of something deeper and more essential but which are represented as terminating in themselves. The latter distinction differentiates "natural" character-drawing from caricature, as in *Hudibras*. The earlier distinction, between natural manners and the merely verisimilar, marks the difference between the significantly realistic and the merely "graphic." It is presumably the latter quality that Cunningham has in mind in his remarks about the "scandal" given by specific circumstances.

CONCEPTS AND PERCEPTS

If the values which Johnson attaches to particularity and to generality, respectively, are not inconsistent, but exist rather, as I hope I have shown, as complementary points of emphasis within a single synthetic notion of the nature of literary portraiture, why does Johnson fail to give expression to that synthesis by establishing the relationship between its components? Johnson's failure to deal adequately with the relationship between concept and percept can probably be attributed to his acceptance of a naively Baconian model of cognition. For Bacon all conceptual knowledge is derived from the examination of individuals and is only as good as the accuracy of the perceptions on which it is based. In his eagerness to stress the importance of accurate observation, Bacon helped give rise to what may be termed the myth of the unconditional perceiver, who is supposedly able to know individuals directly, without the mediation of concepts of any kind. The ideal is expressed in Bacon's metaphor of the mind as a mirror—"a clear and equal glass, wherein the beams of things should reflect according to their true incidence"—and persists in the eighteenth-century empiricists' equation of ideas with "faint images" of individuals as given in sensory experience. In Bacon's cognitive theory, the influence of concepts upon perception is almost invariably portrayed as prejudicial: they are the Idols of the Mind, unconsciously and arbitrarily limiting perception, or perhaps substituting for it altogether. Thus the necessary role of concepts in making acts of perception possible—their function in synthesizing sense data and in guiding inquiry by providing principles of discrimination, for example—went largely unrecognized. (In later empiricist theory, such as Hume's, many of the cognitive functions of concepts were described as habits or, in modern terms, "conditioned responses," a subterfuge which rescued the ideal of the unconditioned perceiver, able in principle to escape such habits.)[17]

Now for Johnson a chief—perhaps the ultimate—test of the moral knowledge afforded in fiction is the accuracy or objectivity of its perceptual content: realistic detail is valuable not only as the means through which the reader discovers (or rediscovers) what he knows, but as proof that the author's knowledge is grounded in unbiased perception. And the language in which Johnson attempts to account for the presence of such detail in a given work of fiction often betrays the influence of Baconian assumptions. For example, Johnson sometimes writes as though the process of fictive invention merely duplicates or reenacts the process of ordinary moral cognition, both processes being conceived as essentially perceptual rather than conceptual. Thus in Johnson's view the original genius takes his descriptions "immediately from knowledge"; Shakespeare "exhibited only what he saw before him"; the realistic novelist is "at liberty, though not to invent, yet to select" from his acquaintance with the world such individuals as fiction may usefully portray; and so forth. Though Johnson admittedly sometimes overstates his case, such statements are to be taken, I believe, not as the expression of a naive literary realism, but merely as a way of characterizing fictional detail as the product of firsthand and accurate observation. In general, such statements seem intended to describe the local texture of a work, not the nature of the fiction as a whole. For other critical remarks reveal Johnson's awareness that fiction is, after all, fiction— something made, a transformation of the author's concrete experience into a novel synthesis. Imagination, Johnson remarks in *Idler* 44, "selects ideas from the treasures of remembrance" and produces novelty "by varied combinations." In the *Life of Butler* he comments on "how much labour it will cost to form such a combination of circumstances, as shall have at once the grace of novelty and credibility, and delight fancy without violence to reason." In *Rambler* 121 he speaks of the "boundless regions of possibility, which fiction claims for her dominion," and in which there are "a thousand fountains unexhausted, combinations of imagery yet unobserved, and races of ideal inhabitants not hitherto described" (*Works*, 7:175; *Lives*, 1:211; *Works*, 5:322).[18]

Moreover, there is an occasional indication that Johnson recognized the hypothetical character of fiction, its specification of probabilities which are not merely statistical but which flow from the question, What if...? In the *Life of Butler* he comments that "poetical action ought to be probable upon certain suppositions," though he does not explain what these suppositions are. And his actual taste shows more tolerance than might be expected of a strict literary realist. His remarks on Caliban, for example, suggest the provenance of realistic detail within an obviously hypothetical or "romantic" framework: "Even where the agency is supernatural the dialogue is level with life. . . . Shakespeare approximates the remote, and familiarizes the wonderful; the event which he represents will not happen, but if it were possible, its effects would probably be such as he has assigned; and it may be said, that he has not only shewn human nature as it acts in real exigencies, but as it would be found in trials, to which it cannot be exposed" (*Preface*, pp. 64–65).[19]

Such statements as these implicitly acknowledge the conceptual nature of the inventional process, just as Johnson's notions of "general nature" and the "species" quite explicitly acknowledge the conceptual significance of literary characters. But if Johnson had a notion of the necessary role played by concepts in the invention and disposition of fictional materials, he did not explain what it was. To attribute Shakespeare's success in representing the "species" to the objectivity of his perceptions, as Johnson appears to do in the *Preface*, does not come to terms with the problem. For it is not, strictly speaking, objective perception which is at issue here; it is discriminating perception. Johnson's notion of the "species" functions, as we have seen, to emphasize the difference between significant and insignificant detail. But what enables us to make this distinction in the process of actual perception? It may be that, as regards the dynamics of actual moral inquiry, there is a defensible (I do not say universally valid) empiricist answer to this question. That is, one learns gradually to distinguish general from incidental traits by noting the differences and similarities among many individuals of the same species. Thus comedy, as Boswell reports Johnson saying on one occasion, "exhibits the character of a species, as that of a miser gathered from many misers" (*Life*, 2:95). But then it is the species—the relevant universals—which the author knows, and which guide his selection and combination of perceptions. To say that Shakespeare exhibited only what he saw before him begs the question, for Johnson does not say clearly enough either what Shakespeare saw or what enabled him to see it.[20]

When Johnson does speak of the conceptual side of invention it is usually, as with Bacon, to stigmatize the conceptual intellect as idolatrous and prone to error. Johnson's emphasis on Shakespeare's perspicacity may be seen as his way of insisting upon the Baconian principle (which, however, never gets explicitly stated) that concepts have valid meaning only in and through the percepts which they make intelligible. When they have meaning of this kind, their presence in a mimetic work does not call attention to itself. That is, they do not strike the reader as concepts—as fabrications of the mind—but appear instead simply as the objective intelligibility of ''Nature.'' Thus it is general nature which Shakespeare represents, not a ''view'' of general nature. We may say that the adequate concept is congruent with its perceptual content as disclosed in its full empirical reality; the inadequate or ''subjective'' concept exists apart from its perceptual content, or is manifest in the indistinctness or distortion of the empirical reality which it subsumes. Lacking in content, it is apprehended as an abstraction. *It is the truly abstract concept of which Johnson, as a mimetic theorist, disapproves.*

In mimetic writing the abstract or empty concept appears most often as an unrealized convention. For Johnson the idea of the hero (''Shakespeare has no heroes; his scenes are occupied only by men'') exemplified such a convention; so did the stories of classical mythology and of medieval romance; so did everything, in fact, which in his practical criticism he describes as ''fictitious'' in the pejorative sense of the term discussed earlier. He usually took the presence of such conventions as a sign of literary imitation, as opposed to the imitation of ''nature''— and properly so, since the literary imitator can be defined as one who (when he is not simply plagiarizing perceptual details) abstracts from his model those conceptual elements which he can turn to use in inventing and disposing his own fictional material. Literary imitation need not, of course, be a bad thing:

if, as is often said today, all art is conventional, then successful works of art must reflect the adequate realization of their concepts or conventions. But Johnson was not inclined to see the matter in this light. He distrusted the conceptual imagination even in authors whom he greatly admired and in whom it could not be traced to the influence of specific traditions or models. He regretted, for example, that Milton saw nature " 'through the spectacles of books'; and on most occasions calls learning to his assistance.'' Though he did not presume to define the mode of Milton's sublimity, he was aware that "the appearances of nature and the occurrences of life did not satiate his appetite of greatness" and that "reality was a scene too narrow" for Milton's mind; this explained for him why Milton "knew human nature only in the gross" and "would not have excelled in dramatick writing"; why, not only in *Paradise Lost* but in Milton's other works, "the want of human interest is always felt"; and in large part why the perusal of the greatest modern epic was finally "a duty rather than a pleasure" (*Lives*, 1:178, 177–78, 189, 183). Again, we are told in the *Life of Pope* that Dryden was superior to Pope in "acquired knowledge," having had a "more scholastick" education. But this is a qualified advantage. "Dryden knew more of man in his general nature, and Pope in his local manners. The notions of Dryden were formed by comprehensive speculation, and those of Pope by minute attention. There is more dignity in the knowledge of Dryden, and more certainty in that of Pope'' (*Lives*, 3:222).

For the most part Johnson saw the recognizably conceptual in art as arbitrarily borrowed and conventionally applied by minds unwilling or unable to keep in touch with empirical reality. Most fiction, he believed, could be explained—and dismissed— as having originated in this way. In the *Preface to Shakespeare*, where Johnson tries to measure Shakespeare's achievement against the full range of ancient and modern literature, Homer and Chaucer are the only authors mentioned as being in any way comparable to Shakespeare in their ability to hold the mirror up to nature; the other authors and genres to which Shakespeare is compared put Johnson in mind of the Roman schools of declamation as their prototype. It was observed of these schools, Johnson says, "that the more diligently they were frequented, the more was the student disqualified for the world, because he found nothing there which he should ever meet in any other place. The same remark may be applied to every stage but that of Shakespeare" (*Preface*, p. 63). The other dramatists, who gain attention by portraying heroes and heroines, "fabulous and unexampled excellence or depravity," hyperbolical joy and outrageous sorrow," evidently invent according to the principles ascribed in *Rambler* 4 to the authors of "heroick romance," Johnson's generic name for the prose fiction written before the advent of the modern realistic novel. Once a man had learned the conventions of which such fiction was composed—"almost all the fictions of the last age will vanish, if you deprive them of a hermit and a wood, a battle and a shipwreck"—and "had by practice gained some fluency of language, he had no further care than to retire to his closet, let loose his invention, and heat his mind with incredibilities; a book was thus produced without fear of criticism, without the toil of study, without knowledge of nature, or acquaintance with life" (*Preface*, pp. 64, 63; *Works*, 4:20-21).

Johnson's failure to find a necessary or positive role for the conceptual intellect in the inventional process explains why his distinction between the literary imitator and the original genius is so sharply categorical. For in his view the mimetic writer confronts two possibilities: either he works a priori, with concepts borrowed from other men's books (in which case his representations are "fictions," not knowledge), or he begins, Baconian fashion, *tabula rasa*, with the contemplation of his concrete experience, and, like Shakespeare, "gives the image which he receives, not weakened or distorted by the intervention of any other mind" (*Preface*, pp. 89-90). But the mind's innate proclivity to abstraction makes induction, so conceived, enormously difficult. Hence Johnson's inclination toward the only form of contemporary primitivism he was willing to countenance:

> It may be observed, that the oldest poets of many nations preserve their reputation, and that the following generations of wit, after a

> short celebrity, sink into oblivion. The first, whoever they be, take
> their sentiments and descriptions immediately from knowledge; the
> resemblance is therefore just, their descriptions are verified by
> every eye, and their sentiments acknowledged by every breast.
> Those whom fame invites to the same studies, copy partly them,
> and partly nature, till the books of one age gain such authority,
> as to stand in the place of nature to another, and imitation, always
> deviating a little, becomes at last capricious and casual. [*Preface*,
> p. 89]

Only "first" poets can be unconditioned perceivers; later writers learn more from tradition than from "nature," and what they learn does not enhance but rather replaces their power of observation. Paradoxically, they enrich their art at the expense of knowledge. In such passages as the above we can trace the issue of Baconian principles in an esthetic individualism as radical in its demands as the Cartesian individualism implicit in the Port-Royal Logic of Arnauld. Here Johnson is the spokesman for a view of the artist and his art which is wholly modern.[21]

CONCLUSION: JOHNSON'S CONCEPT OF MIMESIS AND THE SPLIT BETWEEN RES AND VERBA

We need to keep in mind that unlike most of his contemporaries Johnson repeatedly emphasizes the cognitive value of fiction. Though he agrees with other eighteenth-century critics in making pleasure the criterion of poetic value, he is careful to insist that "nothing can please many, and please long, but just representations of general nature," and that "the mind can only repose on the stability of truth." Thus, for Johnson, Richardson is great for having "enlarged the knowledge of human nature," and Shakespeare's fictions are a source from which "so much instruction is derived" (*Works*, 5:164; *Preface*, p. 62). This emphasis on mimetic writing as a source of knowledge justifies us, I think, in considering Johnson's concept of mimesis in the light of a solution to the ancient problem of the divorce between matter and words, and a solution, moreover, to the problem particularly as conceived by Bacon and Locke.

These philosophers express, as we have seen, a profound

distrust of abstract language and the forms of inquiry which such language characteristically serves. "Men believe," says Bacon, "that their reason governs words; but it is also true that words react on the understanding," with the result that "the high and formal discussions of learned men end oftentimes in disputes about words and names." It would be better to begin with such disputes and "by means of definitions reduce them to order"; but the definitions themselves "consist of words, and those words beget others," so that in the end "it is necessary to recur to individual instances."[22] While Bacon stressed the futility of verbal disputes in natural philosophy, Locke illustrated their consequences for political and moral inquiry, and although he considered a faith in the possibility of adequate definition indispensable to progress in these studies, his objective analysis of the nature of language strongly supported Bacon's skepticism about definition.[23]

As for Johnson, his awareness of the ease with which beguiling forms of words can draw the mind away from its concrete knowledge, enabling it to repose in purely abstract solutions to historical or moral problems, is one of the most familiar features of his thought. We may recall his attack on the "Leibnitzean reasoning" of the deist Soame Jenyns, his similarly motivated disputes with the followers of Rousseau, and the persistent skepticism with which he greeted the various historical theories of his Scottish hosts during his tour of the Hebrides. Or we may consider the empiricist methodology of his own moral essays, which, though "abstract" in a certain sense, normally consist in generalizations derived from and appealing to observation and experience. Johnson's distrust of theory appears as well in certain striking passages in the *Preface to Shakespeare*. The critic, for example, who rejects tragicomedy as a genre is persuaded by reasoning "so specious, that it is received as true even by those who in daily experience feel it to be false." The defender of the unities of place and time "assumes, as an unquestionable principle, a position, which, while his breath is forming it into words, his understanding pronounces to be false" (*Preface*, pp. 67, 76).

Johnson's perception of this conflict between abstract theory and the knowledge won from "daily experience" conditions—really almost determines—his own approach to criticism. "There is always an appeal open," he writes in the *Preface*, "from criticism to nature"—from theory to experience. He refutes the conservative defenders of the neoclassical dramatic rules, not by referring to principles and definitions, but simply by describing the experience of seeing or reading plays. He trusts in the effectiveness of this appeal to experience because he trusts that his opponents' responses as readers are the same as his own; it is only their theorizing which distracts them from what they would otherwise know. In this context, then, we can see the great value of realistic fiction for Johnson—for fictions which imitate "things really existing and actions really performed" derive from and recall to mind that concrete knowledge which the abstract intellect tends to oversimplify or suppress. The "original genius," such as Shakespeare or Richardson, thus writes out of his most reliable source of moral knowledge, and by providing "individual instances," to use Bacon's phrase, instead of formulary plots or characters governed by an abstract morality, he ensures that his readers in turn will respond out of their own particular experience—out of their own most certain knowledge.

When plot and character are shaped to reflect observed objects, behavior, and events, language too will be required to meet a perceptual standard. Mimetic writing is therefore for the empiricist the mode of expression in which the divorce between *res* and *verba* can be most successfully overcome. Mimetic fiction finally forces the writer, not only to create out of reliable knowledge, but to express his perceptions in language which preserves as much as possible of their original form.[24]

4

"Natural" Style in the Neoclassical Era

Up to now we have been considering the value of particularity and literary realism as a means of solving certain problems concerning the status of the arts of language as liberal disciplines. But Johnson's practical criticism cannot be understood with reference to his philosophical position alone (nor can the whole movement toward a more perceptually oriented criticism be understood in these terms). We have seen that Johnson's concept of mimesis is congruent with his adherence to empiricist principles of inquiry, and in discussing Fénelon we have noted that certain stylistic desiderata emerge logically from an empiricist approach to representation, namely, concreteness and transparency of style as qualities necessary for the accurate recording of particular observations. But while Johnson, like Fénelon, applies standards of poetic style which are in most ways responsive to his empiricism, these standards were developed in a specifically literary context and were thus immediately and complexly conditioned by the tradition of neoclassical stylistic criticism; and this tradition modified the simple objectivist demands of empiricism in important ways. The terms in which Johnson evaluates poetic style are in large part the product of this tradition, and they reflect its history; to recover a sense of their connotative potency in their own time, therefore, we must survey the issues and attitudes representative of the discussion of poetic style in the later seventeenth and eighteenth centuries.

Individualism and Objective Fidelity
to Nature

To discuss these issues and attitudes is to return to subjects already treated in connection with Fénelon's *Dialogues*, a work representative of most of the tendencies in the stylistic criticism of the later seventeenth century. The leading concepts in seventeenth-century discussions of "natural" style are *enargeia*, verisimilitude, and *ut pictura poesis*, all of which ask the poet for a "truth to nature" objectively conceived. The stress falls on "images" and "pictures." Among many similar *loci* we can note Dryden's definition of a play as "a just and lively image of human nature, representing its passions and humours, and the changes of fortune to which it is subject"; Robert Wolseley's assertion that "to make a very like Picture of any thing that really exists is the perfection as well of Poetry as Painting"; and Sir William Temple's remark that "whoever does not affect and move the same present Passions in you that he represents in others, and at other times raise Images about you, as a Conjurer is said to do Spirits, Transport you to the Places and to the Persons he describes, cannot be judged to be a Poet."[1]

Probably the term "verisimilitude" seldom if ever connoted for such critics the standard of empirical realism associated with later figures such as Dubos, Warton, or Johnson. In the *Essay of Dramatic Poesy* (1668), Dryden has Neander remark that "serious plays" present "nature wrought up to an higher pitch. The plot, the characters, the wit, the passions, the descriptions, are all exalted above the level of common converse, as high as the imagination of the poet can carry them, with proportion to verisimility."[2] Still, in many of the contexts in which the ideal of verisimilitude appeared, it necessarily connoted an empirical standard, since it was invoked in criticism of styles which were felt to distort or transform unacceptably the objects which they imitated; and in such cases the critic can only appeal to the nature of the objects as given in ordinary experience, demanding that the representation conform more closely to the original. To this extent the ideal of "natural" style represented the claims of the perceptual as against those of the conceptual; of the spontaneous observation as opposed to the studied "conceit"; of the fluid and dramatic as against the obviously assembled and contrived; and, in characterization, of the lifelike and sympathetically appealing as against the static products of abstraction.[3] So Dryden, for example, is at his most empirical in those portions of the *Essay of Dramatic Poesy* in which to the stereotyped characters of Roman and French comedy, the barren regularity of French declamation (Corneille's *Cinna* and *Pompey* are ''not so properly to be called plays, as long discourses of reason of state''), Neander opposes the greater variety and realism of Johnson and Shakespeare. The French plays, says Neander, have the ''beauties of a statue, but not of a man, because not animated with the soul of poesy, which is imitation of humour and passions.''[4] Ben Jonson's superiority to the French is to be traced to his skill in ''the description of . . . humours, drawn from the knowledge and observations of particular persons,'' while to Shakespeare ''all the images of nature were still present,'' so that ''when he describes any thing, you more than see it, you feel it too.''[5]

The style conducive to such effects was often described as the opposite of those conceited styles whose ornaments draw the reader's attention from the objects represented to the cleverness of the poet. Thus in the preface to *Annus Mirabilis* (1666) Dryden anticipates the terms of Fénelon's later and more developed discussion of the differences between conceited or ''analytic'' and mimetic ''portraiture,'' respectively, in remarking that true wit ''is not the jerk or sting of an epigram, not the seeming contradiction of a poor antithesis (the delight of an ill-judging audience in a play of rhyme), nor the jingle of a more poor paranomasia; neither is it so much the morality of a grave sentence, affected by Lucan, but more sparingly used by Virgil; but it is some lively and apt description, dressed in such colours of speech, that it sets before your eyes the absent object, as perfectly, and more delightfully than nature.''[6]

More general definitions of ''natural'' style in the later seventeenth century were commonly modeled on Horace's dictum in the *Ars Poetica* that ''once the matter is in hand, words will follow of their own accord'' (*verbaque provisam rem non invita sequentur*) or upon passages of similar import in Quintilian.[7] ''When a man's thoughts are clear,'' said Swift, ''the properest words will generally offer themselves first, and his own judgment will direct him in what order to place them, so they may be best understood. Where men err against this method, it is usually on purpose, and to show their learning, their oratory, their politeness, or their knowledge of the world."[8] Swift is speaking here of pulpit oratory and may be thought to have a peculiar interest in defending the plain style of which he was so great a master; but in fact the same standard, frequently bolstered with citations from the Roman rhetoricians, is often applied to poetic style during this period with little or no qualification.[9]

Properties of style can scarcely be defined without reference to the qualities of intelligence which they are taken to mirror, and the more thoughtful stylistic criticism of the period normally makes some attempt to describe "wit written," in Dryden's distinction, in terms of "wit writing." Such discussions typically develop the topics of what we have earlier called "individualism" in discussing Fénelon and Arnauld. The so-called libertine critics in particular—writers such as Temple, St.-Evremond, La Bruyère, and Bouhours— stress the poet's need to free himself from the pedantry of "method" and rules and to seek for truth in the resources of his own experience. Whoever goes about to subject poetry to the constraint of rules, says Temple, "loses both its Spirit and Grace, which are ever Native, and never learnt, even of the best masters": like Seneca's bees, poets must be allowed to "range through fields as well as Gardens, choose such Flowers as they please, and by Proprieties and Scents they only know and distinguish."[10] St.-Evremond rejects the "Precepts" of the old logic and rhetoric, and in particular its "Rules of Definition and Division," on the ground that "the Source and Original of the Exactness of Reasoning, whether in Thoughts or Expressions, consists in the Independence and Liberty of the Soul. Nature has not been wanting on her part to give us Ideas enough of Truth, neither do we want Phrases proper enough to express it, if a Man would rather follow his own Conceptions, than those of other Men."[11] And Bouhours compares wit in the writer (*le bel esprit*) to the wit of the freethinker (*l'esprit fort*), provided, he says, that the latter term is understood to mean not one who believes in nothing and opposes all established truths, but one who has the power of reasoning well, of penetrating the principles of knowledge, and of discovering the most securely hidden truths.[12] This sounds rationalistic, but it has its urbane and skeptical side: wit writing, Bouhours explains, is a power of good sense (*bon sens*) which makes things known as they are in themselves, neither stopping short at superficial appearances, nor going too far, like those "refined" wits who, owing to their "subtlety," evaporate into vain and chimerical fancies (*s'évaporent en des imaginations vaines & chimériques*).[13]

For these and other critics of the time a second and not less important prerequisite for *bel esprit* is the study of the best ancient models, in general those of the Roman Golden as opposed to the Silver Age. But the neoclassical concern with the study of sound models must be viewed in the light of what Morris Croll has said about the decline of the doctrine of literary imitation in the seventeenth century: by the time of Arnauld most critics understood Quintilian's warning to the effect that imitation means not the emulation of specific mannerisms but the appreciation of the general virtues of a given style. It was, in the common neoclassical view, the wrong imitation of bad models that was primarily responsible for the characteristic defects of modern poetic style since the revival of learning—this, together with too great an emphasis on the tropes and figures. Thus St.-Evremond, for example, advises the student of rhetoric that "the orations of *Demosthenes*, or of *Cicero*, may very well supply the Room of the finest Reflexions upon Eloquence," but reminds his reader that the ancients differ from the moderns—for the worse—in many matters of religion, morals, and even style, and that ornaments derived from these differences (as, for example, from their "absurd and fabulous Theology") are anachronistic and offensive in modern writing.[14] The best ancients exemplify excellences of intelligence and expression which are perennial and universal, and which the moderns may therefore seek to imitate without cost to anything that is genuine in their own individuality or modernity.[15] Though the "libertine" critics gave the most emphatic expression to the values represented by the terms "individualism" and "liberalism," the values themselves were in no way peculiar to their critical "school" (conventionally the "School of Taste" in histories of neoclassicism). They were, in fact, broadly characteristic of the literary criticism of the time, and transcended the usual categories of the historians, belonging alike to partisans of the ancients and partisans of the moderns, to Aristotelians in philosophy and to followers of Bacon and Descartes. The case of René Rapin is illustrative. Known today as a conservative neo-Aristotelian (the "rules" announced in the *Poetics*, he claimed, merely "reduce Nature into Method"), as a critic and theorist of rhetoric Rapin is nearly as liberal as Fénelon, with whom he agrees on a wide variety of issues. Thus Rapin's devotion to the ancient rhetorical authorities, especially Aristotle, Cicero, Quintilian, and Longinus, is tempered by the belief that even these liberal theorists exaggerated the importance of art (for "there is still less of Art than of Genius" in eloquence), and in returning "to the Fountains" of classical doctrine Rapin finds more to commend in Aristotle's opening of human nature in Book II of the *Rhetoric* and in Cicero's stress upon the importance of general education than in the more systematic and mechanical aspects of their teaching. In the same spirit Rapin warns against the "Scholastick Way" in oratory, against "curious Methods and quaint Distributions in Sermons," and against all use of "Logick in its own Stiffness and dry Formality"; for although an orderly disposition of the subject matter is essential to effective speaking, the ruling principle of disposition is "Decorum," which, like the other principles of true eloquence—"grace," "good judgment," and the "wonderful Secret of moving the Heart"—are much easier to conceive than to express, cannot be taught, and depend ultimately upon talent and an acquaintance with the best models, namely, Cicero and Demosthenes. Like Fénelon, Rapin brings oratory to the test of a strictly utilitarian standard—"Eloquence that amuses the Head, without affecting the Heart, does not deserve its Name"—and, like Fénelon again, in his reflections on pulpit oratory Rapin condemns those who "preach themselves'' rather than the Holy Spirit and ''had much rather shew themselves Witty than make their audience Wise.'' Such preachers, he implies, are ignorant of the truth of Longinus's teaching that sublimity is owed ''rather to the things of which [the speaker] treats, to the Noble Ideas which he forms of them, and to the Elevation of his Genius, than to the Boldness of Expression, or the Pomp and Splendour of Words.'' ''For it is not in a confus'd Heap of many Tropes and Figures, with which Books are so stuffed, nor in a Pompous Arrangement, or in a vain, empty Splendour of many extraordinary thoughts, which surprize and dazzle us with a Glaring Lustre, that this Art of Persuasion consists. For good Sense, which is always most Persuasive, does not sparkle so.''[16]

In philosophy Rapin is an Aristotelian, mistrustful and even contemptuous of moderns such as Copernicus, Gassendi, and Descartes. Yet his conservatism, like that of Temple and Swift, appears to proceed less from a blind reverence for antiquity than from the skeptical supposition that the problems which Plato and Aristotle were unable to solve probably establish the limits of speculative reason. From this point of view Rapin writes a brief critical history of philosophy from Plato to his own day which has this in common with similar histories written by Cicero, Bacon, and Sprat, that it is a history of the fragmentation of a learned discipline. The philosophy of the good ancients was grave and modest, peaceable and quiet: ''Constancy, Fidelity, Resolution, and good Sense, was what was meant by Philosophy in *Plato*'s Days.'' Its subsequent decline—first at the hands of Sophists and logic-chopping Stoics in the Hellenistic era, later in the medieval schools of Thomism, Scotism, and nominalism—Rapin attributes to ''art,'' ''Cunning,'' ''Subtlety,'' ''Refinement,'' ''Imagination,'' to ''the idleness of the Age, the ill humour that Reigned by the ignorance of good letters, and the excessive fancy of disputing,'' which had ''left the Reins so loose to vain subtilties, that Philosophy lost thereby almost all its credit.''[17] For philosophy ''never becomes abstracted till it ceases to be solid. Men retire to forms when they have nothing real to advance; and take shelter in Subtlety,

when they despair of carrying an Argument by Simplicity. . . .
Those who would refine upon all things, says *Seneca*, are in the
sure Method of spoiling all things. Through a vain Ostentation
of Wit Men relinquish what is most essential to Knowledge:
They weaken the Truth of Things by the Artifice of Words, and
fly to Sophistry when deficient in good Reason."[18]

Rapin's remark about the "Artifice of Words" echoes, we
may recall, Quintilian's judgment of Seneca (*si rerum pondera
minutissimis sententiis non fregisset*), to which Bacon alluded
in describing the fragmentation of Scholastic philosophy.

To move from Rapin's criticism of philosophy to his literary
criticism is to encounter a use of the terms "art" (in its
pejorative sense), "subtlety," and "refinement" which is
clarified, I think, by the meaning of these terms in the former
context. Thus, for example, the genuine eloquence of Thucydides is for Rapin an art of *enargeia*, of concrete and objective
representation: Thucydides "*fixes* the Mind of his Reader upon
the *Action* he describes, by so dazzling Colours and lively
Images, representing to his Eyes, as it were, rather than his
Understanding, the things he speaks of, moving his Passions,
raising his Attention, and filling him full of the matter he's
Expressing: whilst the Mind, *dragg'd* along with a pleasing kind
of *Violence*, lets go its hold, and is willingly carried away."[19]
Tacitus, on the other hand, is censured for want of connection,
for "glaring" figures, and for failing to "speak of *plain* things
in a *plain* Manner"; he appeals rather to "Men of strong
Imaginations" than to the "deepest Judgments." His faults are
faults of "Ostentation" which reflect the "too exquisite Subtlety of his Reasonings and Reflections," the "fine Thoughts,
which are spun out of the Author's Brain, and which the Reader
has not always Capacity enough to disentangle from the main
Thread of the Story."[20]

In both philosophy and belles lettres, then, "art," "subtlety," and "refinement" connote the abuse of conceptual or
analytic reason, working in isolation from empirical reality and
perhaps distorting it. St.-Evremond put Rapin's point succinctly in remarking that Tacitus "robs us of the true Objects, to

leave us pleasing Idea's in their room.''[21] And in opposing objects to ideas, and preferring the former, most seventeenth-century critics express their standard of poetic verisimilitude in a language which reflects the persistence of Aristotelian or realist assumptions about knowledge. These critics, however diverse their announced philosophical leanings, stressed the objective dimension of mimesis over the subjective: they were more interested in the writer's fidelity to objects or ''things'' than in his fidelity to his perception of objects or things. They were not unaware of the latter but tended to take it for granted that the two would or ought to coincide: poetry told the truth when the poet's concept of the thing and the thing in itself were the same—when, in effect, the poet knew its essence.

To think, says Bouhours, ''is to Form in ones self the Picture of any Object spiritual or sensible. Now Images and Pictures are true no further then [*sic*] they resemble: so a Thought is true when it represents things faithfully: and it is false, when it makes them appear otherwise than they are in themselves'' (*Art of Criticism*, pt. 1, p. 7). Here Bouhours is trying to explain what he means by truth in poetry and the belles lettres generally; elsewhere in the same work similar terms serve to define the ''natural'' and the ''simple'' in thought and style. By a ''natural'' thought, says Eudoxus, Bouhours's spokesman in the dialogue, I mean ''something which is not far fetch'd, which follows from the nature of the Subject; I mean a kind of simple Beauty, plain without Art, such as the Ancients describe true Eloquence; one would say, that a Natural Thought should come into any body's Mind, and that it was in our Head before we read it; it seems easie to be found and costs nothing where e'er we meet it; *they come less in some manner out of the Mind of him that thinks than of the things that was spoke of*'' (ibid., 1, p. 156; emphasis mine). This is Pope's standard of ''what oft was thought'':

> *Something*, whose Truth convinc'd at Sight we find,
> That gives us back the Image of our Mind.

True wit gives us back the image of our minds because it deals in universals, in what everyone knows latently if not self-consciously; and in the critical period terminating with Pope the concept or mental category is readily identified with its existential referent, so that the subject-object distinction remains relatively unimportant.

Esthetic Criticism and the Subjective Approach to Mimesis

What is new in the stylistic criticism of the eighteenth century springs from a different set of assumptions. According to Boswell, Johnson praised Bouhours for showing "all beauty to depend on truth" (*Life*, 2:90). But the premises which led to innovation in eighteenth-century thinking about style are best described as esthetic; and that, we may remember, is a term whose historical function has been to separate beauty from truth, "taste" from knowledge, and to group together all those responses to literature and the fine arts which can be discussed as imaginative, sympathetic, emotional, or something other than cognitive.[22] In chapter 2 we had occasion to consider some of the theoretical disjunctions which stemmed from this separation of the esthetic and the cognitive in eighteenth-century criticism— the separation of sympathy from judgment, for example, and also the pragmatic or quasi-Ramist theory of verbal ornament which Addison derived from his sharp distinction between the pleasures of the imagination and those of the understanding (see pp. 66–77). Now, however, we must turn our attention to other theoretical developments which, though arising in part from the principles of Addison's estheticism, and from Lockean psychology as presented by Addison, led eventually to a view of the nature and function of poetic language quite contrary to Addison's own.

In Addison's *Spectator* essays, then, the pleasures of the imagination are treated as independent of cognition. As we read through the papers on imagination we discover that Addison's approach to the subject is conditioned by certain Lockean principles which we have also had occasion to mention earlier. Do words (poetic or otherwise) give us knowledge of things? We know, said Locke, our own ideas of things, not things themselves; we know not real essences but nominal essences, aggregates of sense impressions which may vary considerably from perceiver to perceiver. Do words communicate ideas from writer to reader? Not, said Locke, unless they are qualified by extensive definition. Their ordinary function is not to transmit ideas but to excite them, so that, as James Harris correctly inferred from Locke's principles, there is no ''real'' Eve in *Paradise Lost*, but rather there is Milton's Eve, your Eve, and my Eve, depending upon the ideas each of us summons to give meaning to Milton's words. This view of knowledge and language informs the most important premise of Addison's esthetics, namely, that the pleasure afforded by mimetic works is to be traced not to that delight which accompanies all acts of cognition (where Aristotle had traced it), but to ''that *action of the mind*, which compares the ideas arising from the original objects, with the ideas we receive from the statue, picture, description, or sound that represents them'' (*Spectators* 416, 418; emphasis mine). In itself the difference between Addison and Aristotle may seem slight, but its historical consequences for theory and taste were enormous. Addison's ''action of the mind'' becomes in Joseph Priestley, for example, a ''moderate exertion of the faculties''—a far more comprehensive expression.[23] Priestley's comprehensiveness, however, was allowed for by Addison himself: we recall the value Addison attached to verbal suggestiveness, and the Proustian observation in *Spectator* 417 that ''any single circumstance of what we have formerly seen, often raises up a whole scene of imagery, and awakens numberless ideas that before slept in the imagination; such a particular smell or colour is able to fill the mind, on a sudden, with the picture of the fields or gardens where we first met with it, and to bring up into view all the variety of images that once attended it.''

The logic which links Locke and Addison with Archibald Alison, writing at the end of the century, is thus simple and direct. What Addison called the pleasure of imagination, says Alison, is in reality the ''emotion of beauty,'' which arises from ''the union of the pleasure of SIMPLE EMOTION, with that which is annexed, by the constitution of the human mind, to the Exercise of IMAGINATION.'' The emotion of beauty (also called the ''emotion of taste'') is the ''peculiar pleasure'' which results when ''THE IMAGINATION IS EMPLOYED IN THE PROSECUTION OF A REGULAR TRAIN OF IDEAS OF EMOTION.''[24] From this it follows that poetical descriptions are beautiful in proportion to their power to stimulate associations charged with emotion. What we mean when we call a description ''picturesque,'' Alison explains, is that we feel its power to ''suggest an additional train of conceptions, besides what the scene or description itself would have suggested.... They are, in general, such circumstances, as coincide, *but are not necessarily connected*, with the character of the scene or description, and which at first affecting the mind with an emotion of surprise, produce afterwards an increased or additional train of imagery.''

In Alison we find a theory of poetry as revery or mood, and what may fairly be called critical solipsism. After quoting a passage from Milton, Alison comments:

> In these [lines] and a thousand other instances that might be produced, I believe every man of sensibility will be conscious of a variety of great or pleasing images passing with rapidity in his imagination, beyond what the scene or description immediately before him can of themselves excite. They seem often, indeed, to have but a very distant relation to the object that at first excited them; and the object itself, appears only to serve as a hint, to awaken the imagination, and to lead it through every analogous idea that has place in the memory. It is then, indeed, *in this powerless state of reverie, when we are carried on by our conceptions, not guiding them*, that the deepest emotions of beauty or sublimity are felt, that our hearts swell with feelings which language is too weak to express, and that, in the depth of silence and astonishment, we pay to the charm that enthralls us, the most flattering mark of our applause.[25]

Poet and reader are as hopelessly cut off from one another as the characters in *Tristam Shandy*, each bound by the arbitrary and mechanical workings of his own mind.

Midway between the moderate subjectivism of Addison and

the extreme subjectivism of Alison lies Burke's analysis of poetic language in the *Enquiry*, perhaps the subtlest development of Lockean premises achieved by an eighteenth-century British critic. Accepting the Lockean equation between idea and image, Burke attacks the notion of *ut pictura poesis* by denying that *words* are the images of things. We do not, he argues, ordinarily visualize words of the class which he calls ''simple abstract'' (e.g., terms for simple qualities, such as red, blue, round, square, etc.) when we hear or read them, nor does their meaning depend in any way upon our visualizing them, nor do they gain in force when we visualize them. The same is true for words of the class called ''aggregate words'' (e. g., Locke's terms for ''substances'': man, horse, castle, etc.). As for the third class of ''compounded abstract'' words (e. g., virtue, honor, persuasion, docility: Locke's ''mixed modes''), these cannot be visualized, since they stand primarily for aggregates of what Locke called ''notions'' as opposed to ''ideas'' (images); moreover, as ''Mr. Locke has somewhere observed with his usual sagacity,'' words of this class are usually taught ''before the particular modes of action to which they belong are presented to the mind,'' so that they acquire a power to affect us before we attach specific notions to them, and in fact continue to affect us even when we do not call up any part of the meaning which we might legitimately attach to them. And to some words and phrases it is nearly impossible to assign any specific meaning at all: when we read in Milton the phrases ''universe of Death'' or ''angel of the Lord'' we summon neither images nor specific sets of ''notions''; yet the phrases are affecting and, in context, sublime.[26]

In the second place, Burke argues that even when poetic descriptions are meant to be visualized, their force depends much less than is commonly thought upon their excellence *as descriptions*. We do not sufficiently distinguish, Burke remarks, ''between a clear expression, and a strong expression. . . . The former regards the understanding; the latter belongs to the passions. The one describes a thing as it is; the other describes it as it is felt.'' What critics have not noticed is that ''we yield to sympathy, what we refuse to description. The truth is, all verbal description, merely as naked description, though never so exact, conveys so poor and insufficient an idea of the thing described, that it could scarcely have the smallest effect, if the speaker did not call in to his aid those modes of speech that mark a strong and lively feeling in himself. Then, by the contagion of our passions, we catch a fire already kindled in another, which probably might never have been struck out by the object described" (*Enquiry*, ed. Boulton, pp. 163–76, passim). In the third place, an accurate and detailed knowledge of any object, precisely represented (as far as that is possible) in words, is in the nature of the case relatively unaffecting. We not only yield to sympathy what we refuse to description; we refuse to description what we yield to ignorance. "It is our ignorance of things," says Burke, "that causes all our admiration, and chiefly excites our passions. Knowledge and acquaintance make the most striking causes affect but little" (ibid., p. 61).

These arguments support Burke's conclusion, already noted, that the business of rhetoric and poetry "is to affect rather by sympathy than imitation; to display rather the effect of things on the mind of the speaker, or of others, than to present a clear idea of the things themselves" (ibid., p. 172). In the *Enquiry* Burke will not allow that this mode of "display" constitutes an imitation; taking the latter term in the narrowest sense possible, he restricts it to the drama only.[27] But for many other critics Burke's "display" came to be included in the notion of imitation, so that all animated writing could be seen as implicitly dramatic—imitative not primarily of things in themselves, but of the writer's perceptual process and of the particular consciousness engendered by his perceptions.[28]

A MIMETIC THEORY OF VERBAL ORNAMENT

The assumption that what is sublime or pathetic in writing proceeds from the representation of subjective states of consciousness led to a theory of verbal ornament very different from the pragmatic view characteristic of seventeenth-century criticism. The newer view was a mimetic one, and found its classical authority in Longinus, a critic whose subjectivism complements that of the post-Lockean critics and estheticians at every point.

Aristotle's theory of metaphor, we recall, is cognitive and ontological in emphasis. Metaphors, he says, are agreeable when they enable us "to get hold of new ideas easily": "when the poet calls old age 'a withered stalk', he conveys a new idea, a new fact, to us by means of the general notion of 'lost bloom', which is common to both things." For Aristotle metaphor involves the discovery of objective similarities—similarities founded on the real properties of things.[29] In Cicero and Quintilian the pragmatic or rhetorical emphasis is primary: metaphors are a source of novelty, variety, liveliness; they illustrate or clarify.[30] Longinus too is concerned with effect, and for him too the immediate justification of metaphor is rhetorical: metaphors dazzle, move, or please. But Longinus differs from the other classical authorities in tracing the power of metaphor to the sympathetic appeal of apparently spontaneous utterance. Metaphors and the other tropes are, he says, best used to "counterfeit" or imitate "spontaneous emotion," and the "right moment" for metaphor is "when emotion sweeps on like a flood and inevitably carries the multitude of metaphors along it." For art, as Longinus insists, "is only perfect when it looks like nature," that is, when it creates the illusion of unself-conscious "artless" speech (*On the Sublime*, 18, 32, 22). Otherwise the use of tropes will seem manipulative, for there is "an inevitable suspicion attaching to the unconscionable use of figures. It gives a suggestion of treachery, craft, fallacy" (*On the Sublime*, 17). In this context, it should be noted, the word "nature" acquires a relatively precise significance, meaning, ultimately, consciousness and the normal expression of consciousness.[31]

Despite the growth in Longinus's popularity after Boileau's translation of *Peri Hupsous* in 1674, the Longinian view of ornament made little headway in England before the eighteenth century. Dryden and even the otherwise Longinian John Dennis are among the critics who, thinking Ramistically of ornament as something added to plain speech, or as an alternative to normal expression, continued to uphold the common view that tropical language is out of place in the poetic representation of spontaneous expression (as in dramatic dialogue, for example), on the grounds that the use of tropes "showes remoteness of thought, or labour in the Writer."[32] In Trapp and Addison, however, and later in Husbands and Manwaring, the Longinian approach to metaphor begins to legitimize the use of tropes in emotive utterance, appearing often in connection with the growing critical interest in "Hebrew poetry," whose figurative extravagance is now seen as the "natural" and appropriate expression of Oriental sensibility. This development reaches a kind of climax in the publication of Bishop Lowth's *Lectures on the Sacred Poetry of the Hebrews* (in Latin, 1753), after which time the mimetic doctrine of ornament occurs in such writers as Kames, Blair, Beattie, Gerard, Gibbon, Adam Smith, and, at least by implication, Johnson.[33]

M. H. Abrams has traced the role of Longinian assumptions in the evolution of expressive theories of poetry.[34] For Longinus himself the orator or poet was a mimetic artist, counterfeiting, not expressing, passion. But if poetry can be identified with figurative style, and if, as Longinus had suggested, the language of passion is naturally figurative, then it follows that passionate speech is inherently poetical. "Civil society," wrote Richard Hurd in 1749, "*tames us to humanity*, as Cicero expresses it," and "brings us down to one dead level" in speech as well as in manners. But when the violent passions arise, "we return again to the free and ferocious state of Nature. And what is the expression of that state? It is (as we understand by experience) a free and fiery expression, all made up of bold metaphors and daring figures of Speech." Hurd concludes that "Poetry, *pure Poetry*, is the proper language of Passion, whether we chuse to consider it as ennobling, or debasing the human character" (*Works*, 1:104). Such assumptions received support from the contemporary pioneers of historical linguistics, who stressed the radically metaphoric character of all language. The figures, Blair wrote about 1760, "are commonly considered as artificial modes of speech devised by orators and poets after the world had advanced to a refined state. The contrary of this is the truth. Men have never used so many figures of style as in those rude ages, when, besides the power of a warm imagination to suggest lively images, the want of proper and precise terms for the ideas they would express obliged them to have recourse to circumlocution, metaphor, comparison, and all those substituted forms of expression which give a poetical air to language.''[35] In 1772 the great linguist Sir William Jones explicitly rejected the notion of poetry as imitation, remarking that cultures such as the Moslem, with a theological ban on imitation in any form and a consequent lack of dramatic literature, nevertheless value and cultivate poetry of other kinds. Poetry, Jones believed, is the expression of feeling, and ought to be ''sincere'': ''Petrarch was, certainly, too deeply affected with real grief, and the Persian poet [unidentified] was too sincere a lover, to imitate the passions of others.''[36]

Such a climate of opinion was conducive to the spread of the Longinian and Fénelonian doctrines of negative capability. Horace's dictum, *si vis me flere, dolendum est/Primum ipsi tibi* (''if you would have me weep, you yourself must first be moved''), a commonplace of seventeenth-century criticism, was now taken with a new literalness. Blair believed that ''there is no possibility of speaking properly the language of any passion, without feeling it,'' and that it is not to a want of art but rather to ''the absence or deadness of real emotion, that we must ascribe the want of success in so many Tragic Writers, when they attempt being pathetic'' (*Lectures*, 2:312, 507–8). The dramatist who would write ''natural'' dialogue, Kames explains, must ''assume the precise character and passion of the personage represented,'' adding that this is the ''only difficulty; for the writer, who, annihilating himself, can thus become another person, need be in no pain about the sentiments that belong to the assumed character: these will flow without the least study, or even preoccupation; and will frequently be as delightfully new to himself as to his reader.''[37]

So conceived, imitation is indistinguishable from expression, and Art is swallowed up in Nature: the ''natural'' style is seen not as the product of skill, but as the direct manifestation of ''genius.''[38] Wordsworth's 1802 preface to the *Lyrical Ballads* aptly illustrates the ambiguities in which the notion of art had involved itself, under the pressure of Longinian attitudes, by the end of the century. For Wordsworth poetry is on the one hand expression, "the spontaneous overflow of powerful feelings," produced by "obeying blindly and mechanically" the "impulses" of those habits of mind which the poet has acquired through the attentive contemplation of man and nature. On the other hand poetry is imitation, or something very like it, inasmuch as in his own poems Wordsworth intends to trace "the primary laws of our nature," to "illustrate the manner in which our feelings and ideas are associated in a state of excitement," choosing incidents and devising fictions which will manifest the general in the particular. And qualifying Wordsworth's emphasis on the spontaneous and impulsive is his recognition of the need to deal artistically not only with the exigencies of rhyme, but with language, which, though it is to be "as far as possible ... the very language of men," must be purified of "triviality and meanness" and "all lasting and rational causes of dislike and disgust." Still, the role allotted to art is a small one, for even in the treatment of fictional situations the poet can speak with the voice of Nature, in the literal language of emotion, only by an act of negative capability. For it will be the poet's wish "to bring his feelings near to those of the persons whose feelings he describes, nay, for short spaces of time, perhaps, to let himself slip into an entire delusion, and even confound and identify his own feelings with theirs; modifying only the language which is thus suggested to him by a consideration that he describes for a particular purpose, that of giving pleasure." Guided by this sole consideration, Wordsworth goes on, the poet will feel "that there is no necessity to trick out or to elevate nature: and, the more industriously he applies this principle, the deeper will be his faith that no words, which *his* fancy or imagination can suggest, will be to be compared with those which are the emanations of reality and truth."[39] Poetry here aspires to a standard of literal truthfulness with which not even the strictest Baconian devotée of fact could quarrel.

Although what I have called the mimetic theory of verbal ornament shades off into an expressivist literalism when pushed to an extreme, we shall continue to call it mimetic, partly on the ground that the term legitimately preserves our sense of the poet as a conscious artist (as the term "expressive" does not), and partly in order to reveal the inherent advantages of considering figurative language in mimetic rather than in pragmatic terms. The advantages are implicit in the fact that the mimetic theory of ornament obviates most of the problems which arise when poetry and rhetoric are conceived as alternatives to dialectic. To the Ramist or Platonic supposition that dialectic is the expression of thought itself, unadulterated by suasory considerations, the mimetic theorist replies that dialectic is the expression merely of one mode of thinking, and that there are other modes, and consequently other styles of expression organic to them. Figurative style is not to be conceived as an alternative to dialectic, or as dialectic-plus-ornament, but as the proper and indeed inescapable expression of a way of thinking which is neither better nor worse but simply other than abstract and logical.[40]

This point of view, which makes us think of Coleridge, is in fact as old as the Port-Royal Logic. We have seen Arnauld reject the "Artificial and Rhetorical style compos'd of false Imaginations, Hyperboles, and forc'd Figures," whose vogue he associates with the Ramist approach to ornament, in favor of a "less Pompous, and more Barren" style adapted to exact reasoning. This sounds Cartesian. But the Port-Royal Logic contains not merely a mimetic theory of rhetoric, but a detailed analysis of the function of figurative language based on the subjectivist conception of mimesis which we have associated with Longinus and the literary theory of the later eighteenth century.[41] The chief aim of the orator, declares Arnauld, is "to conceive things strongly and clearly in the Mind, and being conceiv'd to express 'em in such a manner, that they may imprint in the Breasts of the Hearers a clear and lively Image of the things express'd, *which not only represents the things barely as they are, but also the Motions and Affections with which they are conceiv'd*"

(*Logic*, pt. 2, p. 139; my emphasis). The figures of thought (and by implication the tropes as well) exist to portray the "Motion and Gesture of him that speaks." It is significant that Arnauld's most extensive discussion of figurative language occurs in a chapter of the *Logic* devoted to kinds of definition, for Arnauld is concerned with the ways in which ornament embodies meaning, and thus enters into the conceptual process of the speaker.

Arnauld notes that many words have the potential for two distinct kinds of meaning and may thus be defined in two ways. Philosophic definition gives the technical meaning of a term as it is used in scientific discourse, lexical definition the meaning as determined by common usage. The orator is usually concerned with the second kind, since he normally treats moral subjects in the context of ordinary experience rather than philosophically. The grammarians, Arnauld remarks, who are responsible for lexical definition, seldom give a complete account of the ordinary meanings of words because they neglect what today would be called their connotations.[42] Arnauld's terms for the distinction between denotation and connotation are "principal" and "accessory" ideas, and he goes on to illustrate this distinction by explaining that the statement, *You lie*, is not equivalent to the statement, *You know the contrary of what you affirm*, because the former includes, in addition to the "principal" idea, the "accessory" ideas of scorn and contempt. The "accessory" aspect of meaning, Arnauld continues, is what chiefly determines the difference between a plain and a figured style, and he explains why one is often more "lovely" than the other:

Which proceeds from hence, that figur'd expressions, besides the principal thing, signifie the Motion and Gesture of him that speaks, and imprint both the one and the other *Idea* in the mind, whereas simple expressions set forth only the naked Truth: For example, if this half verse of *Virgil*,

   Usque adeone mori miserum est?

were express'd simply and without a Figure,

   Non est neque adeo mori miserum.

> Without doubt the sentence would not have had that force; and the
> reason is, because the first Expression signifies more then [*sic*] the
> second; for it does not only express the Thought, that it is not so mis-
> erable a thing as Men think to die; but it represents also the *Idea* of a
> Man, as it were provoking death, and undauntedly looking it in the
> face, which, without question is a great and lively Accession to the
> signification of the words. [Ibid., pt. 1, pp. 142–55]

The first expression signifies more than the second. Pragmatic
theories of rhetoric obscure the relationship between the twin
issues of right rhetoric, truth and persuasiveness, by treating
them in separate frames of reference. Truth is abstract, a matter
of logic and of the commonplace tradition; ornament, on the
other hand, is said to please or move on account of its novelty,
variety, or vividness. Arnauld reunites the issues of truth and
persuasiveness in arguing that, if the ornamented expression is
more pleasing or moving than its plain "equivalent," this is
because it is more significant, and significant not only of the
speaker's "feeling" or "emotion"—as though "emotion"
were ever really separable from "thought"—but of a complex
attitude or awareness on his part. This is the full meaning, then,
for rhetorical theory, of Arnauld's maxim that "there is nothing
lovely but what is true." The essential function of verbal
ornament is not to persuade but to disclose—artistically to
"imitate"—a complex act of apprehension. Conception and
expression, invention and style, are here seen as aspects of one
another, and figurative language as an instrument of thought.[43]
Implicit in this mimetic view of eloquence is a denial that moral
truth is to be identified with logic or purely conceptual
thinking; Arnauld's theory of ornament complements Pascal's
esprit de finesse and Burke's conception of moral knowledge as a
complicated and semi-intuitive "wisdom of the heart."[44]

We have seen that subjectivist critical theory in eighteenth-
century England tended to be esthetic in emphasis, in the sense
that literary effects such as the beautiful, the pathetic, and the
sublime were often treated without regard to questions of truth.
The example of Arnauld shows clearly that this separation of
pleasure from truth is not naturally incident to a subjectivist
approach to mimesis. And after Arnauld, Fénelon shows the
same thing more clearly still. In chapter 1 we stressed the

objectivist character of Fénelon's rhetorical thought, with its emphasis on "portraiture," or the concrete and dramatic rendering of the experience of people other than the speaker himself. But the *Dialogues on Eloquence* contain a subjective counterpart to "portraiture" in the theory of what Fénelon calls "movements," which refer to the depiction, in language or physical gesture, of the speaker's emotional response to his subject. In reply to the question, "What movement can there be in words?" Speaker A, Fénelon's principal spokesman, quotes from the *De Oratore* an asyndetic passage from a speech attributed to Gracchus ("Wretched: Where shall I go? What sanctuary remains to me? The Capitol?" etc.). Put these "broken sentences which so well mark nature in the transports of grief" into connected, declarative prose, says Speaker A, and they will lose their mimetic vivacity. For "the manner of saying things makes visible the manner in which one feels them, and it is this which strikes the listeners the more."[45] In Fénelon the aims of "portraiture" and "movements," taken together, define the function of figurative language, which is, accordingly, to assist in registering the speaker's total (i. e., "objective") concrete reality. This distinction between objective and subjective mimesis reappears in Fénelon's *Letter to the French Academy*, where, after setting forth his ideal of poetic self-effacement in the interests of dramatic objectivity, Fénelon remarks that "the ancients did not think it enough to copy nature exactly: their pictures were moving, as well as true" (*Letter*, p. 49). When the poet speaks about himself, for example, let it be with the "tender simplicity" of a Catullus: "Odi, et amo: quare id faciam fortasse requiris. / Nescio, sed fieri sentio, et excrucior."[46] "How much," asks Fénelon, "are the elaborate witty conceits of Ovid and Martial inferior to these negligent words; where the distracted heart alone speaks in a kind of despair?" (ibid., p. 56). Fénelon's point of view here is that of Johnson or Wordsworth: the "natural" expression of subjective experience has the objective truth of dramatic probability. Conversely, the conceited style falsifies the process of subjective apprehension as well as the nature of what the speaker apprehends.

English critics were late to grasp the advantages of the mimetic theory of ornament developed by Arnauld and Fénelon. In 1762, however, exactly a century after the appearance of *L'Art de Penser*, Adam Smith explicitly rejected the pragmatic view of ornament in favor of an Arnauldian approach to the nature of persuasive speaking. The ancients, said Smith, finding that what they called tropes and figures of speech were frequently met with in the most striking and beautiful passages of poetry and prose, unwisely concluded that the figures gave the passages their beauty. "But the case is far otherwise. When the sentiment of the speaker is expressed in a neat, clear, plain, and clever manner, and the passion or affection he is possessed of and intends, *by sympathy*, to communicate to his hearer, is plainly and cleverly hit off, then and then only the expression has all the force and beauty that language can give it." The figures of speech contribute to the beauty of expression "only so far as they happen to be the just and natural forms of expressing ... sentiment." "When they are more proper than the common forms of speaking, then they are to be used; but not otherwise" (*Lectures*, pp. 22–23). The ornaments, in short, are not ornaments when correctly used, but expressions as proper as the so-called proper ones from which they are distinguished in traditional rhetoric. They are proper because the "passion or affection" which they express is as vital a part of what is being communicated as the thought ("sentiment") of the speaker.[47]

By regarding conception and style as inseparable, then, the mimetic theory of ornament overcame that "undoubtedly absurd and unprofitable and reprehensible severance between the tongue and the brain" which Cicero had so long ago complained of and freed rhetoric and poetry (considered as modes of discourse) from the awkward position of being in potential competition with dialectic.[48] The influence of the theory upon critical practice was gradual, and did not manifest itself completely until the end of the eighteenth century. During the period between Lowth and Wordsworth, critics interested in describing the structure of "natural" styles in prose and poetry gave almost all of their attention to syntax.

Discussions of "natural" style in poetry emphasized the drama, Shakespeare being the universal favorite as a model of natural dialogue. The issues continued to be those raised by Dryden and the other seventeenth-century critics of declamation and conceit, and Shakespeare's "nature" was typically opposed to the connected "artificial" rhetoric of Dryden, Rowe, Corneille, and sometimes Racine.

Critics like Kames and Gerard elaborate the differences between these two general kinds of style with a new minuteness born of their fascination with the descriptive possibilities of associationism. For a mimetic style simply registers the motions of the mind, and the mind moves according to the laws of association, as *Hamlet* is often called upon to demonstrate:

> to die; to sleep;—
> To sleep? Perchance to dream! Ay, there's the rub . . . [49]

But the laws of association are not to be taken as abstract principles which make unnecessary the poet's imaginative participation in his characters' feelings. Dramatic poetry fails, says Gerard, when the poet,

> having conceived some of the objects strictly connected with a passion, considers that object only in general and abstractly as a present perception; he therefore allows himself to run into such a train of thought as that object present to the mind would dictate if it were unconnected with any passion; he goes on coolly imagining such ideas as it suggests by means of any of the principles of association; and he makes the person possessed by the passion to express all these ideas. He feels not the passion, he has not the force of genius or sensibility of heart sufficient for conceiving how it would affect a person who felt it, or for entering into the sentiments which it would produce in him. The sentiments which he makes him utter might all be very proper in a description, a discourse, or a meditation occasioned by the view of such an object; but they are not natural to a person in whom that object produces a suitable passion. In order to conceive sentiments natural to him, the poet ought to have confined himself to the consideration of the object in this one point of view, as strictly connected with a passion and suggested by it; he ought to indulge only such a train of thought as it would lead to in these circumstances, or such a train as the passion with which it is presently

connected would introduce into the mind of a person under the power of that passion.[50]

The bad dramatic poet considers his object ''only in general and abstractly'': it is again the problem of conceptual overdetermination, the failure of negative capability, but described in a new and, in its way, very precise vocabulary. The effect of the new criticism is a sharpening of emphasis, a clarification of the demand for a perceptive and perceptual style in poetry.

A MIMETIC APPROACH TO ''NATURAL'' STYLE: THE PROBLEM OF ''POETIC DICTION''

We are apt to feel now that if spontaneity is the hallmark of ''natural'' style, that style should be spontaneous in diction as well as in syntax, and we are puzzled to find critics of the later eighteenth century paying so little attention to the problem of coterie language. There are, to be sure, signs of dissatisfaction with contemporary poetic diction, and the increasing taste for naturalistic and ''minute'' description bespeaks a demand for a more perceptive language than descriptive writing in the tradition of Pope normally affords. Nevertheless, Wordsworth's two prefaces to the *Lyrical Ballads* (1800, 1802), taken together, constitute the first thorough-going Longinian criticism of poetic diction in English. Here at last the principle of verisimilitude is separated from the classical and neoclassical doctrine of the three levels of style, and the latter doctrine—the main theoretical support of eighteenth-century ''poetic diction'' in Wordsworth's sense of the term—is repudiated, along with the pragmatic view of ornament with which Wordsworth rightly associates it. Thus to condemn ''poetic diction'' it is enough simply to identify it as such; it is not the ''natural'' language of imagination or feeling, but a specialized vocabulary of ''phrases and figures of speech which from father to son have long been regarded as the common inheritance of poets.'' Its uses have been rhetorical rather than mimetic: ''to elevate the style, and raise it above prose''; to minister to a cultural expectation that metrical writing will employ a ''particular language''; to impress (as Wordsworth shrewdly says) ''a notion of the peculiarity and exaltation of the Poet's character, and [to flatter] the Reader's self-love by bringing him nearer to a sympathy with that character." But these purposes conflict with mimetic truth. The genuine ornaments of poetry—"the emanations of reality and truth"—are to be sought in the nature of the subject, which, if "judiciously chosen," will "naturally, and upon fit occasion, lead him to passions the language of which, if selected truly and judiciously, must necessarily be dignified and variegated, and alive with metaphors and figures. I forbear to speak of an incongruity which would shock the intelligent Reader, should the Poet interweave any foreign splendour of his own with that which the passion naturally suggests."⁵¹

But as Wordsworth's critical thinking matured he came to approach the problem of poetic diction from a somewhat different point of view. For lack of verisimilitude is neither the only nor the primary fault of eighteenth-century poetic diction. The principal difficulty with the eighteenth-century stock phrase—or "kenning," as Professor Tillotson significantly calls it—especially when it purports to imitate feeling or describe physical objects, lies precisely in its difference from the real kenning as found in *Beowulf* or Homer. The real kenning is a form of public language; in its unchanging conventionality it is an emblem of continuity and community of feeling, and therefore of the ritual or ceremonial function of the so-called primary epic. The modern reader does not wish it away, nor does he merely savor its quaintness; instead, because the experiences and concerns which epics celebrate—courage, death, national destiny—are universal, he participates in the community which the epic defines, if only self-consciously and temporarily, by a partially willed act of imagination; thus the kenning keeps for him some measure of its emblematic power. The neoclassical kenning is a form of public language too, inviting the reader to rehearse feelings and attitudes preestablished by and definitive of a community. But in this case the community is composed of certain poets and their readers; it is a coterie. A reader contemporary with it may wish to include himself in it or not. If he does, he will no doubt be moved by the conventionalities of its style in somewhat the same way as the participant in the larger community of the epic. But here we are dealing, not with universals, but with fashions in language and feeling; and fashions in both change, and the mannerisms which give the feelings currency become dated. For the reader who survives the coterie, its kennings must lose their power (if they do not, indeed, become objects of disgust), for they are emblems now of the unworthy, of a community which found its identity in feelings now discarded or outgrown.

Such a reader will then perceive the essential difference between the two kinds of kenning, namely, that the valid kenning appears to be the product of a culture, while the literary kenning too obviously originates with a particular writer. Homer and the *Beowulf* poet are effaced and anonymous; it is not their voices we hear but the voices of their communities. But the eighteenth-century kenning is simply a characteristic and rather intrusive ornament imitated or plagiarized from Milton or Spenser or Pope or Virgil or someone else. The reader who has outgrown its community (as Wordsworth and Coleridge did in their twenties) reads these poets and their imitators as individuals, and in the context of individualism the kenning is merely a piece of stock diction asking for a stock response. It is neither public language nor private (in the sense of individual), for it registers merely an absence, a failure in experience or perception. It is a formula in the common and modern pejorative sense of the word, an abstract or empty universal, imitated and imitable, which is to say capable of repeated and mechanical use as a substitute for genuine intuition.

Wordsworth came increasingly to regard the mannerisms of eighteenth-century verse in this light as he became increasingly aware of the dependence of style upon perception. In the prefaces of 1800 and 1802, as we have seen, he stresses the Longinian principle of verisimilitude: eighteenth-century diction is faulty because it is not "a selection of language really used by men." Yet even here a concern for perceptual accuracy is evident; Wordsworth has "at all times endeavoured to look steadily at [his] subject," and hopes that there is in the *Lyrical Ballads* "little falsehood of description." His later criticisms of eighteenth-century diction stress its imperceptiveness. "The poetry of the period intervening between the publication of the Paradise Lost and the Seasons," he writes in a supplement to the preface of 1815, "does not contain a single new image of external nature; and scarcely presents a familiar one from which it can be inferred that the eye of the Poet had been steadily fixed upon his object" (*Poetical Works*, 2:419–20). So too the period diction and predictable syntax of Pope's epitaphs, which Wordsworth examines in his *Essay on Epitaphs* (1810), convict Pope of writing out of habits which replaced an intuitive, sympathetic understanding of his subject. That the epitaph by its nature admits little more than the restatement of commonplaces is no objection in Pope's favor, for the poet's task is to rescue the commonplace from mere abstraction by experiencing it in language peculiarly his own: "it is required that these truths should be instinctively ejaculated or should rise irresistibly from the circumstances; in a word that they should be uttered in such connection as shall make it felt that they are not adopted, not spoken by rote, but *perceived* in their whole compass with the freshness and clearness of an original intuition."[52] Where Pope's style is mechanical, language is all too obviously the "dress" of thought, and Wordsworth rejects the favorite neoclassical metaphor in rejecting the style: words "are not what the garb is to the body but what the body is to the soul, themselves a constituent part and power or function in the thought." "If words be not . . . an incarnation of the thought, but only a clothing of it, then surely will they prove an ill gift; such a one as those possessed vestments, read of in the stories of superstitious times, which had power to consume and to alienate from his right mind the victim who put them on."[53]

In the *Biographia Literaria* Coleridge criticizes Wordsworth's principle of verisimilitude in poetic diction by remarking that "were there excluded from Mr. Wordsworth's poetic compositions all, that a literal adherence to the theory of his preface *would* exclude, two-thirds at least of the marked beauties of his poetry must be erased.'' No one but a poet would have called a singing bird ''busy,'' or have translated a beautiful May-day into ''Both earth and sky keep jubilee''; the most perceptive diction is, in context, extraordinary, not commonplace, the expression of extraordinary powers of observation or imagination.[54] But in his preface of 1815, two years before the *Biographia* was published, Wordsworth had already turned away from verisimilitude in favor of an emphasis upon the privileged power of imaginative perception expressed in terms similar to those of Coleridge. For Wordsworth now, as for Coleridge in the *Biographia*, the most valuable poetic effects are produced by language which records, not merely the motions of an excited mind, nor the objective appearances of external nature, but the transformation of natural appearances which occurs when the mind responds actively to what it sees. The imagination creates a second nature which is not, in Coleridge's distinction, a copy of the first but an imitation of it, an ''interfusion of the SAME throughout the radically DIFFERENT, or of the different throughout a base radically the same.''[55] In its most characteristic operations, Wordsworth explains in the preface, the imagination confers additional properties upon its objects, abstracts from them some which they actually possess, juxtaposes them in striking ways so that their individual natures are partly lost in a novel *tertium quid*, consolidates numbers into unity, or dissolves and separates unity into number. As one would expect, the quotations from Virgil, Milton, and his own poems with which Wordsworth illustrates these generalizations call attention not to the poetical value of common speech but to the power of novel metaphor as a principle of creative perception.[56]

After 1815 Wordsworth and Coleridge both bring poetic diction to the test of a perceptual standard, but the standard is informed by a theory of perception markedly different from any common in the eighteenth century. Their ideal poet is not, for example—or not merely—an accurate observer of nature in the Baconian sense, because he is not a recorder of normal appearances. Such observation is, in the Romantic view, passive and mechanical, whereas the observer who is moved by what he sees transfigures it. Their view that in its most valuable form perception is a creative activity of the mind carries Wordsworth and Coleridge equally far beyond the subjectivism of Burke's *Sublime*, with its implied antithesis between "distinct ideas" or accurate perceptions ("little," familiar, unimpressive) and "sublime" impressions which (when they are not produced by words alone unaccompanied by ideas of any kind) arise from acts of incomplete apprehension or simply misapprehension. For, although there is a place for the Burkean sublime in Wordsworth if not noticeably in Coleridge, both writers insist that the imaginative transformation of natural objects is not a misperception or distortion but a superior realization of what is there. The imaginative recreation of nature is to them inconceivable without that discriminating and captivated attention to the objects of vision or memory which is the source of the poet's precision of language.

Wordsworth insisted throughout his life that poetic descriptions ought to betray the marks of fresh and exact observation.[57] Coleridge admired in Wordsworth

> the perfect truth of nature in his images and descriptions, as taken immediately from nature, and proving a long and genial intimacy with the very spirit which gives the physiognomic expression to all the works of nature. Like a green field reflected in a calm and perfectly transparent lake, the image is distinguished from the reality only by its greater softness and lustre. Like the moisture or the polish on a pebble, genius neither distorts nor false-colours its objects; but on the contrary brings out many a vein and many a tint, which escapes the eye of common observation, thus raising to the rank of gems what had been often kicked away by the hurrying foot of the traveller on the dusty high road of custom. [*Biographia Literaria*, 2:121]

Thus the imaginative modification of natural appearances which Wordsworth and Coleridge have in mind is not an imposition of form from without but the disclosure of an immanent beauty which escapes ordinary observation. "Remember," says Coleridge in his essay "On Poesy or Art" (1818), "that there is a difference between form as proceeding, and shape as superinduced;—the latter is either the death or the imprisonment of the thing;—the former is its self-witnessing and self-effected sphere of agency'' (ibid., 2:262). The artist who proceeds from a fixed concept, a ''given form, which is supposed to answer to the notion of beauty,'' produces ''emptiness'' and ''unreality''—*mere* abstractions, ... outlines drawn according to a recipe'' (ibid., 2:257, 187). In contrast to this, the kind of imagination which Coleridge celebrates in Wordsworth is able to work directly upon perceptual materials, as an energy of focused response, contemplating ''the ANCIENT of days and all his works with feelings as fresh, as if all had then sprang forth at the first creative fiat'' (ibid., 1:59).

To describe the effect which this produces in Wordsworth's poetry, Coleridge employs the same radical formula that Johnson had used to describe true wit: natural and new. It is ''the prime merit of genius and its most unequivocal mode of manifestation, so to represent familiar objects as to awaken in the minds of others a kindred feeling concerning them and that freshness of sensation which is the constant accompaniment of mental, no less than of bodily, convalescence.'' Thus Wordsworth is able ''to give the charm of novelty to things of every day,'' not by an art which declares its abstracted separateness from the visual experience on which it draws, but simply ''by awakening the mind's attention from the lethargy of custom, and directing it to the loveliness and the wonders of the world before us; an inexhaustible treasure, but for which, in consequence of the film of familiarity and selfish solicitude we have eyes, yet see not, ears that hear not, and hearts that neither feel nor understand'' (ibid., 1:60; 2:6).

The effect here attributed to Wordsworth's poetry is the effect which distinguishes the landscapes of his great contemporaries, Constable and Turner, from the many conventionally idealized landscapes of the eighteenth century. With the latter, studied form keeps the viewer within the boundaries of the work of art; natural objects are not only idealized but formulated—''drawn according to a recipe.'' With the former, and in Constable especially, the representation returns the observer to his own experience, giving him the sense that he knows intimately what he is beholding and that the painter has, as it were, merely revived his awareness of his own powers of observation. This effect has been celebrated in our time by Wallace Stevens, whose "necessary angel" represents (at least in part) the power to produce it. Responding to the claim that "poetry has to do with matter that is foreign and alien," Stevens replies, "On the contrary, its function, the need which it meets and which has to be met in some way in every age that is not to become decadent or barbarous, is precisely this contact with reality as it impinges upon us from outside, the sense that we can touch and feel a solid reality which does not dissolve itself into the conceptions of our own minds."[58] In a broader context which includes the imitation of "the scenes of life" as well as "the prospects of nature," the effect described by Coleridge and by Stevens is the highest effect of poetry for Johnson too.

5

The Prismatic Glass

In the *Life of Cowley* Johnson follows Bouhours and other neoclassical critics in defining true wit as "at once natural and new, that which though not obvious is, upon its first production, acknowledged to be just."[1] Wit here is treated as a limited effect of poetry, implicitly distinguished, for example, from the pathetic and the sublime. The formula "natural and new," however, is not restricted to wit in Johnson's criticism but describes the essential esthetic value of a wide range of poetic effects. Thus Shakespeare "approximates the remote, and familiarizes the wonderful," making the new seem natural; and *The Rape of the Lock* exhibits "in a very high degree the two most engaging powers of an author: new things are made familiar, and familiar things are made new" (*Preface*, p. 65; *Lives*, 3:233). To make familiar things new is for Johnson the finest local achievement of poetry, regardless of genre, and the highest excellence available to the shorter poetic forms. "He who reads these lines," says Johnson of his favorite passage in Congreve, "enjoys for the moment the powers of a poet: he feels what he remembers to have felt before, but he feels it with great increase of sensibility; he recognizes a familiar image, but meets it again amplified and expanded, embellished with beauty, and enlarged with majesty" (*Lives*, 2:230). If there is an effect still higher, it is when the natural and familiar is genuinely new, not made to seem novel by art or special sensibility, but discovered and articulated for the first time. The four stanzas of Gray's *Elegy* beginning "yet even these bones" are, says Johnson, "to me original: I have never seen the notions in any other place; yet he that reads them here persuades himself that he has always felt them. Had Gray written often

thus it had been to vain to blame, and useless to praise him''
(*Lives*, 3:441–42).

This effect—the evocation of a kind of knowledge which is, as
Keats said, ''almost a reminiscence''—Johnson conceived of as
imitative rather than discursive: the poet gives us back the
image of our minds by representing—dramatizing—a process of
thought, by creating an *image* (in one common neoclassical
sense of the word) of a mind in action.[2] In Johnson as in
Wordsworth the mimetic principle is adapted to apply not only
to plotted works such as plays, epics, and novels, but also to
many of the shorter poetic forms. Johnson has the latter in mind
when he writes of the metaphysical poets, for example, that ''if
the father of criticism has rightly denominated poetry $\tau\acute{\epsilon}\chi\nu\eta$
$\mu\iota\mu\eta\tau\iota\kappa\acute{\eta}$, *an imitative art*, these writers will without great
wrong lose their right to the name of poets, for they cannot be
said to have imitated any thing: they neither copied nature nor
life; neither painted the forms of matter nor represented the
operations of intellect''(*Lives*, 1:19).

This broad notion of imitation enabled Johnson (again like
Wordsworth in the *Prefaces* of 1800 and 1802) to subsume both
the objective and subjective dimensions of mimesis under the
standard of probability or objective truth. That is, the poet may
wish to depict ''the forms of matter,'' for example, either
objectively and accurately, as they ''really are,'' or as subjec-
tively misapprehended by a distracted or agitated observer,
depending upon the requirements of his poem. As I show in
appendix A, Johnson tacitly understands that in either case it is
the process of perception, rather than the object perceived,
which is being imitated, and that accordingly it is the depiction
of this process that the reader will judge as probable or
improbable, true or false, within the context of the whole. To
paint the ''forms of matter'' or of anything else is, finally, to
represent ''the operations of [the perceiving] intellect,'' and the
poet's task, especially in the lyric or pathetic genres, is to paint
truthful pictures of subjective states of mind.[3] The metaphysical
poets ''cannot be said to have imitated anything'' because their
addiction to certain mannerisms of style led them into ways of

thinking and speaking that were improbable from a mimetic or dramatic point of view. The same standard of mimetic naturalism which is explicit in Wordsworth's *Prefaces* is implicit in the *Life of Cowley*. Whatever differences may appear between Johnson and Wordsworth in their criticism of the "pathetic" genres of the short poem are differences not of principle but of taste.

The implications of Johnson's mimetic approach to the short poem will become clearer as we pursue our present concern, which is to understand how Johnson adapted the mimetic principle to serve as a means of describing poetic unity, and particularly as a means of criticizing the fragmentary effect produced by the obtrusive ornaments of mannered or coterie styles such as the metaphysical style. Here we shall have an opportunity to observe the synthetic character of Johnson's liberal neoclassicism and to specify his indebtedness to the rhetorical and literary theory of antiquity. For the terms which Johnson applies in the *Life of Cowley* to the fragmentation of metaphysical style have a specific history in neoclassical and classical tradition and draw their connotations from these sources; yet they are made to express standards which reflect the influences of modern empiricism and anticipate Romantic developments. So in Johnson the tradition is subtly modified, and the way prepared for its evolution into something new.

POETIC FORM IN NEOCLASSICAL CRITICISM

Apart from Imlac's brief remarks on the tulip, Johnson's criticism affords two major statements on the problem of fragmentation in style. The first occurs in *Rambler* 158, where Johnson is contending that most of the rules of poetry have been arbitrarily derived from established poetic practice rather than from "any settled principle or self-evident postulate, or adapted to the natural and invariable constitution of things," and have therefore often hindered the improvement of the art. So with the rules of lyric poetry:

> The imagination of the first authors of lyrick poetry was vehement and rapid, and their knowledge various and extensive. Living in an

age when science had been little cultivated, and when the minds of their auditors, not being accustomed to accurate inspection, were easily dazzled by glaring ideas, they applied themselves to instruct, rather by short sentences and striking thoughts, than by regular argumentation; and finding attention more successfully excited by sudden sallies and unexpected exclamations, than by the more artful and placid beauties of methodical deduction, they loosed their genius to its own course, passed from one sentiment to another without expressing the intermediate ideas, and roved at large over the ideal world with such lightness and agility, that their footsteps are scarcely to be traced.

From this accidental peculiarity of the ancient writers the criticks deduce the rules of lyrick poetry, which they have set free from all the laws by which other compositions are confined, and allow to neglect the niceties of transition, to start into remote digressions, and to wander without restraint from one scene of imagery to another.

A writer of later times [presumably Montaigne] has, by the vivacity of his essays, reconciled mankind to the same licentiousness in short dissertations; and he therefore who wants skill to form a plan, or diligence to pursue it, needs only intitle his performance an essay, to acquire the right of heaping together the collections of half his life, without order, coherence, or propriety.

Yet "confusion and irregularity," Johnson continues, "produce no beauty, though they cannot always obstruct the brightness of genius and learning. To proceed from one truth to another, and connect distant propositions by regular consequences, is the great prerogative of man. Independent and unconnected sentiments flashing upon the mind in quick succession, may, for a time, delight by their novelty, but they differ from systematical reasoning, as single notes from harmony, as glances of lightning from the radiance of the sun" (*Works*, 6:108–10).

Johnson appeals here to a rhetorical, not a mimetic, ideal of coherence. Strictly speaking, of course, it is a logical standard: in the lyric as in the essay, coherence is a matter of "regular argumentation," "methodical deduction," "systematical reasoning." These terms, so applied, are unusual both in Johnson and in his tradition. Johnson speaks elsewhere of the art of "reasoning in verse" as being of recent invention and limited interest; he appears to restrict it to expressly didactic poems such as Davies's *Nosce Teipsum* and *Religio Laici*.[4] Nor do his own odes exhibit "methodical deduction" or "systematical reasoning." The terms, in context, seem hyperbolic and are somewhat misleading.

They express, however, a concern which is one of the chief characteristics of neoclassical criticism. Johnson is right in saying that the neoclassical tradition made room for the unconnected style of Pindar, and even embraced it; the defense of Pindar does reflect the authoritarian side of neoclassical taste. But even here an effort was made to reconcile Pindaric "enthusiasm" with an ideal of coherence. Edward Young found Pindar to have "as much Logic at the Bottom as *Aristotle* or Euclid."[5] Few critics went so far. But when the wave of English Pindarizing set off by Cowley had subsided a compromise was struck, and most eighteenth-century discussions of ode couple a description of Pindaric enthusiasm with a warning against its imitation and often too with a stated preference for the more regular odes of Horace.[6] If we are to consider neoclassicism as a distinct and definable movement in the history of English criticism, we must place its essence not in a concern for neo-Aristotelian rules nor even in its responsiveness to the critical authority of the French, but rather in its orthodoxy of taste; and the principle of that orthodoxy was an admiration for the clarity and coherence of Greek and especially of Golden Age and Augustan Roman style, as seen in sharp and no doubt occasionally exaggerated contrast to the tendencies in modern writing which we describe today as Baroque. "Perhaps there is nothing," wrote Charles Gildon in 1718, "in which the Ancients excelled the Moderns more, than in always forming some Plot, Plan or Design to their Poems, which guided and led them from the Beginning to the End, while every Verse depended on the former, and continued to carry on the said Design. Whereas the Moderns have thought it sufficient to throw together a Company of Rhimes independent of each other, and directed to no manner of End, so that the Antients were Poets indeed, the Moderns generally speaking are Versifyers."[7]

But the neoclassical critics considered "Design," in the

short poem and in belletristic writing generally, as implicitly
rather than overtly logical, and avoided using logical terminology to describe it. As we have seen, they associated the literary
use of ''Logick in its own Stiffness and dry Formality,'' to repeat
Rapin's phrase, with scholasticism and pedantry, with the
substitution of machinery for insight, and with certain Renaissance and Baroque forms from which they wished to dissociate
themselves, such as the ''metaphysical'' sermon, with its mechanical and ingenious methods of textual division.[8] ''The
Beauty of Order,'' said Henry Felton in 1709, ''is its Freedom
and Unconstraint: It must be dispersed and shine in all the Parts
thro' the the whole Performance, but there is no necessity of
Writing in Trammels, when we can move at ease without
them.'' Proportion in writing, he explained, is not to be
measured out mechanically, like the proportions of a horse in a
drawing, but ''is to be taken by the Mind, and formed upon a
general View and consideration of the Whole.''[9] In the epistles
and satires of the Romans, Shaftesbury pointed out, it is ''the
concealment of order and method [which] makes the chief
beauty of the work.'' ''Even the satiric or miscellaneous manner
of the polite ancients, required as much order as the most
regular pieces. But the art was to destroy every such token or
appearance, give an extemporary air to what was writ, and make
the effect of art be felt without discovering the artifice.''[10] The
Roman poets exemplified a concept of form which was difficult
to describe, and about which little practical advice could be
given, since it contained no fixed prescriptive elements.[11] In the
concrete, such form was practically inseparable from the individual work which embodied it. Only in a very abstract sense
could it be said to preexist the work, as the author's ''general
View and Consideration of the Whole.'' It appeared to come
into being in and through the actual process of composition,
and to exist completely only as the realized entelechy of the
whole. Thus it was conceivable in abstraction from the work less
as a collection of structural features which could be isolated and
described than as the principle or principles (whatever they
might be) which gave order to the author's intelligence. The

"artifice," therefore, in Shaftesbury's sense of the word, which produced such form was best described mimetically: the poet imitates a free but orderly process of thought.[12]

It was, in short, the classical ideal of organic unity which the neoclassical critics made the cornerstone of their stylistic theory. This concept asks to be described in metaphor, and organic metaphors, on the model of those suggested in the *Poetics*, are not uncommon in neoclassical criticism.[13] When considering form in relation specifically to style, however, the neoclassical critics preferred, until well into the eighteenth century, spatial and plastic analogies drawn from the arts of painting, sculpture, or architecture; and in this too they were following the practice of the ancients.[14] Near the beginning of the *Ars Poetica* Horace describes the problem of fragmentation in style in terms of sculptors who excel in representing particular parts of the body—the nails or the hair—but who cannot achieve beauty in the whole figure.[15] Pope's description of what contemporary critics often called "simplicity of design" in poetry alludes to Horace, then turns to architecture:

> In Wit, as Nature, what affects our Hearts
> Is not th' Exactness of peculiar Parts;
> 'Tis not a *Lip*, or *Eye*, we Beauty call,
> But the joint Force and full *Result* of *all*.
> Thus when we view some well-proportion'd Dome,
> (The *World*'s just Wonder, and ev'n *thine* O *Rome*!)
> No single Parts unequally surprize;
> All comes *united* to th' admiring Eyes;
> No monstrous Height, or Breadth, or Length appear;
> The *Whole* at once is *Bold*, and *Regular*.[16]

Addison, who was especially fond of comparing the effect of a poetic simplicity of design to the unified visual impression produced by ancient buildings, popularized the analogy between Gothic architecture and conceited style. "As the eye," says Hume, in a particularly concise version of the comparison, "in surveying a Gothic building, is distracted by the multi-plicity of ornaments, and loses the whole by its minute attention to the parts; so the mind, in perusing a work overstocked with wit, is fatigued and disgusted with the constant endeavour to shine and surprise."[17]

Equally common was a version of *ut pictura poesis* which, following Aristotle, makes form equivalent to the drawn outline, and style equivalent to the coloring in a picture. Among the ancients Dionysius of Halicarnassus had compared the Attic simplicity of the Greek orator Lysias to "old paintings which are worked in simple colours without any subtle blending of tints but clear in their outline, and thereby possessing great charm," while the more sophisticated art of later orators such as Isaeus and Demosthenes resembles "later paintings [which] are less well-drawn but contain greater detail and a subtle interplay of light and shade, and are effective because of the many nuances of colour which they contain." The speeches of the latter seem to Dionysius "suspect because of their great rhetorical skill," those of Lysias "genuine and just" because "straightforward and simple."[18]

Hobbes revives the terms of this double comparison in praising the description of love in Book II, Canto 7 of Davenant's *Gondibert*: "Poets are Painters: I would fain see another Painter draw so true, perfect, and natural a Love to the Life, and make use of nothing but pure Lines, without the help of any the least uncomely shadow, as you have done."[19] In the Port-Royal Logic, Arnauld compares the language and verbal ornaments of oratory to "the shadows of Colouring" in painting, and remarks that the power of true eloquence—that of imprinting "in the Breasts of the Hearers a clear and lively Image of the Things express'd"—may be found "in persons not so diligent in sorting their words, and adjusting their Figures; but is rarely seen among those who are over-curious in streining their words and similitudes; for that same curiosity calls off their minds from the consideration of Realities, and weakens the vigour of our thoughts, as Painters observe, that they who are excellent for Colouring, are seldom good Designers; the mind not being capable to study two things at once, and the one disturbing and hindring the other" (*Logic*, pt. 2 , p. 139). In the *Discourses* Reynolds describes the studied chiaroscuro effects of the Venetian school of Titian and his followers, and criticizes the Venetian style in terms remarkably like those which Johnson applies to the metaphysical poets. The Venetian painters show ''more copiousness than choice, and more luxuriancy than judgment''; they seem ''more willing to dazzle than to affect,'' and their work is marked by ''capricious composition,'' ''violent and affected contrasts,'' and a ''total inattention to expression.'' They excel, says Reynolds, in the mechanical part of the art which is called *the language of painters*,'' but it is a ''poor eloquence which only shews that the orator can talk. Words should be employed as the means, not as the end: language is the instrument, conviction is the work'' (*Discourses*, ed. Mitchell, pp. 45–47). The Roman and Florentine schools, which to Reynolds represent the highest standard of the grand style in painting, avoid ''all trifling or artful play of little lights'' and ''variety of broken and transparent colours,'' preferring instead ''a breadth of uniform, and simple colour'' which contributes to the effects of ''simplicity'' and ''grandeur.''[20] In this respect, these schools correspond to the style of painting to which Dionysius compares Lysias.

Specialized and Unspecialized Styles in Classical Rhetoric

Such criticisms help to specify the neoclassical concern for coherence and unity of design as a preference for strong, simple structures over subtle or minutely elaborated ones; and in associating simple, uniform colors with unity of total effect and broken, transparent colors with the violent, dazzling, and capricious, they also bring us closer to the particular metaphoric tradition upon which Johnson draws both in the criticism of fragmented style cited above from *Rambler* 158 and in the famous paragraph on the ''analytick'' attempts of the metaphysical poets, which constitutes his second major statement of the problem of fragmentation in poetic style. In *Rambler* 158 the ''independent and unconnected sentiments'' characteristic of the lyric and of the essay in the manner of Montaigne ''may, for a time, delight by their novelty, but they differ from systematical reasoning, as single notes from harmony, as glances of lightning from the radiance of the sun." In the *Life of Cowley* Johnson remarks that the metaphysical poets "broke every image into fragments, and could no more represent by their slender conceits and laboured particularities the prospects of nature or the scenes of life, than he who dissects a sun-beam with a prism can exhibit the wide effulgence of a summer noon" (*Lives*, 1:21). Johnson's metaphors—the lightning, the prism, the radiance of the sun—have a definite history in classical and neoclassical criticism, and one which throws considerable light on the standards against which the school of Donne is implicitly judged in the *Life of Cowley*.

This history may be said to begin with Aristotle's distinction in the *Rhetoric* (III. xii) between the styles of written prose and spoken oratory.[21] Aristotle associates the former with epideictic oratory, "for it is meant to be read"; the oral style is best seen in the deliberative oratory of the assembly; the forensic style falls between the two, but is nearer to the style of written prose. The written style, says Aristotle, is the more finished, the oral style more dramatic. Written speeches "sound thin in actual contests," while those of the orators "are good to hear spoken, but look amateurish enough when they pass into the hands of the reader" precisely because "they are so well suited for an actual tussle, and therefore contain many dramatic touches, which, being robbed of all dramatic rendering, fail to do their own proper work, and consequently look silly." They are full of asyndetic passages and "strings of unconnected words" which would be out of place in written composition, but which are expressive of character and emotion, and which must be "acted," not simply delivered. Aristotle's emphasis on the essentially dramatic nature of oral style (in the literal or mimetic sense of "dramatic," that is, to be *acted*) is repeated by Cicero, Quintilian, Demetrius, and especially Longinus, and, among the moderns, by Fénelon, who appeals to these authorities, as we have seen, in illustrating the mimetic character of figurative language.[22] Significantly, Aristotle himself illustrates the dramatic qualities of oral style with a passage from the *Iliad*.

Now the style of oratory addressed to public assemblies is "really just like scene-painting" (*skiagraphia*, or "painting with shadows and shading").[23] The skiagraphic picture is a kind of public art, meant to be seen at a distance, in an outdoor setting, and appealing to a wide audience. "The bigger the throng," Aristotle continues, "the more distant is the point of view: so that, in the one and other, [that is, in the skiagraphic picture and the deliberative speech], high finish in detail is superfluous and seems better away." Like skiagraphic painting, deliberative oratory relies upon certain broad dramatic effects which can bridge the psychological distance between the public speaker and his audience, a distance in which subtler "literary" effects are lost.[24] Thus the forensic style, addressed to a more limited and more expert audience of judges and jurors in the law courts, is "more highly finished," and "still more so is the style of language addressed to a single judge, with whom there is very little room for rhetorical artifices, since he can take the whole thing in better, and judge of what is to the point and what is not." The epideictic style, addressed to an audience of readers who have the time to note subtleties, is, as remarked above, the "most literary" of all. These differences between written and oral composition, Aristotle says in conclusion, explain why the same speakers do not distinguish themselves in all branches of oratory at once. Very different kinds of talent are required.

Most of the differences which for Aristotle distinguish the spoken from the written style reappear in Cicero as differences between the style of genuine eloquence and the styles of various coteries. That oral composition differs from written (that is, from writing intended *only* to be read) Cicero takes for granted; he fails to emphasize this particular distinction in part, perhaps, because he insists that oral style can and should carry the highest possible finish: when his ideal Attic orator employs the *genus tenue* his phrasing may occasionally appear negligent, but it is in reality a "careful negligence" (*neglegentia ... diligens*).[25] More to the point for Cicero (and here he approaches Aristotle's distinctions by another route) is the question of breadth of appeal. Cicero's ideal orator will be master, first of all, not of one specialized style but of all three styles described in the rhetoric textbooks, the high, the middle, and the low; he will have the flexibility and range which the varied purposes of rhetoric demand, and will be able to adapt his language to the peculiar requirements of each rhetorical situation.[26] Of the three styles, however, the most excellent and by far the most difficult is the high style, the *genus grande*, in which Demosthenes alone has come near to perfection; and this style, suited to deliberative oratory and adapted to the widest possible audience, is like the agonistic style described by Aristotle. When a master speaks in the high style ''the listening throng (*audiens multitudo*) is delighted, is carried along by his words, is in a sense bathed in deep delight … They feel now joy now sorrow, are moved now to laughter now to tears; they show approbation detestation, scorn aversion; they are drawn to pity to shame to regret; are stirred to anger wonder, hope fear; and all these come to pass just as the hearers' minds are played upon by word and thought and action.'' To gain such effects eloquence must be ''adapted to the ears of the multitude'' (*nostra oratio multitudinis est auribus accommodanda*); it cannot afford to cater to specialized tastes. In other arts ''that is most excellent which is furthest removed from the understanding and mental capacity of the untrained,'' but the art of oratory ''lies open to the view, and is concerned in some measure with the common practice, custom, and speech of mankind,'' so that for it the cardinal sin would be to depart ''from the language of everyday life, and the usage approved by the sense of the community'' (*in dicendo … vitium vel maximum sit a vulgari genere orationis, atque a consuetudine communis sensus abhorrere*).[27]

The coterie styles to which Cicero opposes his own ideal of Attic eloquence are not more highly finished than the Attic style, for Cicero's Attic orator is an artist who overlooks nothing. Rather, they are devoted to kinds of refinement which lack public appeal. Some of these styles profit more by being read than listened to, but even then they are of limited interest.

Thus, for example, the Stoic style, "though possibly subtle (*subtile*) and undoubtedly penetrating," is too entangled in logical distinctions, and too "meagre, spiritless, cramped, and paltry" in diction (*exile, aridum, concisum ac minutum*) to be of use to the orator (*De Oratore*, III.xviii.65–66; II.xxxviii.157–59; *Brutus*, 118–20). Resembling the Stoics in their disdain for emotional appeals are the Roman *Attici*, the coterie against whom the *Brutus* and *Orator* are primarily directed. The "Atticists" erred in taking the style of Lysias (which, though precise and urbane, is also, in Cicero's opinion, "meagre," "dry," and "impoverished") as the sole standard of Attic purity and good taste, much as the sixteenth-century Ciceronians took Cicero to be the sole standard of good Latin. Lysias's real virtues are not to be despised, for there is room, in an art as varied as oratory, even for "such small refinements of workmanship" (*huic minutae subtilitati*). But the result of Roman Atticism has been at best a cold correctness whose merits escape the general public: Cicero says of the style of Calvus, the founder of the movement, that "while scholars and careful listeners recognized its quality, the multitude and the forum, for whom eloquence exists, missing its finer flavour gulped it down whole."[28]

Ignorant of the emotive power of the rounded period, or unable to achieve it, the *Attici* are typically "broken" and "choppy" (*infracta, amputata*), and puerile in their affectation of balance and antithesis (*Brutus*, 287; *Orator*, 170, 226). In the last respect they resemble the Sophists, inventors of the third mannered style to which Cicero gives detailed critical attention. Like Fénelon, Cicero associates sophistic eloquence with epideictic tradition and with Isocrates in particular.[29] Sophistic style differs from the style of true oratory in this, that because the object of the Sophists "is not to arouse the audience but to soothe it, not so much to persuade as to delight, they are on the look-out for ideas that are neatly put rather than reasonable [*concinnas magis sententias exquirunt quam probabilis*]; they frequently wander from the subject, they introduce mythology, they use far-fetched metaphors and arrange them as painters do colour combinations [*verba altius transferunt eaque ita disponunt ut pictores varietatem colorum*]; they make their clauses balanced and of equal length, frequently ending with similar sounds" (*Orator*, 65). This description recalls Fénelon's description of seventeenth-century "conceited" oratory, and even more strongly Bacon's description in the *De Augmentis* of the fashion for Silver Latin mannerism that had replaced Ciceronianism as the latest version of "delicate learning" in his own time.[30]

To heighten the contrast between his ideal of unspecialized eloquence and the specialized styles just described, Cicero uses certain metaphors which were to become conventional among later critics of Silver Latin excess. The oratorical style is associated with full sunlight, the dust and heat of battle—metaphors for the world of public affairs. The coterie styles are associated with tranquil and shaded settings, the rhetorical schools, the porches and groves of the philosophers. At last, says Crassus in the *De Oratore*, after the preliminary training is completed, "must our Oratory be conducted out of this sheltered training-ground at home [*hac domestica exercitatione et umbratili;* lit., "shaded"], right into action, into the dust and uproar, into the camp and the fighting-line of public debate; she must face putting everything to the proof and test the strength of her talent, and her secluded preparation must be brought forth into the daylight of reality [*in veritatis lucem*]."[31] So the epideictic style is "fitter for the parade than for the battle; set apart for the gymnasium and the palaestra, it is spurned and rejected in the forum," just as Isocrates himself, its greatest master, "shrank from the broad daylight of the forum" and won his fame "within the walls of his school" [*intraque parietes aluit eam gloriam*).[32] Again, the Athenian orator Demetrius of Phaleron "entertained rather than stirred his countrymen; for he came forth into the heat and dust of action, not from a soldier's tent, but from the shady retreat of the great philosopher Theophrastus" (*e Theophrasti doctissimi hominis umbraculis*). As for the style of philosophy itself (of which both the Stoic and the Roman "Atticist" styles are in a sense subspecies), it is "gentle and academic [*mollis . . . et umbratilis*]; it has no equipment of words or phrases that catch the popular fancy; it is not arranged in rhythmical periods, but is loose in structure; there is no anger in it, no hatred, no ferocity, no pathos, no shrewdness; it might be called a chaste, pure and modest virgin. Consequently it is called conversation [*sermo*) rather than oratory."[33]

In the following century similar metaphors appear in a variety of authors. Quintilian, for example, speaks of the Roman *Attici* as a "withered, sapless and anaemic band" who, because they "cannot endure the dazzling rays of the sun of eloquence [*clariorem vim eloquentiae velut solem*], hide themselves beneath the shadow" of the mighty Attic name.[34] The principal context now, however, is the decadence of Silver Latin and the conditions which produced it. In the opening pages of the *Satyricon* Petronius attributes the decline of eloquence to the influence of the schools of declamation, where training in *controversiae* and *suasoriae* merely produces the result that "a pupil who steps into a court thinks that he has been carried into another world." In the days when Pindar was too modest to steal Homer's lines, "no cloistered pedant [*umbraticus doctor*] had yet ruined young men's brains" (*Satyricon*, pp. 3–4). Messala, in Tacitus's *Dialogue on Oratory*, contrasts the contemporary practices of the schools with the rhetorical training of an earlier time, when students were taken to the law-courts to form their judgment of good speaking from firsthand observation of what succeeded and what did not; "they carried on their studies in the light of open day [*in media luce*], and amid the very shock of battle" (*Dialogue*, 34–35). Similar criticisms of the schools appear in the rhetorical collections of the elder Seneca, where, for example, the orator Votienus Montanus explains that, "as a person coming out of a shady and darkened place is blinded by the splendour of the full light of day, those who come from the schools to the forum are troubled by all the unexpected things they see."[35] The associations of these metaphors were quite alive for the neoclassical period, and appear in Johnson's prose and even in his verse.[36]

METAPHORS FOR COHERENT STYLE IN
CLASSICAL AND NEOCLASSICAL CRITICISM

The metaphors which Johnson uses in the passages on fragmentation cited above find quite specific *loci classici* in Longinus and Quintilian. In *On the Sublime* the distinctions we have been tracing in Aristotle and Cicero between the public and agonistic grand style of oratory and the more subtly finished styles of written composition return as differences between sublime speaking or writing and two opposing styles, the "puerile" and the Attic, the latter coming under attack as represented in its most correct and polished form by Lysias and especially by Hypereides. Longinus associates sublimity predominantly, though not exclusively, with oral composition: in poetry it is found especially in Homer and the Greek tragedians, and it is the finest effect of oratory, not merely persuading the audience but transporting them out of themselves.[37] Its primary causes are "weighty thought" ("full-blooded ideas") and "vehement emotion," though it may also be produced by a happiness in verbal ornament or skillful composition. It is a public effect, pleasing "all people at all times," and, as we shall see, Longinus, like Aristotle, occasionally thinks of it in terms of distance (ibid., 7–8, 17). It is on the whole attributable to Nature or "genius" rather than Art, a distinction which explains why sublimity is opposed to high finish. For Nature is "good fortune," Art merely "good judgment"; art alone, therefore, can aspire only to correctness, and while Longinus admits that art in league with genius "may ... result in perfection," he notes that "perfect precision runs the risk of triviality, whereas in great writing as in great wealth there must needs be something overlooked." Those who have aimed at what is greatest in writing have in fact "scorned detailed accuracy."[38]

Hence the conflict between the sublime and both the puerile style and the Attic refinement of Lysias and Hypereides. Longinus describes puerility in the same terms that first-century critics of the schools of declamation apply to Silver Latin mannerism. It is an ''academic attitude,'' characterized by overelaboration and frigidity. All the improprieties of the puerile style ''are weeds sprung from the same seed, namely that passion for novel ideas which is the prevalent craze of the present day'' (ibid., 3, 5). These are the charges brought against Baroque mannerism by the neoclassical critics of the late seventeenth century, and by Johnson against the metaphysical style in the *Life of Cowley*. The correct Attic style is, by contrast, tasteful and modest; but it too is cold. Hypereides has ''an untold store of polished wit, urbane sarcasm, well-bred elegance, supple turns of irony, . . . clever satire, plenty of pointed ridicule,'' but these beauties, many as they are, ''lack grandeur; they are dispassionate, born of sober sense, and do not trouble the peace of the audience.'' Demosthenes, who lacks most of Hypereides' peculiar virtues, nevertheless ''shows the merits of great genius in their most consummate form, sublime intensity, living emotion, redundance, readiness, speed . . . and his own unapproachable vehemence and power''(ibid., 34).

These distinctions had an increasing influence on eighteenth-century taste from Addison onwards. In *Spectator* 160 Addison distinguishes two kinds of great genius, those ''prodigies of mankind'' who have produced immortal works ''by the meer strength of natural parts, and without any assistance of art or learning,'' and those who have ''submitted the greatness of their natural talents to the corrections and restraints of art.'' Shakespeare exemplifies the former type, Bacon the latter, and although Addison disclaims any preference his bias is obvious: ''There appears something nobly wild and extravagant in these great natural geniuses, that is infinitely more beautiful than all the turn and polishing of what the French call a *Bel Esprit*, by which they would express a genius refined by conversation, reflection, and the reading of the most polite authors. The greatest genius which runs through the arts and sciences, takes a kind of tincture from them, and falls unavoidably into imitation.'' For Joseph Warton, as we have seen, the sublime and the pathetic are the two chief nerves of genuine poesy; ''the most solid observations on human life expressed with the utmost elegance and brevity are MORALITY, and not PO- ETRY,'' and Pope is a man of sense and wit (like Donne, Warton suggests) but not a true poet.[39]

The significance for Johnson of Longinus's distinction be- tween the great and the polished styles is suggested by the two rather different contexts in Johnson's criticism which depend on it. Earlier we noted Johnson's comparison of *Othello* to Ad- dison's *Cato*. The former is the ''vigorous and vivacious off- spring of observation impregnated by genius''; the latter belongs among ''the fairest and noblest progeny which judg- ment propagates by conjunction with learning,'' but shows us ''nothing that acquaints us with human sentiments or human actions.'' The diction of *Cato*, it will be recalled, is ''easy, elevated and harmonious, but its hopes and fears communicate no vibration to the heart.'' Immediately after these remarks Johnson develops a comparison which Addison had used before him in a passage of Longinian criticism: ''The work of a correct and regular writer is a garden accurately formed and diligently planted, varied with shades, and scented with flowers; the composition of Shakespeare is a forest, in which oaks extend their branches, and pines tower in the air, interspersed some- times with weeds and brambles, and sometimes giving shelter to myrtles and to roses.''[40] Then Johnson changes the figure: ''Other poets display cabinets of precious rarities, minutely finished, wrought into shape, and polished unto brightness. Shakespeare opens a mine which contains gold and diamonds in unexhaustible plenty, though clouded by incrustations, de- based by impurities, and mingled with a mass of meaner minerals.''[41]

The second context is from the *Life of Cowley*, and includes the paragraph on the ''analytick'' attempts of the metaphysical poets. Johnson disagreed with Warton's restriction of poetry to the pathetic and sublime, but he did not hesitate to use Warton's categories in accounting for the limitations of meta- physical verse: the paragraph on the fragmentation of meta- physical style is intended to explain why it failed to achieve sublimity; the immediately preceding paragraph explains its failure to reach "the pathetick" (*Lives*, 1: 20-21). Johnson's respect for the poetry of wit and sense (and his admiration for Pope's Homeric translations) kept him from depreciating Pope as Warton had done, but the contexts just cited from the *Preface to Shakespeare* and the *Life of Cowley* reveal Johnson's tendency to think, with Addison, of minutely finished styles—whether vicious like Cowley's, or genuinely elegant, like the style of Cato—as the product of "art" and literary imitation, activities which (it is implied) at once estrange the poet from his own immediate knowledge of men and nature and cut him off from the highest effects of his art.[42]

As to the precise nature of sublimity itself, Longinus may seem on first reading somewhat inconsistent. On the one hand, the sublime is described as a purely local effect, distinct from the effects of rhetorical amplification, for example, because often found "in a single idea" (*On the Sublime*, 12). It is associated with novelty and wonder,[43] and is opposed at one point to the virtues of form: "inventive skill and the due disposal and marshalling of facts do not show themselves in one or two touches: they gradually emerge from the whole tissue of the composition, while, on the other hand, a well-timed flash of sublimity scatters everything before it like a bolt of lightning and reveals the full power of the speaker at a single stroke" (ibid., 1).

Fénelon, who has high praise for Longinus in other respects, censures him for applying himself "more to the admirable than to the useful," and in the passages referred to Longinus may seem indeed to be an exponent of "the pleasures of sudden wonder"—pleasures which, Johnson reminds us, are "soon exhausted." Wonder is "the effect of novelty upon ignorance"; it is "a pause of reason, a sudden cessation of the mental progress, which lasts only while the understanding is fixed upon some single idea" (*Lives*, 2: 303; *Works*, 5: 417). As such, wonder is in radical conflict with the "placid beauties of methodical deduction" which Johnson wished even for the ode; it is an esthetic based on novelty and wonder that Johnson is opposing in *Rambler* 158. But in the *Life of Cowley* Johnson defines the sublime as "that comprehension and expanse of thought which at once fills the whole mind, and of which the first effect is sudden astonishment, and the second rational admiration" (*Lives*, 1: 20–21). The phrasing suggests that in the truly sublime the wonder is only momentary: the mind moves from "sudden astonishment" to "rational admiration" by finding a context for the isolated idea, by discovering its meaning in relation to a larger whole. The "independent and unconnected sentiments" which flash upon the mind in *Rambler* 158 like "glances of lightning" are a kind of false sublime. Rapin uses the same lightning metaphor to characterize the brokenness and extravagance of Tacitus's style, and John Oldmixon uses it to describe metaphysical conceit.[44]

But Longinus also describes sublimity in terms quite compatible with Johnson's conception of it. *On the Sublime* places a central emphasis on organic unity and on order and connection in style; Longinus considers these qualities essential, not perhaps to every type of sublimity, but to many types which he especially values. The sublime writer is known by his gift for making a consistently happy choice of the most striking features of his subject, and has "the power of combining them together as it were into an organic whole." Demosthenes' achievement in his descriptions and narations "is to make a clean sweep . . . of all the main points by order of merit, and to bring them together, allowing nothing affected or undignified or pedantic to intervene."[45] This requires for the most part a periodic style in which the individual effects of grandeur can be "united into a single system and embraced moreover by the bonds of rhythm" so that "they gain a living voice." There is such a thing as a proper brevity or conciseness, but "absolutely short sentences," Longinus warns, have a mutilating effect, and are to be avoided as "the small change of literature" (ibid., 40–42).

Altogether, then, sublimity is a local effect, but an effect which is *composed*: there is a synthesis of elements, and a unity involved which is partly due to syntax and rhythm, partly to the speaker's "enthusiasm," which, infecting the listener by sympathy, carries him rapidly along and blends discrete details into a single impression. The composition as such, Longinus implies, is as much the result of art as of genius; but the genius hides the art. The figures of speech, when brought to the listener's attention, carry, as we have seen, a suggestion of "treachery, craft, fallacy," but when they find their place in a fabric which is sublime throughout, "the effrontery of the artifice is somehow lost in its brilliant setting."

> Much in the same way that dimmer lights vanish in the surrounding radiance of the sun, so the all-embracing atmosphere of grandeur obscures the rhetorical devices. We see something of the same kind in painting. Though the high lights and shadows lie side by side in the same plane, yet the high lights spring to the eye and seem not only to stand out but to be actually much nearer. So it is in writing. What is sublime and moving lies nearer to our hearts, and thus, partly from a natural affinity, partly from brilliance of effect, it always strikes the eye long before the figures, thus throwing their art into the shade and keeping it hid as it were under a bushel. [Ibid., 17]

True wit gives us back the image of our minds: the sublime is that which is so congruent with our sympathies that when we encounter it "we are filled," as Longinus says earlier, "with a joyful pride, as if we had ourselves produced the very thing we heard" (ibid., 7). Thus sublimity leaps the psychological distance between speaker and audience, capturing our attention so that lesser effects, along with all traces of artifice, fail to reach us. And Longinus's metaphor of "the radiance of the sun," whose meaning is developed by the *ut pictura* comparison which follows it—a comparison which implicitly directs attention to the value of coherence or unity of effect—is apposite to the similar figures in the two passages from Johnson.[46]

Longinus's metaphor is apposite, but Quintilian's is (though indirectly) an actual source of Johnson's figures, and more apposite still. It occurs in a discussion not of the sublime but of *sententiae* or *lumina*, the epigrams or striking antitheses which contemporary critics of Silver Latin regarded as its characteristic and most abused mannerism.[47] Such ornaments have their uses,

Quintilian declares—''what sin is there in a good epigram?''—but the cult of epigram has brought into vogue a style which is fragmented and ostentatious, for ''every *reflexion* [*sententia*] is isolated, and consequently a fresh start is necessary after each. This produces a discontinuous style, since our language is composed not of a system of limbs, but of a series of fragments'' (*et e singulis non membris sed frustis collata* [*oratio*]). Thus, Quintilian continues,

> although these ornaments may seem to stand out with a certain glitter of their own, they are rather to be compared to sparks flashing through the smoke than to the actual brilliance of flame: they are, in fact, invisible when the language is of uniform splendour, just as the stars are invisible in the light of day [*ut in sole sidera ipsa desinunt cerni*]. And where eloquence seeks to secure elevation by frequent small efforts, it merely produces an uneven and broken surface which fails to win the admiration due to outstanding objects and lacks the charm that may be found in a smooth surface. [*Institutio Oratoria* VIII.v.26-29]

Pope seems to have the above passage in view when he writes in the *Essay on Criticism* that

> *False Eloquence*, like the *Prismatic Glass*,
> Its gawdy Colours spreads on *ev' ry place*;
> The Face of Nature we no more Survey,
> All glares alike, without Distinction gay:
> But true Expression, like th' unchanging *Sun*,
> *Clears*, and *improves* whate' er it shines upon,
> It *gilds* all Objects, but it *alters* none.[48]

Pope's metaphors are remarkably rich in implication. First, Pope brings Quintilian's rather submerged metaphors into prominence by giving them an explicitly mimetic context: Quintilian's ''uneven and broken surface'' and ''outstanding objects'' become parts of a *scene*—the ''Face of Nature'' which we ''survey.'' In Longinus and Quintilian the sun merely represents a style of ''uniform splendour'' in which individual effects of art—in Quintilian *lumina*—do not call attention to themselves as such. In Pope the sun of ''true Expression'' illuminates a world of familiar objects which—as on a day of unusually clear air and unusually brilliant light—appear newly beautiful while remaining unchanged. To grasp the image is inevitably to think of the effects of Wordsworth's nature poetry as Coleridge described them, of Wordsworth's gift for removing the ''film of familiarity'' from commonplace objects and letting them stand forth in the beauty of their own natures, now fully perceived.

The point is not, however, that Coleridge's context is precisely Pope's. The latter's is undoubtedly broader and includes Coleridge's. We note, then, that Pope's terms for coherent style are spatial and perceptual: ''true Expression'' gives us the literary and imaginative equivalent of a coherent visual field, a description or (by metaphoric extension) a dramatic situation which we can take in all at once with the mind's eye. This is the effect of the ancients' *enargeia* and of Fénelon's ''portraiture,'' and it requires the specific properties of style which Fénelon calls for in the *Dialogues*—transparence, descriptive accuracy, vividness, and above all, perhaps, linear momentum, for spatial effects in writing are achieved by a style which moves rapidly and efficiently through mental *time*. Momentum is in particular the result of a well-connected style; a conceited style—Pope's ''false eloquence''—cannot achieve it because by giving ornamental prominence to a great many of its details it isolates them from one another, so that no coherent mental picture emerges (''All glares *alike*, without *Distinction* gay''). The modern reader needs to remind himself that the neoclassical critics perceived the fragmentary effects of conceit in terms of this almost literally visual standard of coherence.

But more than this is implied. ''True expression'' is the vehicle for an intelligence which is fixed upon its subject and sees it for what it is; Pope's poet, like Lucian's historian, has a mind ''like a mirror, clear, gleaming-bright, accurately centred, displaying the shape of things just as he receives them, free from distortion, false colouring, and misrepresentation.''[49] As a metaphor of mind—of false wit issuing in false eloquence—the prismatic glass stands for the distorting conceptual intellect. In the *Essay on Man* the prism is the mind which falsifies its immediate knowledge through the subtlety and abstractions of philosophy: ''Ere Wit oblique had broke that steddy light, / Man, like his Maker, saw that all was right.''[50] In the *Essay on Criticism* the prismatic mind falsifies its knowledge by representing it in glaring colors of speech, ornaments which transform and disguise, instead of clarifying, human experience.[51]

UNITY OF EFFECT IN NEOCLASSICAL TASTE AND PRACTICE

Pope's metaphors have, I believe, a fairly exact application to neoclassical taste and to neoclassical poetic practice. As was said above, one must seek the unity of English neoclassicism in the orthodoxy of its taste, for the central principles of that orthodoxy were all but universally accepted from the time of Arnauld until beyond the middle of the eighteenth century and cut across all other critical divisions, uniting devotees of the Ancients and devotees of the Moderns, libertines and partisans of the Rules, admirers of French classicism and defenders of the English genius. These principles can be summarized as follows: (1) The qualities of good style are timeless and universal, and are to be learned from the best Greek and especially (since it was easier to read) from the best Latin writing, namely, that of the Augustan or so-called Golden Age.[52] (2) Literary cultures, whether ancient or modern, normally exhibit a cyclical pattern of growth and decay, moving, as Johnson remarks in *Idler* 63, ''from rudeness to convenience, from convenience to elegance, and from elegance to nicety.'' Latin literature, from its beginnings through the Silver Latin decadence, manifests the complete cycle, and thus represents the perfection of the possibilities of style, both good and bad. Modern writing since the ''revival of letters'' (variously dated from Dante, Petrarch, or the age of Leo X) has repeated the cycle, but with this difference: in the ignorance of its beginnings it became addicted to the glaring ornaments of Silver Latin, so that its period of growth has had the appearance of a premature decadence. (3) There has been, nevertheless, a gradual progress in knowledge and taste, as witnessed by the present recovery of Augustan standards. The function of criticism, and of stylistic criticism in particular, is therefore to establish the principles of a genuine classicism which will help bring modern writing to its due maturity. This is to be accomplished chiefly in two ways: by exhibiting the virtues of Golden Age models and the vices of Silver Latin style, and by mastering the criticism of the ancients.[53] The ancient critics (it was assumed, and on the whole not unreasonably) provide a consensus on most important matters of practice and taste which illuminates the faults and virtues alike of ancient and of modern styles. (I have tried to bring out certain salient features of this consensus, as the neoclassical critics perceived it, in the above discussion of the classical background of Johnson's metaphors for fragmentation.)[54]

One consequence of these premises was that Quintilian's objections to the Silver Latin cult of *sententiae* were taken as applicable to Baroque conceit, which was regarded as the product of Silver Latin imitation.[55] Quintilian especially emphasizes the fragmentary effect of sententious amplification; in addition to the passage adapted by Pope and considered above, the most important statement occurs in his criticism of Seneca, which became the favorite neoclassical *locus* for the discussion of fragmentation in style. Seneca, says Quintilian in part, is an extremely dangerous model for the young because he abounds in attractive vices (*dulcibus vitiis*). "One could wish that, while he relied on his own intelligence [*ingenio*], he had allowed himself to be guided by the taste [*judicio*] of others. For if he had only despised all unnatural expressions and had not been so passionately fond of all that was incorrect, if he had not felt such affection for all that was his own, and had not impaired the solidity of his matter by striving after epigrammatic brevity [*minutissimis sententiis*], he would have won the approval of the learned instead of the enthusiasm of boys."[56] In the second half of the seventeenth century these remarks were quoted, alluded to, paraphrased or amplified by such critics as Bishop South, St.-Evremond, Dryden, Sprat, and Bouhours; in eighteenth-century discussions of prose style citations of Quintilian on Seneca appear with an utterly predictable regularity until the time of Blair's *Lectures* (1783).[57] These criticisms expressed a concern of which one great practical result was the development of a Restoration prose distinguished by precisely the virtues which Senecan and Silver Latin prose and its Baroque imitations lacked—a polite plainness, order, and connection.[58] But the relevance of Quintilian's criticism of Seneca was not restricted to prose; Baroque poetry exhibited analogous faults. Dryden modeled a criticism of Cowley on Quintilian's judgment of Seneca, and John Oldmixon, paraphrasing Bouhour's objections to Seneca, found them applicable to Cowley too: "Of all ingenious Authors, *Bouhours* tells us, *Seneca* is he who knew least how to keep his Thoughts within due Bounds: He is always endeavouring to please, and so afraid that a Thought, which is of itself beautiful, will not strike, that he puts it into all the Lights it can be seen in, and sets it off with all the Colours that can render it agreeable; insomuch that one may say of him what his Father said of *Montanus* . . . [that by] 'repeating the same thought, and turning it several Ways, he spoils it: Not being contented with having said a good Thing at first, he so manages it, that at last it ceases to be good.'" The secret of knowing "when to leave off when he had done well" was possessed, says Oldmixon, by Addison and Garth, but "as to Mr. Cowley he offends to Enormity, by saying more than he needed, and spoils what was well imagin'd and well said, by turning and winding it, and putting it in too many Lights."[59]

What specific qualities of style does such a criticism denote? When they speak of fragmentation in Baroque poetry the neoclassical critics have in mind, I believe, a kind of form or movement which is not uncommon in English metaphysical verse and which it shares with much prose of the same period. This movement has been sensitively described by Croll, who writes as follows of the "curt style" in the seventeenth century:

[T]here is a characteristic order, or mode of progression, in a curt period that may be regarded either as a necessary consequence of its omission of connectives or as the causes and explanation of this. We may describe it best by observing that the first member is likely to be

a self-contained and complete statement of the whole idea of the
period. It is so because writers in this style like to avoid prearrange-
ments and preparations; they begin, as Montaigne puts it, at *le
dernier poinct*, the point aimed at. The first member therefore ex-
hausts the mere fact of the idea; logically there is nothing more to
say. But it does not exhaust its imaginative truth or the energy of its
conception. It is followed, therefore, by other members, each with a
new tone or emphasis, each expressing a new apprehension of the
truth expressed in the first. We may describe the progress of a curt
period, therefore, as a series of imaginative moments occurring in a
logical pause or suspension. Or—to be less obscure—we may compare it with successive flashes of a jewel or prism as it is turned about
on its axis and takes the light in different ways.[60]

Croll's remarks exactly apply to the kind of verse movement one
finds in Cowley's ''Hope,'' in Herbert's ''Prayer [1],'' in
Vaughan's ''Son-dayes,'' and in the first nine lines of the
latter's ''To His Books,'' to suggest some touchstones. The
same movement achieves an unusually distinguished form in
the middle verse-paragraph of Marvell's ''To His Coy Mistress.''[61] But in its more extreme versions (as in Herbert's
''Prayer'') the method justifies Pope's description of it:

> Some to *Conceit* alone their Taste confine,
> And glitt'ring Thoughts struck out at ev'ry Line;
> Pleas'd with a Work where nothing's just or fit;
> One *glaring Chaos* and *wild Heap* of Wit.[62]

This ''hovering, imaginative order,'' as Croll calls the movement of the curt style, was to be replaced by the powerfully
linear movement characteristic of the mature styles of Dryden
and Pope, as Restoration verse, like Restoration prose, gradually
acquired the virtues of connected composition. Now this change
in poetic structure must be carefully described, for while its
effects were in fact revolutionary, it did not entail the complete
break with the Baroque past which neoclassical critical writing
often seems to call for. The rhetoric of eighteenth-century
couplet verse, especially as practiced by its greatest masters,
Dryden and Pope, remained inescapably Silver and in particular
sententious—for the pursuit of Augustan simplicity could not
mean the abandonment of a whole style and sensibility, the

termination of habits or the denial of forms which, however tainted their origins, had established themselves as part of the basic vocabulary of modern thought and writing. Restoration verse broke no more radically with its past than Restoration prose had done, which, while contemporary criticism cried up the virtues of the periodic style in Cicero and Livy and came close to a categorical condemnation of post-Augustan prose, nevertheless remained committed, if not to an expressly Silver style, at least to the un-Ciceronian syntax which had become habitual to it during the Baroque era.[63] But if Pope's style remained Silver, and in some sense, no doubt, ''minute,'' it was in a form that had profited by the ancients' insistence on the importance of order and connection, for in overcoming the inherent tendency of closed-couplet verse to break up into epigrammatic fragments—in learning, that is, to compose in the long sentence and even in the verse-paragraph—Dryden and Pope created an instrument adapted to just those effects of unified visual and dramatic presentation called for in Pope's description of ''true expression.''

The illustration of this last claim would be endless; to take Pope, for example, at his architectonic best one may look at the sentence structure of the Atticus portrait:

> Peace to all such! but were there One whose fires
> True Genius kindles, and fair Fame inspires,
> Blest with each Talent and each Art to please,
> And born to write, converse, and live with ease:
> Shou'd such a man, too fond to rule alone,
> Bear, like the *Turk*, no brother near the throne,
> View him with scornful, yet with jealous eyes,
> And hate for Arts that caus'd himself to rise;
> Damn with faint praise, assent with civil leer,
> And without sneering, teach the rest to sneer;
> Willing to wound, and yet afraid to strike,
> Just hint a fault, and hesitate dislike;
> Alike reserv'd to blame, or to commend,
> A tim'rous foe, and a suspicious friend,
> Dreading ev'n fools, by Flatterers besieg'd,
> And so obliging that he ne'er oblig'd;
> Like *Cato*, give his little Senate laws,

> And Sit attentive to his own applause;
> While Wits and Templers ev'ry sentence raise,
> And wonder with a foolish face of praise.
> Who but must laugh, if such a man there be?
> Who would not weep, if *Atticus* were he![64]

Here linear momentum is provided by a suspended period of twenty-one lines, which draws the reader's attention steadily forward and enables Pope to bind a sequence of epigrammatic details into a single unit, so that the effect of the whole is not that of witty display—a series of lucky hits on Atticus—but the progressive revelation of a coherent character. The passage has the economy, complexity, and unity which connected composition makes possible, and at the same time the energy, sharpness, and finality of observation typical of more broken Silver styles. The latter effects require the antitheses in which the passage abounds. These give each discrete observation its full weight, but are not allowed to detach themselves from the larger units of thought to which they belong, for Pope is writing in couplets here but not thinking in them: his mode of observation is epigrammatic but it seldom produces full-fledged epigrams. The complexity of the antithetical phrasing and the extraordinary exactness and concentration of meaning no doubt exceed our sense of the conversational, yet the portrait does not seriously disturb the dialogue norm of the poem, for the plainness of the diction preserves a sense of the speaking voice. Such metaphoric language as there is remains quiet, almost inconspicuous, because wholly subservient to the moral discriminations which the speaker is making. This is a mimetic style, and in a double sense. What it produces is not a piece of abstract analysis but quite literally a portrait—Addison, the great man, surrounded by his sycophants, sits there visibly before us—while at the same time the speaker discloses to us his own moral character and is a dramatic presence in the poem.[65]

MIMETIC STANDARDS FOR POETIC STYLE
IN JOHNSON

In the critical portion of the *Life of Cowley* Johnson's context is, like Pope's in the prismatic glass passage, mimetic: the metaphysical poets, as we have seen, "cannot be said to have imitated any thing: they neither copied nature nor life; neither painted the forms of matter nor represented the operations of intellect" (*Lives*, 1:19). The full meaning of this statement is latent—if, for the modern reader, no longer sufficiently explicit—in the famous remarks on "analytick" imagery:

> Nor was the sublime more within [the metaphysical poets'] reach than the pathetick; for they never attempted that comprehension and expanse of thought which at once fills the whole mind, and of which the first effect is sudden astonishment, and the second rational admiration. Sublimity is produced by aggregation, and littleness by dispersion. Great thoughts are always general, and consist in positions not limited by exceptions, and in descriptions not descending to minuteness. It is with great propriety that subtlety, which in its original import means exility of particles, is taken in its metaphorical meaning for nicety of distinction. Those writers who lay on the watch for novelty could have little hope of greatness; for great things cannot have escaped former observation. Their attempts were always analytick: they broke every image into fragments, and could no more represent by their slender conceits and laboured particularities the prospects of nature or the scenes of life, than he who dissects a sunbeam with a prism can exhibit the wide effulgence of a summer noon.
>
> What they wanted however of the sublime they endeavoured to supply by hyperbole; their amplification had no limits: they left not only reason but fancy behind them, and produced combinations of confused magnificence that not only could not be credited, but could not to be imagined. [*Lives*, 1:21]

When we keep before us the connotations which Johnson's figures of the prism and the summer noon would have possessed for him as a result of their history in classical and neoclassical criticism, we recognize that in the above paragraphs Johnson is, like Pope before him, distinguishing in general terms between the properties of a "natural" and those of a coterie style. Sublimity requires a style which, in Reynolds's phrase, "gives us by reflection our own mode of conceiving." Sublime description must mirror for us the unified perceptual field which we enjoy in actual vision. Moral sublimity implies an intellectual comprehension, a power of seeing one's subject as a whole, which Johnson evidently thinks of as analogous to the unity of visual experience. Both kinds of sublimity are the result of composition or, as Johnson says, of "aggregation." The metaphysical, like other coterie styles, sacrifices these effects through ''dispersion,'' the process of seeking distinction in refinements of detail.[66]

Considered from a mimetic point of view, this process presupposes what may be called an artificially cultivated state of mind. Thus metaphysical description involves a ''nicety of distinction'' at odds with our normal perceptual experience: in ''ransacking'' nature for ''illustrations, comparisons, and allusions,'' in scrutinizing it for ''occult resemblances,'' the metaphysical poets neglected simply to look at it and report what they saw. And in endeavoring to be ''singular in their thoughts'' and wishing ''only to say what they hoped had been never said before'' they adopted a style which could not represent the ''operations of intellect,'' that is, which could not trace the normal motions of the mind. Thus the effect of metaphysical conceit as Johnson conceives it is to alienate the reader from the experience which the poet's language purportedly reveals. For the metaphysical style, at least as represented by the specimens collected in the *Life of Cowley*, does not in fact portray a mind focused on its experience. Instead, it illustrates a method of disguising familiar kinds of experience in the interests of rhetorical display.

Most of the samples of metaphysical style offered in the *Life of Cowley* illustrate the adaptation to poetry of rhetorical procedures of the kind attacked by Arnauld and Fénelon. In these stanzas, and in the whole poems from which they are taken, the poet appears to conceive of his subject matter in terms of topics or commonplaces susceptible to certain established methods of amplification. Typically, his subject provides the basis for an argument, often a sophistical one; or it is developed through a series of conceits which put it in various lights—a procedure which, as the examples from Cowley's love poems particularly show, may lend to banal sentiments and postures only the thinnest kind of metaphoric novelty. That these techniques appear as the practical embodiment of a Ramistic or matter-plus-ornament approach to figurative style is presumably not accidental, since, as Joseph Mazzeo has shown, the theoretical apologists for Baroque conceit—Pierfrancesco Minozzi and Cardinal Sforza-Pallavicino—begin precisely with the assumption that the poet's subjects are commonplaces which can be made interesting only when treated in a novel style.[67]

Now Johnson does not absolutely reject these old-fashioned rhetorical methods. Instead, he considers them from what is again essentially a mimetic point of view. It must be confessed, he says, that if the metaphysical poets "are upon common subjects often unnecessarily and unpoetically subtle, yet where scholastick speculation can be properly admitted, their copiousness and acuteness may justly be admired''; and he goes on to praise the "unequalled fertility of invention" which Cowley displays in his poetical declamation against hope. The ornamented dialectic of the metaphysical school does have its use and its value—speculative reasoning is, after all, one of the "operations of intellect" which poetry may undertake to represent (though we must again note Johnson's low estimate of the pleasures afforded by "metrical disputation"—see p. 137). But the metaphysical poets applied dialectical subtlety to subjects requiring a more dramatic treatment. These included the whole range of subjects which Johnson considered sources of "the pathetick," an effect which the imitators of Donne failed to achieve because they "had no regard to that uniformity of sentiment, which enables us to conceive and to excite the pains and the pleasure of other minds: they never enquired what on any occasion they should have said or done, but wrote rather as beholders than partakers of human nature" (ibid., 1:20). The pathetic requires a style which can reproduce the natural language of passion, and in his various critical remarks on this subject Johnson endorses a standard of verisimilitude as naturalistic as Wordsworth's. Like Wordsworth's, indeed, the language in which this standard is described blurs the distinction between the mimetic and the expressive; Johnson was one of those who took literally Horace's advice, *si vis me flere*.... Thus the "amorous effusions" of Prior are unsatisfactory because "not dictated by nature or by passion," and Dryden is "not often pathetick" because "upon all occasions that were presented he studied rather than felt, and produced sentiments not such as Nature enforces, but meditation supplies'' (ibid., 2:202; 1: 457–58).

Johnson's expectations with regard to love poetry are consistent with those of an earlier neoclassicism. Dryden criticized Donne, we recall, for perplexing the minds of the fair sex with nice speculations of philosophy when he should have been entertaining them with the softnesses of love.[68] And in one of the most detailed neoclassical discussions of the love poem William Walsh assumes that the object poets propose in writing love verses is quite simply ''the obtaining the Love of their Mistress,'' which is ''certainly not to be done by forc'd Conceits, far fetch'd Similes, and shining Points; but by a true and lively Representation of the Pains and Thoughts attending such a Passion.''[69]   In a sense this dramatic standard trivialized the genre, restricting it to the expression, in Johnson's usual phrase, of ''gallantry or fondness'' in the tradition of the Cavalier lyric; one understands why Johnson, like other neoclassical critics, placed the love poem near the bottom of his hierarchy of poetic forms. On the other hand, the neoclassical standard required qualities of style that were rarely achieved, and the love poem, like other modes of ''pathetick'' writing, had an ideal value somewhat proportional to the difficulties it was expected to overcome. Johnson mentions Chesterfield as having praised the love elegies of Hammond for ''a very high species of excellence,'' namely, for being ''the genuine effusions of the mind, which expresses a real passion in the language of nature.'' But, alas, Chesterfield was wrong: ''the truth is these elegies have neither passion, nature, nor manners. Where there is fiction, there is no passion; he that describes himself as a shepherd, and his Neaera or Delia as a shepherdess, and talks of goats and lambs, feels no passion. He that courts his mistress with Roman imagery deserves to lose her; for she may with good reason suspect his sincerity. Hammond has few sentiments drawn from nature, and few images from modern life. He produces nothing but frigid pedantry.'' Hammond's love poems are like Prior's, at best the ''dull exercises of a skilful versifier ... trying to be amorous by dint of study.'' Most of Johnson's practical judgments of pathetic writing run to this tune. He found little in the verse of either the preceding or his own century that corresponded to his notion of "simplicity" or "nature."[70]

"Where there is fiction, there is no passion." *Fiction* here bears its typically Johnsonian connotation of conventional or "borrowed" elements of fable or ornament. Fiction has no place in pathetic writing, for reasons that have already been considered. The poet's task in the pathetic genres is to portray— to dramatize—the passions. He can do this perceptively, in images drawn from his own observation, and in language that is his own, or he can do it by literary imitation. Characteristically, Johnson is more sensitive than most of his contemporaries to the moral and epistemological implications of the latter method. He held strictly to the empiricist view that, since borrowed observations can have no authority as knowledge, no poetry that depends on them can have a serious claim to our attention. Thus it is not simply that conventional imagery is otiose (though this, of course, is enough to damn it esthetically); it is rather that the poet who pretends to depict the passions in such language produces a kind of unintentional falsehood. "The basis of all excellence is truth," he remarks in the *Life of Cowley*: "he that professes love ought to feel its power." He goes on to mention that Cowley admitted to writing his *Mistress*, a sequence of love poems, because he thought it expected of him to produce something in that genre, and that, although he pretends in these poems to a great variety of experiences as a lover, according to an early biographer he "in reality was in love but once, and then never had the resolution to tell his passion" (*Lives*, 1:6). For Johnson there are two issues here. When the poet claims to speak or appears to speak *in propria persona* about his own experience he ought really to do so; and if he does not his work will in any case be unsatisfactory, since no one can convincingly dramatize experiences which he has not observed or felt. The compositions comprising Cowley's *Mistress* "are such as might have been written for penance by a hermit, or for hire by a philosophical rhymer who had only heard of another sex" (ibid., 1:42).

These same issues are raised by *Lycidas*, a poem almost

uniquely suited, one might say, to excite Johnson's disgust. Of all the really famous poems in English, *Lycidas* may be the most conspicuously conventional not only in conception but in particular details. It is relentlessly "fictitious." And, as with Cowley's *Mistress*, this fault is compounded by the fact that Milton claims to be expressing real feelings about a real event.[71] "In this poem there is no nature, for there is no truth; there is no art, for there is nothing new." Milton does not "express" his feelings; he does not "imitate" grief. He puts together a poem out of materials "such as a College easily supplies." Johnson, we must remember, knew the pastoral tradition in detail from its Greek origins down to his own time; and he was deaf to the music of Milton's verse.[72] He therefore enjoyed an unobstructed view of Milton's methods, and found them pedantic. "Fame," he wrote in *Rambler* 154, "cannot spread wide or endure long that is not rooted in nature, and manured by art. That which hopes to resist the blast of malignity, and stand firm against the attacks of time, must contain in itself some original principle of growth. The reputation which arises from the detail or transportation of borrowed sentiments, may spread for a while, like ivy on the rind of antiquity, but will be torn away by accident or contempt, and suffered to rot unheeded on the ground."

The metaphysical style and the style of *Lycidas* appear opposite; in one essential respect, however, they are alike. The former seeks distinction in novel combinations of ideas—"the most heterogeneous ideas are yoked by violence together." The latter is for the most part parasitic upon familiar and even classical effects of art. Yet both are learned styles ("the metaphysical poets were men of learning, and to shew their learning was their whole endeavour"), and as such both offer the same kind of escape from the supremely difficult task of recovering what one concretely knows of human nature and human experience and giving it effective verbal form. For Johnson the highest effects of poetry are mimetic. Poetry is not as well suited as prose to the communication of discursive understanding; it is ideally suited to those kinds of awareness which can only be communicated dramatically.[73] It is in this context that Johnson saw the choice between learning and knowledge as radical. It was the choice between words and things.

When we consider Johnson in relation to the critics of antiquity we find that he has preserved the essential substance of their thinking about style, but with a notable sharpening of focus and emphasis in one respect: the element of commonsense empiricism in Ciceronian tradition reappears in Johnson with a prominence and exactness indicative, no doubt, of Johnson's training in the modern tradition of Bacon and Locke. Thus for Johnson the highest virtues of style are the public virtues stressed in particular by Cicero, Quintilian, and Longinus— perspicuity, flexibility, dramatic force, and the power to appeal to the widest possible audience by keeping to what is central in human experience. And like the ancients Johnson opposes these qualities to the "minuteness," "subtlety," or "refinement" of styles adapted to the expression of specialized learning or to the pursuit of verbal novelty. But Johnson is more preoccupied than the ancients with identifying the sources of these virtues and limitations, and here the pattern of his thought is consistently empirical. "Nature" and "simplicity" connote the power to write "immediately from knowledge," to give the image which one receives "not weakened or distorted by the intervention of any other mind." "Subtlety" begins with the desire for elegance, and the desire for elegance, Johnson repeatedly says, reflects the writer's ambition to be not merely understood but admired.

We can understand, then, why "elegance" is an ambiguous term in Johnson's criticism. "All the delicacies of style and subtilties of composition" which the arts of rhetoric and poetry have produced, Johnson says in *Idler* 63, are "useful while they advance perspicuity, and laudable while they increase pleasure, but [are] easy to be refined by needless scrupulosity till they shall more embarrass the writer than assist the reader or delight him." In earlier numbers of the *Idler* Johnson remarks that "figures, criticisms, and refinements, are the work of those whom idleness makes weary of themselves," and speaks of the writer ambitious of elegance as one who "transfers his consideration from words to sounds, from sentences to periods, and as he grows more elegant becomes less intelligible" (*Works*, 7:148, 143).[74] Refinement entails a departure from the intuitive level of experience. And in couching his definition of "conceit"—it is the most precise definition I have found in neoclassical criticism—in terms of this departure, Johnson gives us not only his conception of the dominant features of metaphysical style, but also the grounds of his objections to that style: for conceits are "thoughts not immediately impressed by sensible objects, or necessarily arising from the coalition or comparison of common sentiments" (*Rambler* 143).

6

Antinomies

Johnson is essentially an eclectic critic, as we have seen in the use he makes both of the ancient ideals of right rhetoric and of modern thinking on the empirical basis of genuine knowledge. It is this eclecticism which makes him interesting, not merely as an isolated figure, but as a focal point from which to study certain persistent problems in literary theory, for in Johnson we find reflections of virtually all the ancient and modern critical theory available to his generation, formulated with almost invariable intelligence and comprehension.

In considering the moral and cognitive ends which Johnson wished literature to serve, and the standards for style which he developed in conjunction with those ends, we have found the components of an individualistic view of poetic perception which looks ahead to Wordsworth and Coleridge. At this point, however, we must remind ourselves of the inclusive nature of Johnson's eclecticism and of the unsystematic nature of his thought. Johnson's willingness to use critical premises taken from disparate contexts at best resulted in the harmonious synthesis which we have been examining, but at times it also produced logical inconsistencies. It is important to understand the points of logical conflict in Johnson's criticism for several reasons. They define his limitations as a theorist. They reveal the transitional character of his thought, dependent on the past but at the same time anticipating some of the fundamental values of Romantic criticism. And they help us to view Johnson's criticism in its full complexity, and to minimize the danger of oversimplification.

The antinomies with which we are especially concerned have a common source in the fact that Johnson thinks of poetic ornament both in mimetic terms and in the matter-plus-ornament terms of Renaissance and Ramist tradition. In establishing the significance and provenance of his mimetic vocabulary we have said nothing about the many passages in which his stylistic criticism is governed by more traditional assumptions. These passages are, indeed, well known—it is rather the influence of Johnson's mimetic principles which the modern reader is likely to overlook. Thus, for example, in the allegorical style of *Rambler* 96, Truth is invested with "a loose and changeable robe" named Fiction with which she captivates the admirers of Falsehood. Again, Imlac tells Rasselas that the poet must store his mind with inexhaustible variety because "every idea is useful for the enforcement or decoration of moral or religious truth." And in *Rambler* 139 Johnson observes that "the idea of ornament admits use, though it seems to exclude necessity." Now the matter-plus-ornament phraseology remained habitual even to those critics who, like Hugh Blair, were most active against the assumptions which had originally produced it, so that it is not always to be taken literally. But there are, as we shall see, several important contexts in Johnson's criticism in which it is literally intended and in which the premises which it reflects determine the course of Johnson's arguments. In such contexts moral or religious truth is regarded as something abstract, categorical, and familiar, and poetry or fiction as an optional mode of illustration or decoration. The incompatibility of these notions with the empiricist tendency of Johnson's moral and critical thought has already been noted.

Poetic Diction

The Ramistic strain in Johnson's criticism reveals itself in various ways. In the matter of poetic diction, for example, Johnson's views were conventionally neoclassical. "Language," he declares in the *Life of Cowley*, "is the dress of thought; and as the noblest mien or most graceful action would be degraded and obscured by a garb appropriated to the gross employments of rusticks or mechanicks, so the most heroick sentiments will lose their efficacy, and the most splendid ideas drop their magnificence, if they are conveyed by words used commonly upon low and trivial occasions, debased by vulgar mouths, and contaminated by inelegant applications'' (*Lives*, 1:58–59). In the preceding chapter we considered the mimetic basis of Johnson's objections to metaphysical style, and specifically the fact that for Johnson a ''natural'' style is one which meets a standard of verisimilitude regarding the depiction of the ''operations of intellect'' which embraces both thought and language. We saw, moreover, that the terms in which Johnson expresses this ideal at times suggest a standard as naturalistic as Wordsworth's. But this standard was powerfully qualified by that extreme sensitivity to levels of diction in poetry that is characteristic of neoclassical taste in general. Johnson found in the metaphysical poets the same combination of opposite qualities that the neoclassical period had detected in most European literature written before its own rigid standard of elegance began to prevail: the imitators of Donne were simultaneously rude and overrefined, addicted to decadent forms of ornament but generally ''in very little care to clothe their notions with elegance of dress.'' Cowley, says Johnson, ''makes no selection of words, nor seeks any neatness of phrase; he has no elegances either lucky or elaborate'' (*Lives*, 1:31, 59). Less than thirty years after Johnson wrote the *Life of Cowley*, Coleridge was able to remark that ''in the elder poets, from Donne to Cowley, we find the most fantastic out-of-the-way thoughts, but in the most pure and genuine mother English'' (*Biographia Literaria*, 1:15). Johnson found much in their English that was ''gross,'' ''feeble,'' and ''plebian.'' If the ''curiosity'' and ''minuteness'' of metaphysical ornamentation conflicted with an ideal of spontaneity and dramatic force, there was another sense in which the metaphysical style was all too spontaneous: it was undiscriminating, indifferent to Johnson's distinctions between ''diction scholastick and popular, grave and familiar, elegant and gross'' (*Lives*, 1:420). The modern reader, who may grasp Johnson's objections to ''analytick'' or extended metaphor (especially in the versions cited in the *Life of Cowley*) yet wonder nevertheless at Johnson's lack of feeling for the dramatic power of earlier seventeenth-century verse in its plainer moments, must remind himself that the post-Coleridgean standard of pure and genuine mother English embraces a great deal that Johnson would have found remarkably insensitive and inept. In brief, Johnson's mimetic expectations coexisted with a standard of purity and correctness in poetic diction formed according to principles of a distinctly antagonistic sort and in a combination which it is very difficult to recover imaginatively today.

That Johnson, for all his concern with originality, perceptual freshness, and vividness of language, would find the eighteenth-century kenning, the stock diction which Wordsworth scorned, consonant with his notion of poetic elegance might be inferred from his own poetic practice—though it is always dangerous to infer anything about a critic's taste from the example of his poetry. But the inference is confirmed by his criticism. Dryden found English poetry brick and succeeded in leaving it marble by attempting ''those happy combinations of words which distinguish poetry from prose'' (*Lives*, 1:420). Pope in turn ''searched the pages of Dryden for happy combinations of heroick diction'' and cultivated the language ''with so much diligence and art that he has left in his *Homer* a treasure of poetical elegances to posterity'' (*Lives*, 3:238). This was a treasure to which, in the opinion of Wordsworth and Coleridge, posterity helped itself much too freely: the mannerisms of eighteenth-century style to which the Romantics especially objected were those of the ''school of Pope,'' and of Pope's Homeric translations in particular.[1] The latter owe their stylistic peculiarities in part to the methods Pope employed to give his language a properly epic elevation in accordance with the neoclassical doctrine of levels of style. The critical tradition which supported the principle of elevation, both in classical and neoclassical times, was Ramistic in its willingness to sanction ornaments which, having no organic relation to the writer's thought, functioned solely to throw the language out of prose. Pope ridiculed the doctrine, or at least the absurdities to which it led, in *Peri Bathous* (where ''Shut the door'' becomes in the high style "The wooden guardian of our privacy / Quick on its axle turn"), but followed it in his Homer, as Milton had done before him in *Paradise Lost*.[2]

Johnson defended the refinement of Pope's heroic style against contemporary apologists for Homer's artless simplicity, but it would be difficult to say how much positive pleasure he took from the artifice of Popean elevation.[3] His critical remarks on the subject of levels of style reveal on the whole a pronounced preference for the unspecialized language demanded by Cicero and Quintilian, a style whose durability and breadth of appeal derive precisely from its conformity to the norms of ordinary usage. "If there be," Johnson remarks in the *Preface to Shakespeare*,

> what I believe there is, in every nation, a stile which never becomes obsolete, a certain mode of phraseology so consonant and congenial to the analogy and principles of its respective language as to remain settled and unaltered; this stile is probably to be sought in the common intercourse of life, among those who speak only to be understood, without ambition of elegance. The polite are always catching modish innovations, and the learned depart from established forms of speech, in hope of finding or making better; those who wish for distinction forsake the vulgar, when the vulgar is right; but there is a conversation above grossness and below refinement, where propriety resides, and where [Shakespeare] seems to have gathered his comick dialogue. He is therefore more agreeable to the ears of the present age than any other authour equally remote, and among his other excellencies deserves to be studied as one of the original masters of our language.[4]

Johnson considered Milton's style "formed ... by a perverse and pedantick principle," namely, the desire "to use English words with a foreign idiom," and said of it what Ben Jonson had said of Spenser's, that " 'he wrote no language' " (*Lives*, 1: 189–91). Pope's heroic manner was for Johnson quite another affair, yet in *Idler* 77, on what he calls "easy poetry," Johnson anatomizes the style of Pope's *Iliad* with cold-blooded skepticism if not clear disapproval:

> The first lines of *Pope*'s Iliad afford examples of many licenses which an easy writer must decline:

> *Achilles' wrath*, to Greece the *direful spring*
> Of woes unnumber'd, *heaven'ly* Goddess sing,
> The wrath which *hurl'd* to Pluto's *gloomy reign*
> The souls of *mighty* chiefs untimely slain.

In the first couplet the language is distorted by inversions, clogged with superfluities, and clouded by a harsh metaphor; and in the second there are two words used in an uncommon sense, and two epithets inserted only to lengthen the line; all these practices may in a long work easily be pardoned, but they always produce some degree of obscurity and ruggedness.

The "easy poetry" which Johnson praises in *Idler* 77 he defines as "that in which natural thoughts are expressed without violence to the language." "Where any artifice appears in the construction of the verse, that verse is no longer easy." Johnson goes on to show that ease is compatible with "greatness" by quoting some plain lines from Addison's *Cato*, and that it is compatible with wit by quoting a stanza from Cowley. It has been "so long excluded by ambition of ornament, and luxuriance of imagery, that its nature seems now to be forgotten." Yet, says Johnson in conclusion, "it is less difficult to write a volume of lines swelled with epithets, brightened by figures, and stiffened by transpositions, than to produce a few couplets graced only by naked elegance and simple purity."

Johnson defends the advantages of simplicity and plainness in some detail; he offers little or nothing to justify the use of ornament merely to elevate style. The stylistic principles which seem to claim his deepest allegiance are not, after all, very far from Wordsworth's as described in the 1802 preface—Johnson's norms are polite and urban, Wordworth talks of peasant speech, but both seek the permanent center of the language—yet unlike Wordsworth Johnson sees no need to make a categorical choice between mimetic and Ramistic premises. His stylistic criticism, and probably in some degree his personal taste, reveal the strain of a contradiction which he did not perceive.[5]

Religious and Didactic Verse

We saw in considering Johnson's criticisms of metaphysical style that in certain respects it was the practical results of a matter-plus-ornament conception of the short poem that he found objectionable. On properly argumentative subjects metaphysical subtlety and acuity could be admired, but on "common subjects" they were unnecessary and unpoetical. Passion, Johnson assumes, should be dramatized, not talked about; but the metaphysical poets turned feelings into topics, asserting the existence, perhaps, of a dramatic situation, but actually converting the materials of drama into motives for the pursuit of novel metaphors. If this is a reasonably accurate description of how Johnson perceived the love poetry, for example, of Cowley and Donne, it may seem all the more curious that he failed to conceive of religious poetry in mimetic terms. This failure may be traced both to the "enthusiastic" quality of Johnson's religious feelings and to his habit of thinking of the dramatic in poetry as the literal "effusion" rather than the artful imitation of emotion. When in the *Life of Waller* Johnson briefly considers the subject matter of religious verse in dramatic terms, as the portrayal of the speaker's religious experience, the subject seems to him too private for poetry and, indeed, almost too private for words: "The employments of pious mediation are Faith, Thanksgiving, Repentance, and Supplication. Faith, invariably uniform, cannot be invested by fancy with decorations. Thanksgiving, the most joyful of all holy effusions, yet addressed to a Being without passions, is confined to a few modes, and is to be felt rather than expressed. Repentance, trembling in the presence of the judge, is not at leisure for cadences and epithets. Supplication of man to man may diffuse itself through many topicks of persuasion, but supplication to God can only cry for mercy" (*Lives*, 1: 292).

But Johnson normally thinks of religious poetry as a vehicle for illustrating or adorning abstract religious truths: "The essence of poetry is invention; such invention as, by producing something unexpected, surprises and delights. The topicks of devotion are few, and being few are universally known; but, few as they are, they can be made no more; they can receive no grace from novelty of sentiment, and very little from novelty of expression" (ibid., 1: 291–92). Here Johnson's accustomed dialectic of "natural and new" operates in a starkly Ramistic fashion. Religious truth is too familiar—too commonplace—to be interesting in itself as a poetic subject, while novelty of sentiment and expression is ineffectual for reasons given a few paragraphs later: "Of sentiments purely religious, it will be found that the most simple expression is the most sublime. Poetry loses its lustre and its power, because it is applied to the decoration of something more excellent than itself. . . . The ideas of Christian Theology are too simple for eloquence, too sacred for fiction, and too majestick for ornament; to recommend them by tropes and figures is to magnify by a concave mirror the sidereal hemisphere" (ibid., 1: 292-93).

Religious poems, then, cannot be fictions in the sense in which Shakespeare's plays are fictions; they cannot be just representations of the general nature of religious experience. Once we recognize that this alternative is excluded, and that Johnson is left with the two extremes of a literally "confessional" (and therefore to him indecent) poetry, on the one hand, and a kind of ornamented religious discourse on the other, his rejection of the genre becomes—this is perhaps the most that can be said for it—easier to understand.

The disadvantages of didactic poetry as a genre are nearly those of religious poetry as Johnson conceives of it, for the abstract truths of most didactic writing are, like the truths of religion, commonplaces which "raise no unaccustomed emotion in the mind."[6] Thus, "in a didactick poem," says Johnson in the *Life of Granville*, "novelty is to be expected only in the ornaments and illustrations" (*Lives*, 2: 295). The only apparent difference for Johnson between the religious and the didactic genres is that the truths of the latter are susceptible of decoration. This susceptibility, however, will not necessarily rescue them from their commonplaceness. Pope's *Essay on Man*, for example, "affords an egregious instance of the predominance of genius, the dazzling splendour of imagery, and the seductive powers of eloquence," but Pope's masterful ornaments finally do nothing for his matter. "Never were penury of knowledge and vulgarity of sentiment so happily disguised. The reader feels his mind full, though he learns nothing; and when he meets it in its new array no longer knows the talk of his mother and his nurse'' (*Lives*, 3: 243). The ornaments are excellent, the poem a failure. Johnson tries to account for the failure by emphasizing the ''vulgarity'' of Pope's positions; he runs through a list of Pope's great truths—''that evil is sometimes balanced by good; that human advantages are unstable and fallacious, of uncertain duration and doubtful effect; that our true honour is not to have a great part, but to act it well; that virtue only is our own; and that happiness is always in our power''—and concludes by remarking, ''Surely a man of no very comprehensive search may venture to say that he has heard all this before'' (ibid., 1: 243-44). But this is an irrelevant objection; Johnson has already admitted that novelty is not to be expected in the precepts of didactic poems. Johnson's objections to Pope's *Essay* reveal the failure not of the poem but of the critic. The weakness of the poem to which Johnson wishes to call attention is that in it matter and ornament remain separated: despite the ''blaze of embellishment'' and the ''sweetness of melody'' one sees Pope's truths as truisms, naked and vulgar in their abstractness. Johnson, however, cannot say this because he is arguing from premises which take the separation of matter and ornament for granted. The assumptions which Johnson brings to the criticism of didactic poetry will not allow him to explain the limitations of Pope nor, for that matter, the success of his own *Vanity of Human Wishes*—a poem which enforces some of the same moral truths condemned as banal in the *Essay on Man*.[7]

POETIC JUSTICE AND THE
MORAL VALUE OF THE DRAMA

Besides leading to conflicting terminologies in his discussions of poetic style, Johnson's use of both pragmatic and mimetic premises results in inconsistencies regarding the moral value of poetry; these are most obvious in the *Preface to Shakespeare*. After describing Shakespeare as ''the poet of nature'' who excels all other modern writers by holding up to his readers ''a faithful mirrour of manners and life,'' Johnson observes, ''It is from this wide extension of design that so much instruction is derived. It is this which fills the plays of Shakespeare with practical axioms and domestick wisdom. It was said of Euripides, that every verse was a precept; and it may be said of Shakespeare, that from his works may be collected a system of civil and oeconomical prudence. Yet his real power is not shewn in the splendour of particular passages, but by the progress of his fable, and the tenour of his dialogue''(*Preface*, p. 62). Here Johnson seems content to let the moral significance of Shakespeare's plays arise inductively from the characters, action, and dialogue. But when Johnson comes to enumerate Shakespeare's faults, his ''first defect'' is that

> he sacrifices virtue to convenience, and is so much more careful to please than to instruct, that he seems to write without any moral purpose. From his writings indeed a system of social duty may be selected, for he that thinks reasonably must think morally; but his precepts and axioms drop casually from him; he makes no just distribution of good or evil, nor is always careful to shew in the virtuous a disapprobation of the wicked; he carries his persons indifferently through right and wrong, and at the close dismisses them without further care, and leaves their examples to operate by chance. [Ibid., 7:71]

It is not enough, then, to let the example ''operate by chance'': the moral must be pointed, the universal stated abstractly so that there will be no mistake. The critic who of all others in the eighteenth century best described and praised the complexity, variety, and empirical intelligibility of Shakespeare's fictions at the same time wanted these fictions, in the part if not in the whole, to exemplify a categorical morality.

Although in his notes and commentary to Shakespeare's plays Johnson spends far more time exhibiting Shakespeare's ''skills in human nature'' by noting the complexity and realism of his characters than he does drawing moral lessons from the plots, there is no doubt that Johnson habitually looked for such lessons and saw no incongruity in stating them sometimes in remarkably simple terms. Johnson's perspicacity as an interpreter of ''general nature'' is best seen in the brilliant prose character of Falstaff given in the concluding note to 2 *Henry IV*, but even here he is not content to stay within the boundaries of the play: "The moral to be drawn from this representation [of Falstaff] is, that no man is more dangerous than he that with a will to corrupt, hath the power to please; and that neither wit nor honesty ought to think themselves safe with such a companion when they see Henry seduced by Falstaff" (*Works*, 7:523-24). At his most insensitive, as Jean Hagstrum has noted, Johnson could find in the plot of *Othello* proof that "deceit and falsehood . . . are, in the sum of life, obstacles to happiness" as well as a warning "against the imprudent generosity of disproportionate marriages."[8]

On the other side, it must be noted that Johnson never committed himself to poetic justice. Of all the didactic premises of neoclassicism, this was the most radically incompatible with an empirical approach to the moral value of fiction. At worst, poetic justice sanctions the violation of probability for the sake of a predetermined outcome; at best it severely circumscribes the range of fiction by allowing only those plots in which an outcome conformable to a standard of ideal justice can be made to seem probable. Neoclassical defenses of poetic justice naturally depend on some form of conceptualist approach to fiction: the moralistic defense—that the reward of virtue and punishment of vice will move the audience to virtuous action—makes fiction a form of rhetoric, or as we say now, propaganda; the mimetic argument, such as that of John Dennis, for whom poetic justice on the stage imitates the reality of Divine Justice, makes fiction a kind of allegory, since the "reality" thus "imitated" is merely an article of faith, that is, a concept not derivable from experience. The incompatibility of either doctrine with what seem to be the most general and durable principles of tragedy has been much discussed, and needs no special mention here.

It is not (as R. D. Stock seems to suggest) that Johnson sometimes wrote in favor of poetic justice and at other times against it. His position was more complicated than this.[9] It is true, as Stock notes, that the doctrine of poetic justice is defended in the dedication to Thomas Maurice's *Poems* (1780), which Johnson assisted Maurice in writing, but in no remarks published as his own does Johnson endorse the doctrine or give the traditional reasons for it.[10] Johnson's remark in the *Preface to Shakespeare* that Shakespeare "makes no just distribution of good or evil" may, indeed, stand as an exception to this statement, but this is by no means certain: if Johnson is referring to poetic justice in this phrase, his language is quite imprecise (we must take "good or evil" to mean "reward or punishment"), and one might argue that, if poetic justice is meant, the uncertainty of the expression indicates a reluctance on Johnson's part to commit himself fully to that doctrine. Elsewhere in his edition of Shakespeare, Johnson either skirts the issues raised by the doctrine or severely qualifies the doctrine itself. In his commentary on *Hamlet*, for example, Johnson notes in passing that the play fails to produce poetic justice, but he is more concerned to display its improbability: "The poet is accused of having shewn little regard to poetical justice, and may be charged with equal neglect of poetical probability. The apparition left the regions of the dead to little purpose; the revenge which he demands is not obtained but by the death of him that was required to take it; and the gratification which would arise from the destruction of an usurper and a murderer, is abated by the untimely death of Ophelia, the young, the beautiful, the harmless, and the pious" (*Works*, Yale ed., 8: 1011). The remark about the gratification which would arise from the destruction of Claudius gives us the clue to Johnson's interest in poetic justice, such as it was. When Johnson does object to Shakespeare's violation of poetic justice—and this is a criticism which he only makes a posteriori, on the basis of his response to the individual play—his reasons are esthetic, not moralistic or theological. When for example he comments, a propos of Angelo's pardon in the last act of *Measure for Measure*, that "Angelo's crimes were such, as must sufficiently justify punishment," he is thinking not of the salutary effect of such punishment upon the reader but of two faults intrinsic to the play: the improbability of its resolution, and the fact that the resolution fails, in Coleridge's phrase, to "satisfy the claims of the moral sense''—''every reader feels some indignation,'' says Johnson, ''when he finds [Angelo] spared'' (ibid., 7: 213).

Johnson would have understood Coleridge's phrase to mean —and the principle is as old as the *Poetics*—that fiction ought to respect the reader's sympathies as well as his sense of probability: the best fictions are those in which the emotional expectations created in the reader by his moral response to the characters are gratified in a probable way.[11] This is the assumption underlying Johnson's objection to the death of Cordelia. Shakespeare had no good esthetic reason for having Cordelia killed, and several for keeping her alive; he has, in short, suffered her ''to perish in a just cause, contrary to the natural ideas of justice, to the hope of the reader, and, what is yet more strange, to the faith of chronicles.'' Johnson's defense of Tate's revision of the play then takes this form: ''A play in which the wicked prosper, and the virtuous miscarry, may doubtless be good, because it is a just representation of the common events of human life: but since all reasonable beings naturally love justice, I cannot easily be persuaded, that the observation of justice makes a play worse; or, that if other excellencies are equal, the audience will not always rise better pleased from the final triumph of persecuted virtue'' (ibid., 8: 704). *If other excellencies are equal*—if, that is, the effect can be had without violence to probability—the audience will rise better *pleased* (not instructed or reformed) by having its hope and its sense of justice gratified. Johnson goes on to add that he was himself so ''shocked'' by Cordelia's death when he first read the play that he never picked it up again before becoming Shakespeare's editor. His own ''sensations,'' together with the fact that ''the publick has decided'' in favor of Tate, supply the empirical basis for Johnson's esthetic preference for the revised version of *Lear*.[12]

The modern reader will no doubt find Johnson's defense of Tate unacceptable, but it will be for reasons only indirectly related to the doctrine of poetic justice. It will be because he considers the gratification of our love of justice to have a less prominent place in the experience of tragedy than Johnson thought it should, and because he finds that the death of Cordelia, however ''shocking,'' satisfies deeper and more truly tragic emotional expectations having to do (in Aristotle's terms) with pity, fear, and wonder. The principle that fiction ought to satisfy the emotional as well as the rational expectations of the audience holds with tragedy as with other genres, but Johnson's application of the principle in the case of *King Lear* is superficial.

That he keeps to this principle in *Rambler* 4, where his subject is a form of comedy and where his moralistic interest in literature is given its fullest expression, is, I think, a remarkable instance of the sophistication of Johnson's esthetic thinking relative to his own time. In *Rambler* 4 Johnson is defending the moral value of the modern realistic novel, a form which, he says, ''may be termed not improperly the comedy of romance, and is to be conducted nearly by the rules of comick poetry. Its province is to bring about natural events by easy means, and to keep up curiosity without the help of wonder.'' Now comedy is of all fictional modes the most hospitable to poetic justice, yet Johnson stops short of endorsing poetic justice in *Rambler* 4. Since novels are written ''chiefly to the young, the ignorant, and the idle, to whom they serve as lectures of conduct, and introductions into life,'' their authors ought to take care not only to portray human life and manners faithfully ''but to provide that they may be seen hereafter with less hazard.'' ''If the world be promiscuously described,'' says Johnson, ''I cannot see of what use it can be to read the account: or why it may not be as safe to turn the eye immediately upon mankind as upon a mirrour which shews all that presents itself without discrimination.'' Nevertheless, realistic fiction is to present a selection of characters modeled on contemporary life and manners; it should omit ''many characters [which] ought never to be drawn,'' but it is not to produce allegories of Providential justice. Johnson asks simply that predominantly vicious characters not be portrayed so sympathetically that their vices, borrowing the luster of associated virtues, will be condoned, and that the novelist exhibit ''the most perfect idea of virtue; of virtue not angelical, nor above probability, for what we cannot credit,

we shall never imitate, but the highest and purest that humanity can reach, which, exercised in such trials as the various
revolutions of things shall bring upon it, may, by conquering
some calamities, and enduring others, teach us what we may
hope, and what we can perform.'' In short, he asks principally
that the moral intelligence of the ''implied author'' be clear
and sound and that virtuous characters be credible and probable, but not necessarily always triumphant. And these, after
all, are boundaries within which a great deal of realistic fiction
has flourished from Johnson's time down to our own.

When Johnson does address himself to the traditional arguments for poetic justice he rejects them. Commenting on
Dryden's denial that Adam is the hero of *Paradise Lost* because
he was overcome, Johnson declares that ''there is no reason why
the hero should not be unfortunate except established practice,
since success and virtue do not go necessarily together'' (*Lives*,
1: 176). In the *Life of Addison* Johnson quotes at length from
Dennis's defense of poetic justice, but concludes, ''Whatever
pleasure there may be in seeing crimes punished and virtue
rewarded, yet, since wickedness often prospers in real life, the
poet is certainly at liberty to give it prosperity on the stage. For
if poetry has an imitation of reality, how are its laws broken by
exhibiting the world in its true form? The stage may sometimes
gratify our wishes; but, if it be truly the *mirror of life*, it ought
to shew us sometimes what we are to expect'' (*Lives*, 2: 135).
Significantly, Johnson ignores Dennis's arguments and returns
to the premise of his own partial defense of poetic justice
(''whatever *pleasure* there may be in seeing crimes punished...''), but only to express, now, a preference for the
principle that poetry ought to imitate reality over the rival
principle that it ought to gratify our wishes. The empiricist critic
speaks here: poetry's primary function is to exhibit the real state
of sublunary nature.

It is surely not accidental that the two opposed poetic
functions in the above passage recall Bacon's opposition of
poetry to reason. The discussions of poetry in the *Advancement
of Learning* and in the *De Augmentis Scientiarum* are quoted or

paraphrased so often by critics from Addison to Reynolds and Blair that they may be fairly said to represent the eighteenth century's understanding of the general nature and function of poetry.[13] In citing Bacon, eighteenth-century critics embraced the view that poetry, as Bacon says in the *De Augmentis*, "seems to bestow upon human nature those things which history denies to it, and to satisfy the mind with the shadows of things when the substance cannot be obtained," and, again, that poetry "raises the mind and carries it aloft, accommodating the shows of things to the desires of the mind, not (like reason and history) buckling and bowing down the mind to the nature of things."[14]

Bacon's poetic theory amounts in effect to a psychologized version of Sidney's neo-Platonism. Bacon accepts Sidney's distinction between the golden world which the poets only deliver and the brazen world of experience and explains the appeal of the former by its power to gratify our wishes for "a more ample greatness, a more perfect order, and a more beautiful variety" than we can find anywhere in nature since the Fall. But in addition to Bacon's greater interest in the psychological causes of esthetic pleasure, there is this more important difference between Bacon and Sidney, namely, that Bacon opposes poetry to reason whereas Sidney does not. And this, as we have seen, leaves in considerable doubt the question whether fiction can claim to have any value as truth or knowledge. Sidney could claim on neo-Platonic grounds that poetic fictions were not mere fantasies but embodied intuitions of a higher reality; but such intuitions did not exist for Bacon, who sought truth and knowledge in the empirical world alone. Fictions were, therefore, subjective and arbitrary creations designed to satisfy the mind "with the shadows of things when the substance cannot be obtained." Bacon had no wish to attack poetry; on the contrary, he defends its value as a teaching instrument—that is, as a form of rhetoric. But it is difficult not to consider Bacon's opposition of poetry to reason in the light of his perpetual concern with the Idols of the Mind, that is, with all the ways in which the imagination works to close off the mind from objective reality.

Johnson of course thought habitually of the dangers of fiction in these terms. His profound fear of the "dangerous prevalence of imagination," the tendency of the mind "to indulge the power of fiction" until "fictions begin to operate as realities"; his belief that, because "the power of example is so great as to take possession of the memory by a kind of violence, and produce effects almost without the intervention of the will," literature is apt to be "mischievous or uncertain" in its effects especially upon the young; his extraordinary awareness of the extent to which almost all imaginative works are conventional in substance and in detail, imitations of other imitations in which little is represented as it has been felt or seen—these are only some of the reasons why the process of intellectual maturity, as Johnson describes it in *Rambler* 151, ought to involve the eventual rejection of "imitations of truth, which are never perfect" for the sake of "truth itself."[15] What is remarkable, in view of Johnson's willingness to carry the antipoetic implications of Baconian principles to their farthest extreme, is the subtlety and flexibility of mind reflected in the features of his esthetic theory which we have just been considering. In the rejection of poetic justice quoted above from the *Life of Addison* the Baconian view of poetry as wish fulfillment and the Johnsonian view of poetry as the mirror of life appear for a moment in direct conflict, like the terms "poetry" and "reason" in Bacon's poetic theory. In general, however, Johnson does not accept the logic that posits a necessary conflict between the esthetic and emotional power of fiction and its fidelity to nature. Fiction need not offer us flattering myths or congenial delusions, and it need not pander to our neurotic fears. It can relate the ideal to the actual, as Johnson suggests in *Rambler* 4, by portraying probable virtue and probable vice and deriving its characters from actual observation. And it can excite and gratify a rational sympathy by representations which move us "not because they are mistaken for realities, but because they bring realities to mind" (*Preface*, 7: 78). Unlike many of his contemporaries, Johnson implicitly rejected the Baconian theory of poetry in embracing the formula that "nothing can please many, and please long, but just representations of general nature.'' It is at the very least a likely speculation that Johnson refused to make a rule of poetic justice because he saw that, however plausible in theory, in practice it was a sentimental doctrine, productive of works that showed the reader what he wanted to believe at the expense of what he knew.

NOVELTY AND THE UNIFORMITY OF HUMAN PERCEPTION

The inconsistencies in Johnson's criticism reflect the influence of disparate critical systems and the conflicting implications of disparate terminologies. But they also, in some cases, issue from Johnson's uncertainty whether the kind of poetry he most valued, that which meets a mimetic standard of fidelity to perception, can indeed be written at all periods in the life of a culture. Can the poet who remains true to his firsthand observations of physical nature and human behavior continue to produce reflections which are new as well as natural? This question arose for Johnson because, for all his indebtedness to Locke, Johnson was still under the influence of assumptions which can probably be described as the final esthetic legacy of the realist epistemology of Aristotle and Aquinas. I have in mind, first, the belief in the uniformity of natural appearances —or, to put it in subjective terms, the belief in the uniformity of human perception—which underlay the realist faith in the identity of knowing and the object known and in the existence of a stable world of species.[16] The chief consequence of this belief for esthetics is that art can, in the course of time, literally exhaust the appearances of nature, leaving the artist with no alternative but to produce those ''irregular combinations of fanciful invention,'' as Johnson says in the abstract language of the *Preface to Shakespeare*, those ''accidental compositions of heterogeneous modes,'' which are ''dissolved by the chance which combined them'' (*Preface* 7: 61, 70).

I have stressed the individualistic tendencies in Johnson's thought, especially the high value he attaches to ''perspicacity'' and ''original invention.'' These are the themes of a number of essays in which Johnson takes the optimistic view that ''art and nature have stores inexhaustible by human intellects; and every moment produces something new to him, who has quickened his faculties by diligent observation.'' The foundation of Johnson's empirical approach to the representation of ''general nature'' is, as we have seen, the premise that, though human nature is uniform, it can always be depicted in a way ''at once natural and new'' through the observation of contemporary manners: ''here then is the fund, from which those who study mankind may fill their compositions with an inexhaustible variety of images and allusions.'' And on one notable occasion Johnson extends his faith in perspicacity to the realm of physical description: the poet Thomson, he says ''looks round on Nature and on Life with the eye which Nature bestows only on a poet, the eye that distinguishes in every thing presented to its view whatever there is on which imagination can delight to be detained.... The reader of *The Seasons* wonders that he never saw before what Thomson shews him, and that he never yet has felt what Thomson impresses.''[17]

We have seen that in *Adventurer* 95 Johnson dismisses the common complaint that ''all topicks are pre-occupied'' as ''nothing more than the murmur of ignorance or idleness, by which some discourage others and some themselves'' (see p. 87). But he was not always so sure of this. ''It fills me with wonder,'' says Imlac in chapter 10 of *Rasselas*, ''that, in almost all countries, the most ancient poets are considered as the best,'' and he entertains the possibility that, ''as the province of poetry is to describe Nature and Passion, which are always the same, the first writers took possession of the most striking objects for description, and the most probable occurrences for fiction, and left nothing to those that followed them, but transcription of the same events, and new combinations of the same images'' (*Works*, 3:327). Elsewhere Johnson speaks of the advantage which the ancients enjoy ''merely by priority, which put them in possession of the most natural sentiments, and left us nothing but servile repetition or forced conceits.'' Those who follow the originator of a literary form ''are forced to peep into neglected corners, to note the casual varieties of the same species, and to recommend themselves by minute industry, and distinctions too subtle for common eyes.''[18] This is in particular the dilemma of the literary imitator; but even if one succeeds in imitating nature directly instead of seeing it through the spectacles of books there is the difficulty that ''though nature itself, philosophically considered, be inexhaustible, yet its general effects on the eye and on the ear are uniform, and incapable of much variety of description.'' Physical nature, which does not change, must, if described effectively, always be described in nearly the same way, for poetry ''cannot dwell upon the minuter distinctions'' nor ''dissect the latent qualities of things, without losing its general power of gratifying every mind by recalling its conceptions.''[19] Human nature, on the other hand, appears to us in the perpetual variety of changing manners. Yet Johnson was not always secure in the principles of literary realism which he enunciated so forcefully in *Adventurer* 95; in *Rambler* 36, for example, he argues that pastoral poetry is limited as a genre by the narrow range of the human as well as of the natural appearances which it may properly represent: ''Our descriptions may indeed differ from those of Virgil, as an English from an Italian summer, and, in some respects, as modern from ancient life; but as nature is in both countries nearly the same [!], and as poetry has to do rather with the passions of men, which are uniform, than their customs, which are changeable, the varieties, which time or place can furnish, will be inconsiderable.''

The conflict in Johnson's thinking concerning the perceptual basis of mimesis involves the representation, then, of both ''the prospects of nature'' and ''the scenes of life.'' But it is in certain of Johnson's statements about natural description that it appears most sharply. On the one hand the reader of Thomson ''wonders that he never saw before what Thomson shews him, and that he never yet has felt what Thomson impresses'': the poet's perceptions are extraordinary, unique; the descriptive effect is original. On the other hand, the poet is to gratify every mind by recalling its conceptions, and this can be done only by exhibiting ''those characteristicks which are alike obvious to vigilance and carelessness'' (*Works*, 3:329): the poet imitates normal appearances or the process of ordinary perception.

Now it may be that these positions are reconcilable; I myself believe that they are. But Johnson does not reconcile them, so far as I can discover; the conflict defines a genuine limitation in Johnson's critical thought.[20] This conflict had no real effect, however, on Johnson's expectations as a practical critic. Whatever his doubts about the possibility of continued discoveries about human or physical nature—or their centrality if they are possible—these doubts were never allowed to compromise his demands for freshness of observation and feeling and a transparent language to communicate these: in practice he did not accept conventionality as inevitable. These values lead Johnson to focus on different artistic elements in different forms. In his Shakespeare criticism, he emphasizes the principles of character drawing; in criticizing the short poem, he demands spontaneity in language. But these elements are related: the moral insight which realistic fiction provides by a selection of particular details pointing to central experiences is provided in the short poem by a freshness and flexibility of style which again conveys the individual realization of universal human concerns.

When we consider the antinomies in Johnson's criticism in the light of subsequent Romantic developments, they appear to mark the points at which Johnson failed to pursue consistently and far enough the logic of that individualism whose premises we first explored in connection with Bacon, Fénelon, and Arnauld. Or, to say much the same thing in other terms, they mark the points at which Johnson failed to pursue the logic of his adherence to a perceptual standard of poetic style. Thus he continued to defend the propriety of conventional ornament or ''poetic diction'' in eighteenth-century verse despite the fact that, as Wordsworth pointed out, such ornament has no value as perception. He raised the problem of originality in its acutest —indeed, in an insoluble—form in connection with descriptive writing by restricting the poet to common and obvious appearances, and he raised much the same problem in connection with didactic verse by conceiving of general truths as established commonplaces virtually incapable of being rescued, as Coleridge puts it, "from the impotence caused by the very circumstance of their universal admission."[21]

Wordsworth and Coleridge met these difficulties, as we have seen, by insisting upon the primacy and uniqueness of the poet's powers of observation. The highest effects of poetic description bear witness, in their view, not to the passive impression of normal appearances, but to the selective and creative response of a particular sensibility; in principle, poetic description can always be "at once natural and new," for the good descriptive poet shows us what we have seen or heard before but never noticed so distinctly and at the same time imparts to the properties he selects an emotional coloring which is his own. As for moral truths, these too acquire a new authority whenever they are not merely "adopted" as abstract truisms but instead are "perceived," as Wordsworth says, "with the freshness and clearness of an original intuition."[22] It is not the logical content but the individual experience of truth which supplies the poet's real subject matter.

Conclusion

I have tried in the preceding chapters to reconstruct the logic of Samuel Johnson's taste in poetic style by relating his criticism to the relevant historical background. It has seemed to me desirable to present this background as fully as possible in order to illustrate the perennial importance of the issues involved in Johnson's stylistic criticism and thus the centrality of Johnson's effort and achievement. The history of these issues from the classical period up to and including Johnson supplies us with the terms in which the issues declared themselves to Johnson and enables us to appreciate the values which they represented. Their subsequent history, from Johnson to Wordsworth and Coleridge, reveals the full development and in a sense the completion of the critical logic implicit in Johnson's premises and in those of his age, and this perspective enables us to measure the strengths and weaknesses of Johnson's stylistic criticism against our sense of the potentiality of his critical tools.

I have intended the historical method employed in this book to reflect the principles of the neoclassical approach to the history of taste and style. This approach assumes, as we have seen, that the principles of style are timeless and absolute; that the various epochs in the history of style reflect either approximation to or departure from ideal norms; that the tendency toward mannerism or coterie limitation in the styles of any epoch reflects a recurrent conflict between the dictates of "good sense" and the appeal of novelty and fashion; and that the critic's purpose in studying previous criticism and previous styles is to learn to distinguish, as Johnson said, "that which is established because it is right, from that which is right only because it is established." This cyclical view of literary history inclined the neoclassical critics to seek for parallels rather than differences between earlier periods and their own and to let the past comment on the present wherever possible. It inspired Bacon's parallels between the fragmentation of intellectual life in the sixteenth century and in Roman times; Fénelon's conviction that the ideals which should govern seventeenth-century pulpit oratory had already been defined by Plato, Cicero, and Augustine and that the faults of modern style were as old as Isocrates; and Johnson's use of critical metaphors in the *Life of Cowley* which link the eccentricities of metaphysical style to those of the coterie styles of antiquity.

This view enables us, as modern students of neoclassicism, to find order and continuity in neoclassical stylistic criticism and to locate the principle of its coherence in the reaffirmation and reinterpretation of traditional values rather than in a merely conservative and habitual employment of established terms, methods, and critical opinions. The more thoughtful, at least, of seventeenth- and eighteenth-century stylistic critics persisted in using the critical language of the ancients because they saw the concerns and values reflected in that language as deeply compatible with those accented by the development of modern thought. Thus, in the Roman good sense of Cicero and Quintilian they found attitudes restated with emphasis in the otherwise novel and radical philosophies of Descartes, Bacon, and Locke: a distrust of dogma and of speculative subtlety, of abstract methods and conventional procedures of every kind, which gained in point from the more fully articulated and rationalized skepticism and individualism of the moderns; a concern for the utilitarian values of language—ease of communication and breadth of appeal; and an emphasis upon the fruits of individual observation and experience, made persuasive through a style subordinated to the process of understanding and free from self-conscious artifice.

The pursuit of these themes in neoclassical criticism leads us to a view of that criticism as largely static in values but dynamic in the pressure exerted by these values upon taste, practice, and to some degree upon critical theory. There is little in Fénelon's

Dialogues (1679) which would not have won the assent of Wordsworth in 1800. What occurred in the stylistic criticism of the intervening period was a progressive clarification of the demands of individualism through the evolution of a perceptual standard for poetic style. It is our understanding of these demands that enables us to appreciate the significance of the most important development in the stylistic criticism of the eighteenth century, namely, the emergence of a mimetic theory of ornament which healed the split between matter and words by depicting ornament as the necessary reflection of an individual sensibility and mode of conceiving.

As for Johnson himself, the historical approach undertaken in this study enables us to relate a number of his otherwise apparently disparate critical expectations to their moral and intellectual center. We have found in Johnson's judgments of metaphysical style, of the style of *Lycidas*, and indeed of all learned, as opposed to "natural" or spontaneous, styles in the shorter poetic forms a consistent reflection of the stylistic implications of his central critical premise that fiction ought to strive for the just representation of "general nature." We have resolved that premise, in turn, into a view of mimesis consistent with the epistemology of Bacon and Locke. To appreciate Johnson's view of mimesis we have first had to consider the distinctively empiricist approach to the interpretation of particular moral situations developed in the eighteenth century by Johnson, Gibbon, Burke, and others—an approach in harmony with Pascal's *esprit de finesse* and with Locke's analysis of the "mixed modes" and the limitations of discursive language. This approach dictated the principles of literary realism, inasmuch as it stressed the dependence of moral understanding upon a complex and undistorted view of the particulars of the individual case. And it gave implicit support to the cognitive status of realistic fiction as the vehicle of a moral knowledge more circumstantial and less abstract, hence more adequate to its objects, than could normally be accommodated by the discursive genres of the belles lettres.

These principles of inquiry and expression inform Johnson's

discussions of biography and fiction in the *Rambler* and *Adventurer*, as well as his conception of Shakespeare's success in achieving "just representations of general nature." They support a critical logic which, when understood in its entirety, allows us to interpret Johnson's conception of mimesis as clear and self-consistent within the limits of the empiricist epistemology available to him, to distinguish this conception from the neo-Platonic tradition in neoclassicism and reveal its natural alliance with modern realism in the tradition of Richardson and Austen, and, finally, to appreciate the *Preface to Shakespeare* as an original attempt to find, within the premises of modern empiricism, a solution to the ancient problem of the relation between fictional particulars and general moral truth.

This same critical logic allows us to bridge the gap between Johnson's general principles and his particular criticisms of poetic style. For Johnson's objections to the metaphysical and other learned styles follow in large part from the empiricist demand that the poet write as directly as he can out of his own experience. Johnson looks to the minor poetic genres for the same proof of undistorted perception and detailed contact with reality that he praises in the plays of Shakespeare. Thus he asks for a style distinguished by the virtues of "natural" eloquence best described in the previous century by Fénelon—flexibility, transparency, freedom from mannerism, accuracy in the rendering of perceptual experience and in the imitation of the spontaneous movements of the mind. His sense of what is lost when these qualities are neglected in the interest of verbal ingenuity emerges for us fully and distinctly when we relate his objections to *Lycidas* and to metaphysical style to the tradition of neoclassical commentary on the differences between "natural" eloquence and "conceit." This tradition teaches us to perceive the eccentricities of the metaphysical style in particular as limited in appeal, egocentric in their obtrusive wittiness, and illustrative of a reliance upon the conceptual intellect—the source of fixed methods for securing novel effects through style—at the expense of perception and intuition. Johnson's familiarity with modern empiricism no doubt enhanced his awareness of what these criticisms implied, for his empiricism encouraged him to regard the techniques of metaphysical style as techniques of distortion and evasion leading both poet and reader away from their concrete knowledge of human life.

The neoclassical tradition as a whole, however, judged the mannerisms of seventeenth-century style according to standards which, though supported by modern philosophy, were borrowed from the critics and models of antiquity, and these standards are, as we have seen, implicit in the critical vocabulary of the *Life of Cowley*. Thus in order to appreciate the distinctive synthesis of ancient and modern principles which Johnson's criticism represents, we have described the pattern of critical judgments and concerns which the eighteenth century regarded as defining the central tradition of the classical approach to style. This tradition provided the most complete discussions available to the neoclassical period of the social and moral value of unmannered style and is no doubt the ultimate source of Johnson's preoccupation with the qualities which give style breadth of appeal, "length of duration, and continuance of esteem." It also made available a variety of terms and metaphors for describing the effects of coherent poetic composition and for specifying the kinds of fragmentation produced by specialized or mannered styles—terms which the neoclassical critics used to develop a specific notion of poetic unity. The study of the relevant contexts in classical and neoclassical criticism enables us to read Johnson's criticisms of metaphysical style with a fairly concrete sense of the compositional effects which he required of that style and failed to discover. Thus we reanimate his practical criticism by becoming aware, however partially, of the kinds of perception his formulations originally expressed.

Finally, a historical approach has allowed us to identify and account for the inconsistencies in Johnson's critical thinking. These inconsistencies make Johnson a transitional figure in the development of modern taste and critical theory, as well as the last great interpreter of neoclassical values. By following out the logic of the perceptual approach to poetic style to its completion in the criticism of Wordsworth and Coleridge, we discover the referents of a critical continuum spanning the neoclassical era—a continuum in which Johnson can be placed with some precision. In his criticism we can observe the theoretical limitations, and the consequences for taste, of a reliance upon the matter-plus-ornament conception of style inherited from the Middle Ages and the Renaissance. This side of Johnson looks to the past and to what was, theoretically speaking, weakest in neoclassical tradition. In his use of a mimetic conception of style, and in his appeal to perceptual standards, Johnson looks toward the future.

In emphasizing what is forward-looking in Johnson, I am aware that I make a claim that transcends the historical—for there is no value in innovation, or in progressive rather than conservative thought, in and of itself. The understanding of Johnson's mimetic premises, in their relation to his empiricism, seems to me important because it clarifies the most enduring values celebrated in his criticism as a whole. And these values represent what is best in neoclassical tradition.

APPENDIX A

"The Streaks of the Tulip"

Those who associate Johnson with the neo-Platonic tradition in neoclassical criticism and esthetics usually cite Imlac's advice against numbering the streaks of the tulip as evidence for their point of view. They appear to regard that advice as expressing principles similar to those which inform Reynolds's genuinely neo-Platonic doctrine of "general form" as presented in *Idlers* 79 and 82 and above all in the third *Discourse*.[1] Reynolds indeed invited the comparison with Johnson by borrowing some of the latter's language. In chapter 10 of *Rasselas* Imlac contends that the business of a poet "is to examine, not the individual, but the species; to remark general properties and large appearances; he does not number the streaks of the tulip, or describe the different shades in the verdure of the forest. He is to exhibit in his portraits of nature such prominent and striking features, as recall the original to every mind; and must neglect the minuter discriminations, which one may have remarked, and another have neglected, for those characteristicks which are alike obvious to vigilance and carelessness." In the third *Discourse* Reynolds remarks that the ideal student of painting whom he is trying to describe "will permit the lower painter, like the florist or collector of shells, to exhibit the minute discriminations, which distinguish one object of the same species from another; while he, like the philosopher, will consider nature in the abstract, and represent in every one of his figures the character of its species." And there are verbal echoes of other passages from Imlac's dissertation on poetry elsewhere in the same *Discourse*.[2]

However, a number of commentators have at least implicitly denied that Reynolds's idealism can be taken as a gloss on Imlac in denying that Imlac's remarks express a neo-Platonic esthetic. Jean Hagstrum comments, for example, that "Plato in the *Phaedo* had advised the poet to choose such particulars as remind the reader of universals; Johnson urged the poet 'to exhibit, in his portraits of nature, such prominent and striking features, as recall the original to every mind. . . .' Plato wanted the particular to reveal the general and universal; Johnson wanted the general to recall the particular. Plato's point of view is metaphysical; Johnson's psychological." Hagstrum's interpretation is surely correct, yet the tulip passage has remained a subject of controversy.[3] The following remarks are intended to clarify some of the important differences between Imlac's advice on poetic description and Reynolds's theory of general form and to place the tulip passage in a historical context which may shed some light on its importance.

It may be noted first of all that Imlac's remarks on the tulip pertain only to the poetic description of physical nature. Those who give what amounts to an allegorical account of the tulip passage, taking it as a general defense of abstract representation, do violence to its immediate context. The poet is to examine the species in order to exhibit effective "portraits of nature"—of "nature" as opposed to "life." This distinction, frequent in Johnson, is carefully preserved in the paragraphs surrounding the paragraph on the tulip: "nature" means the world of physical appearances; "life" means human nature. We have already noted Johnson's disapproval of writers who, in their portraits of the latter, record only "general properties and large appearances," "prominent and striking features" (see pp. 78–79, 88). Imlac's remarks on the tulip supply a rule for effective visual description—nothing more.

The rule states that the poet is to confine his description to "such prominent and striking features, as recall the original to every mind," the "original" being evidently a piece of actual, not ideal, nature: Johnson agrees with Hugh Blair in considering poetic description a means "for recalling the images of real objects" (*Lectures*, Harding ed., 1:93). What is recalled is thus an individual, but what prompts the recollection is the description of the species. Why the poet must neglect the "minuter discriminations" is more clearly explained by a remark in *Rambler* 36: "Poetry cannot dwell upon the minuter distinctions, by which one species differs from another, without departing from that simplicity of grandeur which fills the imagination; nor dissect the latent qualities of things, without losing its general power of gratifying every mind by recalling its conceptions." Some of the disadvantages of "minute" or particularized description appear in a passage quoted in the *Life of Cowley*—Cowley's description, in the *Davideis*, of the angel Gabriel:

> He took for skin a cloud most soft and bright,
> That e'er the midday sun pierc'd through with light;
> Upon his cheeks a lively blush he spread,
> Wash'd from the morning beauties' deepest red;
> An harmless flattering meteor shone for hair,
> And fell adown his shoulders with loose care;
> He cuts out a silk mantle from the skies,
> Where the most sprightly azure pleas'd the eyes;
> This he with starry vapours sprinkles all,
> Took in their prime ere they grow ripe and fall;
> Of a new rainbow, ere it fret or fade,
> The choicest piece cut out, a scarfe is made.

Johnson comments:

> This is a just specimen of Cowley's imagery: what might in general expressions be great and forcible he weakens and makes ridiculous by branching it into small parts. That Gabriel was invested with the softest or brightest colours of the sky we might have been told, *and been dismissed to improve the idea in our different proportions of conception*; but Cowley could not let us go till he had related where Gabriel got first his skin, and then his mantle, and then his lace, and then his scarfe, and related it in the terms of the mercer and taylor.[4]

An angel is not, of course, a natural object and cannot be described in a way which will "recall the original to every mind," unless the original might be an image remembered from a statue or painting. But Johnson's point is clear enough: Cowley's minuteness deprives the reader of the pleasure which comes from devising or summoning his own idea of the thing described and substitutes a task of specific imaginative reconstruction which Johnson finds tedious and burdensome. It is again the problem of the radically novel in art: imitations produce pleasure "because they bring realities to mind," but the individuated tulip (whatever the case with the angel) demands attention to its uniqueness and so greets the reader as a new object in its own right instead of as an imitation.

So to the differences between Reynolds's species and that of Johnson. Reynolds's species is Platonic in possessing ontological value; it is an "abstract idea ... more perfect than any one original," that "central form ... from which every deviation is deformity." To conceive it is the work of years of study, both of nature and of art, and a rare and great intellectual achievement; to represent it vividly and distinctly on canvas or in bronze or stone earns for the painter or sculptor "the glorious appellation of Divine" (*Discourses*, pp. 30, 207). Johnson's species involves none of these things, save only that it too is the product of abstraction—a selection of characteristics "alike obvious to vigilance and carelessness." In Lockean terms, the verbal species represents a low-grade "nominal essence": it is what everyone notices about tulips, those properties which, when put into words, will immediately call up the image of the flower. Its value is rhetorical, not ontological; it is a source of pleasure to the widest possible audience, a stimulus to a particular imaginative activity. It represents, in short, an ideal of suggestive brevity.[5]

It also respects certain principles of verbal communication enunciated by John Locke. In the *Essay concerning Human Understanding*, Locke explains at length that the ordinary function of words is not, strictly speaking, to transmit ideas but rather to evoke in one's audience ideas (images) corresponding *in kind* to those which one wishes to convey. (One could speak properly of transmitting a complex idea only when that idea is described in much greater detail than is customary; and even then one could expect no more than a fairly close resemblance between the ideas entertained by the speaker and hearer, respectively.)[6] From this it follows that the species of Reynolds cannot be represented verbally. As James Harris explained in 1744, ''When we read in Milton of Eve, that

> Grace was in all her Steps, Heav'n in her Eye,
> In ev'ry Gesture Dignity and Love;

we have an Image *not* of that EVE, which Milton conceived, but of *such an EVE only*, *as every one*, *by his own proper Genius*, is able to represent, from reflecting on those *Ideas*, which he has annexed to these several Sounds.''[7] The plastic image of the painter or sculptor is single, unique, and there for everyone to see; accordingly, it can in principle possess the attributes which Reynolds ascribes to it. But of the verbal image there are as many realizations as there are readers.

Eighteenth-century theorists of poetic description were more or less sensitive to this difference in media from the beginning. In 1699 Addison praised descriptive touches in the *Georgics* which enable the mind ''to apprehend an idea which draws a whole train after it.'' For here the mind, ''which is always delighted with its own discoveries, only takes the hint from the poet, and seems to work out the rest by the strength of her own faculties.''[8] Addison returned to this effect in his essays on the pleasures of imagination, giving it additional importance as part of a general theory that esthetic pleasure largely consists in the activity to which the imagination is provoked in attempting to realize the pictorial possibilities of language.[9] This view of ''the beautiful'' in poetry was taken up by later critics, and after midcentury it became commonplace to praise Virgil, Horace, and especially Milton for language ''so fortunate,'' as Blair remarked, ''that with a single word or epithet, [it] often conveys a whole description to fancy.''[10]

The theory of sublime (as opposed to beautiful) description required a special application of the same Addisonian principle. The beautiful permitted a certain elaboration of detail, whereas the sublime, as Reynolds said, ''impresses the mind at once with one great idea; it is a single blow.'' Thus, as Blair explains, ''where a sublime, or a pathetic impression is intended to be made,'' the imagination ought ''to be seized at once; and it is far more deeply impressed by one strong and ardent image, than by the anxious minuteness of laboured illustration.''[11] Such remarks return us to Johnson's criticism of Cowley's angel; what might in general expressions be ''great and forcible'' (technical synonyms for ''sublime'') Cowley ''weakens and makes ridiculous by branching it into small parts.'' In *Rambler* 36 the phrase ''that simplicity of grandeur which fills the imagination'' connotes the effect of sublime description as conceived in Addisonian terms.

In *Peri Bathous* (1728) Pope explained that descriptive particularity breeds familarity and so destroys the sublime: the more fully a thing is described the better it is known and the less wonderful it seems.[12] Burke in his *Enquiry* (1757) made obscurity a major cause of the sublime and developed the implications of that principle into a full-scale attack on literary pictorialism. Poetry and rhetoric, he maintains, ''do not succeed in exact description so well as painting does; their business is to affect rather by sympathy than imitation; to display rather the effect of things on the mind of the speaker, or of others, than to present a clear idea of the things themselves.''[13] Burke's position was extreme for his century—''Indeed,'' he says, ''so little does poetry depend for its effect on the power of raising sensible images, that I am convinced it would lose a very considerable part of its energy, if this were the necessary result of all description'' (ibid., p. 170).

British critics writing after the appearance of the *Enquiry* remained on the whole committed pictorialists. But Burke and Harris may have helped make them more aware of the double reference of verbal imitation, that is, of the fact that the poet describes the tulip *as perceived*. Poetic description may, and often should, be faithful to the thing described, but in a sense the immediate object of imitation is the process of perception itself. ''It may be remarked,'' says Reynolds in one of those passages from the later *Discourses* in which his neo-Platonism drops out of sight to be replaced by principles more psychological and Johnsonian, ''that the impression which is left on our mind, even of things which are familiar to us, is seldom more than their general effect; beyond which we do not look in recognising such objects. To express this in painting, is to express what is congenial and natural to the mind of man, and what gives him by reflection his own mode of conceiving." To be needlessly particular, Reynolds goes on to explain, "presupposes *nicety* and *research*, which are only the business of the curious and attentive, and therefore does not speak to the general sense of the whole species" (*Discourses*, pp. 160–61).[14]

This is the doctrine of Imlac's tulip. Johnson, who in general valued the "peculiarities" of Shakespeare's descriptions as proof of perspicacity, nevertheless acknowledged cases where a sublime effect required the imitation of the perceptual act rather than the objects perceived. Geoffrey Tillotson has called attention to Johnson's editorial comment on Edgar's description of the cliffs of Dover in *King Lear*:

> The description [Johnson writes] is certainly not mean, but I am far from thinking it wrought to the utmost excellence of poetry. He that looks from a precipice finds himself assailed by one great and dreadful image of irresistible destruction. But this overwhelming idea is dissipated and enfeebled from the instant that the mind can restore itself to the observation of particulars, and diffuse its attention to distinct objects. The enumeration of the choughs and crows, the samphire-man and the fishers, counteracts the great effect of the prospect, as it peoples the desert of intermediate vacuity, and stops the mind in the rapidity of its descent through emptiness and horrour.

Or, as Johnson put it in conversation, "it should be all precipice,—all vacuum. The crows impede your fall. The diminished appearance of the boats, and other circumstances, are all very good description; but do not impress the mind at once with the horrible idea of immense height. The impression is divided; you pass on by computation, from one stage of the tremendous space to another."[15]

The modern reader of *Rasselas* may wonder why Imlac pauses in the midst of a rapid and comprehensive account of poetry to give so much attention to what seems, after all, a minor subject—visual description. The relative popularity of that subject among Johnson's critical contemporaries makes the tulip digression plausible; but I suggest that its full significance emerges only when it—and the eighteenth-century tradition which it summarizes—is seen as a response to the general problem of stylistic fragmentation which I discussed in chapter 1. The eighteenth-century ideal of suggestive brevity can be traced in part to the influence of Longinus, Petronius, and Lucian, who saw excessively particularized description in prose and verse as a typical expression of the degenerate taste for novelty fostered by the schools of declamation. Longinus, for example, treats description as a major source of the sublime, but tries to distinguish the descriptive sublime itself from the techniques of amplification described in the rhetoric textbooks: "Sublimity lies in elevation, amplification rather in amount; and so you often find sublimity in a single idea, whereas amplification always goes with quantity and a certain degree of redundance" (*On the Sublime*, 11, 12). Sublime effects can be achieved through the piling up of detail, but only the most striking circumstances must be included, and these must be "built into one coherent structure" or, as he says elsewhere, into "an organic whole." Like Pope (who no doubt took the idea from *Peri Hupsous*), Longinus calls attention to the danger of bathos in circumstantial descriptions, and he describes the false esthetic which leads to excessive amplification in terms which Johnson applies to the metaphysical poets. Is not "puerility," he asks, "obviously the academic attitude, where over-elaboration ends in frigid failure? Writers fall into this fault through trying to be uncommon and exquisite, and above all to please, and founder instead upon the tinsel reefs of affectation."[16]

In *How to Write History*—a work notable for its application to historiography of liberal artistic principles similar to those of Cicero and Fénelon—Lucian too associates superfluous description with frigidity, as well as with an inability to distinguish important from trivial detail, and advises that "you need especial discretion in descriptions . . . to avoid the appearance of a tasteless display of your word-power and of indulging your own interests at the expense of the history; you will touch on them lightly for the sake of expedience or clarity, then change the subject, avoiding the limed twig set there and all temptations of this sort, as you see Homer doing in his greatness of mind.'' Of those who succumb to this temptation, he remarks, ''one might rightly say that such people do not look at the rose itself, but accurately observe its thorns that grow along the stem.''[17]

Seventeenth-century criticism affords many parallels to these remarks. Some take the form of general precepts or observations; others are directed specifically against the descriptive exuberance of Baroque poets—a fact which suggests why the principles of good description were given such importance at the time. Thus in his ''Parallel of Poetry and Painting'' (1695), Dryden remarks that as a painter must reject all ''trifling ornaments,'' so must a poet refuse ''all tedious and unnecessary descriptions.'' Rapin complains of wits who ''suffer their *Fancy* to fly out after the pleasing *Images* they find in their way'' and who ''rush into the Descriptions of *Groves*, *Rivers*, *Fountains*, and *Temples.*''[18] As for the Baroque poets, in his *Entretiens* Bouhours speaks of Marino as a poet who in descriptions says everything that his subject might naturally suggest and then goes in search of what it does not; Boileau remarks that St.-Amand spoils his poems on serious subjects by ''the mean Circumstances he mingles with 'em''; and La Bruyère objects that Théophile, whose style is ''loaden with descriptions,'' ''grows heavy in particulars, and gives you an Anatomy.'' For John Dennis ''the wantonness of description is to be accounted at all times (and more especially in a grave way of writing) a most intolerable fault,'' for in a poem where there is action ''it ought always to go forward, and nothing ought to be much insisted on, which can put any considerable stop to that. For which reason all descriptions of persons and places which are any thing large, are extremely faulty.''[19] Later critics did not abandon this seventeenth-century concern for structural coherence and unity of effect, despite their growing interest in realism and vivid circumstantiality, and we are entitled, I think, to regard Imlac's remarks on the tulip as expressing Johnson's way of reconciling both these ideals.

Perceptual Standards in
Romantic Criticism

For our purposes the most interesting and instructive features of Romantic critical thought arise from the attempts of Wordsworth and Coleridge to resolve some of the problems we have encountered in Johnson. We saw in chapter 3 that in the *Preface to Shakespeare* Johnson fails to establish a clear relationship between the accurate observation of particulars and the making of fictional representations of "general nature." I suggested then that this failure may be evidence of his reliance upon the nominalistic theory of perception common in his time; though we may never be able to determine whether or not Johnson consciously adhered to this theory, the phraseology of the *Preface* seems to reflect its influence. In any event, there can be no doubt that the theory itself does give rise to the problem as it appears in the *Preface* (see pp. 92–96, 232 n. 20).

Now Wordsworth and Coleridge saw the problem of reconciling what they felt to be the universality of fictional representations with the empiricist dogma that the mind knows nothing but particulars as crucial to a group of stylistic problems with which Johnson had also been concerned, but which he had framed in other terms. To describe the Romantic critics' approach to these problems will, I think, throw a valuable light on the continuity of English criticism between Johnson and Coleridge, and it will also enable us to contemplate the first fully explicit formulation of the perceptual standard for poetic style toward which English theory and taste appear to be moving throughout the eighteenth century.

In the preface to his *Poems* of 1815 Wordsworth quotes from Taylor's *British Synonyms* the definition of imagination to which Johnson implicitly subscribes in the *Preface to Shake-*

speare: "a man [says Taylor], has imagination in proportion as he can distinctly copy in idea the impressions of sense: it is the faculty which *images* within the mind the phenomena of sensation. A man has fancy in proportion as he can call up, connect, or associate, at pleasure, these internal images ... so as to complete ideal representations of absent objects. Imagination is the power of depicting, and fancy of revoking and combining. The imagination is formed by patient observation; the fancy by a voluntary activity in shifting the scenery of the mind."[1] To these definitions Wordsworth objects that "it is not easy to find out how imagination, thus explained, differs from distinct remembrance of images; or fancy from quick and vivid recollection of them: each is nothing more than a mode of memory" (*Poetical Works*, 2:435–36). Wordsworth and Coleridge both conceive of memory-images as transcriptions of ordinary appearances, exhibiting "merely a faithful copy ... of absent external objects" (ibid., 2:436). Precisely because they are the products of ordinary perception (which from the Romantic point of view is imperception), the images of memory are in themselves flat and unimpressive. They may become interesting through the novelty of their arrangement, but they cannot be conceived as supplying the materials of fiction in the truest sense of the word. They are "fixities and definites," "materials ready made" which, because they retain their separate identities in combination, restrict the poet to effects which are indistinguishable from those of factual reporting. In the *Biographia Literaria* Coleridge finds fault with certain descriptive passages in Wordsworth's poetry for being based upon memory alone. The result is a "laborious minuteness" which destroys the effect of the whole. Reading such descriptions, says Coleridge, is "like taking the pieces of a dissected map out of its box. We first look at one part, and then at another, then join and dove-tail them; and when the successive acts of attention have been completed, there is a retrogressive effort of mind to behold it as a whole. The poet should paint to the imagination, not to the fancy; and I know no happier case to exemplify the distinction between these two faculties."[2] We are reminded of Johnson's objections to the "laboured particularities'' of metaphysical imagery and to the minuteness of the description of the cliffs of Dover in *King Lear*. Coleridge and Johnson evidently bring similar expectations to poetic description; the difference between them concerns theory rather than taste, and it is an ironic difference: Coleridge invalidates the eighteenth century's theory of the imagination by pointing out, in effect, that it can account for features of style of which the eighteenth century disapproved, but not for those which it most valued.

The imagination as the neoclassical era conceived it is for both Wordsworth and Coleridge, then, the fancy, ''a mode of Memory emancipated from the order of time and space'' (*Biographia Literaria*, 1:202). Though capable of descriptive effects of the kind indicated above, the fancy is not, as Wordsworth and Coleridge represent it, typically employed in description. More often it produces the effect of *discordia concors* which Johnson found characteristic of metaphysical wit. ''Fancy,'' says Coleridge in *Table Talk*, ''brings together images which have no connection *natural or moral*; are yoked by the poet by means of some accidental coincidence.''[3] Crabbe Robinson, trying to interpret Wordsworth's view, noted in his diary that ''fancy forms casual and fleeting combinations'' and has its principle in ''a voluntary power ... which only expresses the fact of the combination with little or no import beyond itself.''[4] Thus Milton, as Coleridge remarks, ''had a highly *imaginative*, Cowley a very *fanciful* mind (*Biographia Literaria*, 1:62). In the 1815 preface Wordsworth associates fancy with ''conceit'' and gives an illustration from Chesterfield: ''The dews of the evening most carefully shun, / They are the tears of the sky for the loss of the sun.'' Wordsworth explains that the lines are fanciful rather than imaginative, because although concrete objects are brought into metaphoric relation they remain unrealized, both individually and considered as a whole: they are mentioned rather than described, and nothing prompts the reader to visualize them. The effect, then, is purely verbal, ''a flash of surprise, and nothing more; for the nature of things does not sustain the combination'' (*Poetical Works*, 2:442).

Again, in *The Statesman's Manual* (1816), Coleridge associates fancy with the making of allegory, which he describes as being "but a translation of abstract notions into a picture-language which is itself nothing but an abstraction from objects of the senses." Such abstractions, he goes on, are "empty echoes" of a reality which only the imagination can apprehend and these "the fancy arbitrarily associates with apparitions of matter."[5] Fancy emerges from the varied contexts in which it is discussed as the faculty which subordinates concrete particulars to the abstract or conceptual intellect and so displays them not as being interesting in and for themselves but as a means of achieving an effect. It is a valuable but inferior power for much the same reason that the metaphysical poets' *discordia concors* is for Johnson a valuable but inferior species of "wit": fancy is the source of optional ornaments of style.

Like fancy, the imagination too produces a variety of effects. According to Wordsworth it can modify objects of sense perception by conferring new properties upon them, by abstracting from them some which they actually possess, by consolidating numbers into unity, and by dissolving unity into number. Coleridge observes at one point in the *Biographia Literaria* that poetic images "become proofs of original genius only as far as they are modified by a predominant passion; or by associated thoughts or images awakened by that passion; or when they have the effect of reducing multitude to unity, or succession to an instant; or lastly, when a human and intellectual life is transferred to them from the poet's own spirit,

> 'Which shoots its being through earth, sea, and air.' "

Such passages show Romantic theory at its weakest. The description is so abstract and the processes described so various that their subsumption under the common term "imagination" seems unjustified. But there is in Wordsworth, and more especially in Coleridge, a tendency to limit the term to effects which are directly opposed to those of fancy and so to sharpen the distinction. Thus for Coleridge the imagination is above all, perhaps, an "esemplastic" or unifying power, whose effects he describes in terms with which we are now familiar. The imaginative poet "gives us the liveliest image of succession with the feeling of simultaneousness"; he paints "with such co-presence of the whole picture flash'd at once upon the eye, as the sun paints in a camera obscura" (*Biographia Literaria*, 2:18, 103). The imagination, in short, "acts chiefly by creating out of many things, as they would have appeared in the description of an ordinary mind detailed in unimpassioned succession, a oneness, even as nature, the greatest of poets, acts upon us, when we open our eyes upon an extended prospect."[6] Thus the unified visual field which Pope and Johnson see as the natural result of undistorted observation and unaffected expression becomes in Wordsworth and Coleridge the sign of a particular creative faculty, and the basis for a theory of fiction and a theory of style.

In the 1815 preface Wordsworth discusses imagination and the fictional process in a context which remains psychological and subjective. Here the term "imagination" denotes "operations of the mind upon [sensory] objects, and processes of creation or composition, governed by certain fixed laws" (*Poetical Works*, 2:436). Wordsworth confines himself for the most part to distinguishing the stylistic traits of imagination from those of fancy in an attempt to prove his thesis that the conventional view of imagination cannot account for the distinctive properties of fiction in its highest forms. He is thus especially concerned to show that the imagination must be conceived as a special faculty of the mind which, unlike the fancy, "recoils from everything but the plastic, the pliant, and the indefinite" and that it works by bringing into metaphoric or visual juxtaposition images which "invariably modify each other." "The law," he says, "under which the processes of Fancy are carried on is as capricious as the accidents of things, and the effects are surprising, playful, ludicrous, amusing, tender, or pathetic, as the objects happen to be appositely produced or fortunately combined." But the metaphors produced by imagination depend "less upon outline of form and feature than upon expression and effect; less upon casual and

outstanding, than upon inherent and internal, properties"
(ibid., 2:441). These distinctions are intended to acknowledge
the capacity of fiction to achieve a seamless unity, sometimes as
vivid and coherent as vision itself, which is both more and other
than an aggregation of atomic images copied from normal
appearances.

But in concentrating upon the description of imaginative
processes and effects Wordsworth neglects the question of their
value. He speaks of the imagination as being given "to incite
and support the eternal" part of human nature, as fancy is
given "to quicken and to beguile the temporal part." He
speaks of the imaginative modification of appearances as "proceeding from, and governed by, a sublime consciousness of the
soul in her own mighty and almost divine powers," and again
as an activity which the mind undertakes "for its own gratification" (ibid., 2:442, 439, 436). In these rather heterogeneous
remarks we have the vague association of the imagination with
the eternal part of human nature and the "almost divine" powers
of the soul, but the only explicit value assigned to the products of
imagination is "gratification," or, in the prefaces of 1800 and
1802, their capacity to reflect the operations of the mind. We
know, chiefly from what he says in his poetry, that Wordsworth
valued the imagination for other reasons than these, but he
seems never to have incorporated them into a coherent theoretical statement.[7]

Coleridge, on the other hand, kept the question of the value
of fiction always in view. He rejected the critical hedonism of
the later eighteenth century, and he rejected the subjectivist
principle that fiction is "true" simply to the intellectual and
psychological processes which produce it or to the spiritual
needs which it expresses. Like Johnson, he claimed for fiction
the power of disclosing general and objective truth, and he did
so in a way which addressed itself to all of the principal critical
problems with which the present essay has been concerned.
Thus, for example, he tried to heal the split between matter and
words by establishing the primacy of the perceptual intellect
("reason" or "imagination") over the abstract intellect or

"understanding." "Of the *discursive* understanding," he says in *The Statesman's Manual*,

> which forms for itself general notions and terms of classification for the purpose of comparing and arranging phaenomena, the Characteristic is Clearness without Depth. It contemplates the unity of things in their *limits* only, and is consequently a knowledge of superficies without substance. So much so, indeed, that it entangles itself in contradictions in the very effort of comprehending the *idea* of substance. The completing power which unites clearness with depth, the plenitude of the sense with the comprehensibility of the understanding, is the IMAGINATION, impregnated with which the understanding itself becomes intuitive, and a living power. [Appendix C, p. 69]

The imagination is the "living Power and prime Agent of all human Perception" to which Coleridge attributes a capacity to know general truth in and through the individuals presented to sensory experience (*Biographia Literaria*, 1:202). It knows such individuals as symbols, and by a symbol is meant "not a metaphor or allegory or any other figure of speech or form of fancy, but an actual and essential part of that, the whole of which it represents." A symbol is not the fabrication of a particular mind but the concrete object itself as it stands revealed in its full reality and significance: "it always partakes of the Reality which it renders intelligible; and while it enunciates the whole, abides itself as a living part in that unity of which it is the representative" (*Stateman's Manual*, pp. 79, 30). Corresponding to the "primary imagination" just described is the "secondary imagination" or poetic faculty, which Coleridge regards as "identical with the primary in the *kind* of its agency, and differing only in *degree*, and in the *mode* of its operation. It dissolves, diffuses, dissipates, in order to recreate; or where this process is rendered impossible, yet still at all events it struggles to idealize and to unify" (*Biographia Literaria*, 1:202). Thus it preserves the autonomy and integrity of fictional particulars by regarding them as symbols analogous and indeed equivalent to those apprehended by the primary imagination, that is, as objects "consubstantial with the truths, of which they are the *conductors*" (*Stateman's Manual*, p. 29). The problem of fiction and the problem of style both find their solution within a single theoretical synthesis. But this synthesis, though it makes possible a more unified critical point of view than the eighteenth century was able to achieve and obviates the need for compromises among conflicting critical principles, depends upon an idealist theory of knowledge which raises at least as many questions as it answers.

Notes

INTRODUCTION

1. "The Metaphysical Poets" (1921), in *Selected Essays*, 2d ed. (1960; reprint ed., New York: Harcourt, Brace & World, 1964), p. 250.

2. *Lives of the English Poets*, ed. George Birkbeck Hill (Oxford: Oxford University Press, 1905), 1:20, 21, 35. All future references will be to this edition, cited as *Lives*.

3. It is true that Johnson supplies explicit standards for description (*Lives*, 1:51, 53) and comparison (*Lives*, 1:45). But even these are incomplete and need to be supplemented by other passages from his works and, ultimately, by the general historical context.

4. *The Yale Edition of the Works of Samuel Johnson*, vol. 7: *Johnson on Shakespeare*, ed. Arthur Sherbo (New Haven, Conn.: Yale University Press, 1968), pp. 61–62. All future references to the *Preface to Shakespeare* will be to this edition, cited as *Preface*; future references to other portions of this volume will be cited as *Works*, Yale ed., 7.

5. For the terms "liberal" and "conservative" as used here and throughout, see Wesley Trimpi, "The Ancient Hypothesis of Fiction: An Essay on the Origins of Literary Theory," *Traditio* 27 (1971): 3–9 and, by the same author, "The Quality of Fiction: The Rhetorical Transmission of Literary Theory," *Traditio* 30 (1974): 1–9. These monographs will be cited hereafter as *AHF* and *QF*, respectively. My debt to them is great. Greater still is my indebtedness to Trimpi's outline of Johnson's relationship to the liberal tradition of classical stylistic criticism in *Ben Jonson's Poems* (Stanford, Calif.: Stanford University Press, 1962), pp. 251–52, n.77. My treatment of this relationship, as developed primarily in chapters 1 and 5, is in part a test, confirmation, and specification of Trimpi's suggestions.

CHAPTER 1

1. "The Baroque Style in Prose," in *Style, Rhetoric, and Rhythm: Essays by Morris Croll*, ed. J. Max Patrick and Robert O. Evans with John M. Wallace and R. J. Schoeck (Princeton, N.J.: Princeton University Press, 1966), pp. 208, 209–10. Croll generalizes about such "Baroque" writers as Henry Wotton, Montaigne, Burton, Pascal, and Browne:

> "Their purpose was to portray, not a thought, but a mind thinking, or, in Pascal's words, *la peinture de la pensée*. They knew that an idea separated from the act of experiencing it is not the idea that was experienced. The

"

ardor of its conception in the mind is a necessary part of its truth; and unless it can be conveyed to another mind in something of the form of its occurrence, either it has changed into some other idea or it has ceased to be an idea, to have any existence whatever except a verbal one. It was the latter fate that happened to it, they believed, in the Ciceronian periods of sixteenth-century Latin rhetoricians. The successive processes of revision to which these periods had been submitted had removed them from reality by just so many steps. For themselves, they preferred to present the truth of experience in a less concocted form, and deliberately chose as the moment of expression that in which the idea first clearly objictifies itself in the mind, in which, therefore, each of its parts still preserves its own peculiar emphasis and an independent vigor of its own—in brief, the moment in which truth is still *imagined*.'' [P. 210]

2. For representative statements on the similarity of poetry and oratory, see Gerardus Joannes Vossius, *Opera* (Amsterdam, 1697), 3:7; *Fénelon's Dialogues on Eloquence*, trans. Wilbur Samuel Howell (Princeton, N.J.: Princeton University Press, 1951), pp. 93–94; and Joseph Trapp, *Lectures on Poetry* (London, 1742), pp. 34–35. Trapp paraphrases Vossius. If a common term denotes a common essence, then, as Wilbur Samuel Howell points out, the appearance and eventual broad currency of the term ''belles lettres'' in the later seventeenth and eighteenth centuries as a collective noun for all genres of artistic writing suggests that its users saw important similarities between poetry and artistic prose; see W. S. Howell, *Eighteenth-Century British Logic and Rhetoric* (Princeton, N.J.: Princeton University Press, 1971), pp. 524–33.

3. *Gorgias*, trans. W. D. Woodhead, Bollingen ed. (New York, 1964), passim, but esp. 458e–66; *Phaedrus*, trans. Hackforth, Bollingen ed., 259e–79.

4. *De Oratore*, trans. E. W. Sutton and H. Rackham, Loeb Classical Library (hereafter LCL) (1942; reprint ed., London: Heinemann, 1967), II.xxx.130–xl.176; III.xviii.67–xix.73, xxvii.107–xxxi.125; see also *Orator*, trans. H. M. Hubbell, LCL (1939; rev. and reprint ed., London: Heinemann, 1962), xiv.45–47, xxxvi.125–27. All future references will be to these editions.

5. *De Oratore*, III.xxxiii.132–xxxv.143; *Orator*, iii.11–v.19. For a concise account of the quarrel between philosophy and eloquence in Greece, see H.-I. Marrou, *Histoire de L'Education dans L'Antiquité* (Paris: Editions du Seuil, 1948), chap. 7, ''Les Maîtres de la tradition classique: II. Isocrate''; see also Werner Jaeger, *Paideia: The Ideals of a Greek Culture*, trans. Gilbert Highet (Oxford: Oxford University Press, 1944), vol. 3, chaps. 2, 6, and 8. For a concise discussion of the Isocratean values to which Cicero is indebted, see Trimpi, *AHF*, pp. 9–15.

6. *Causa, controversia,* and *consultatio* are, according to Cicero, Peripatetic and Academic terms (*De Oratore*, III.xxviii.109). In *Orator* Cicero designates the general or unlimited question by the Greek term θευις [*thesis*] (xiv.46). Quintilian prefers *thesis* for the *quaestio infinita, causa* for the *quaestio finita* (*Institutio Oratoria*, trans. H. E. Butler, LCL [1920; reprint ed., London, 1963], III.v.5–16). Quintilian reaffirms Cicero's views on the value of the *thesis* in practical oratory, but without special emphasis. All future references to Quintilian will be to the Loeb edition.

7. See *AHF*, pp. 1–8 and passim. I am deeply indebted to Trimpi's

monograph for my understanding of the relationships briefly indicated here and developed elsewhere in this essay.

8. *Satyricon*, trans. M. Haseltine, LCL (1913; rev. and reprint ed., London: Heinemann, 1951), secs. 1-5; cf. Tacitus, "A Dialogue on Oratory," in *Tacitus: Dialogus, Agricola, Germania*, trans. Sir William Peterson, LCL (Cambridge, Mass., 1920), pp. 30-35. Future references to Petronius and Tacitus will be to these editions.

9. *Institutio Oratoria*, X.i.130. Specimens of the style promoted in the rhetorical schools early in the first century A.D. were available to the neoclassical critics in the collections of *controversiae* and *suasoriae* of the elder Seneca, ed. Muretus (1585), Gronovius (1649), and others. See the modern edition with French translation by Henri Bornecque, *Sénèque le Rhéteur, Controverses et Suasoires*, 2 vols. (Paris: Garnier Frères, n.d.); see also S. F. Bonner, *Roman Declamation in the Late Republic and Early Empire* (Liverpool: University Press of Liverpool, 1949). For Renaissance applications of Quintilian on Seneca, see Trimpi, *Ben Jonson's Poems*, p. 242, n.27.

10. *The Works of Francis Bacon*, ed. James Spedding, R. L. Ellis, and D. D. Heath (London, 1857-74), 3:283. All future references to Bacon will be to this edition, cited as *Bacon*. The reader should compare Ben Jonson's stylistic position, as set forth in *Timber, or Discoveries*, to the critics discussed in this chapter. Though Jonson has important similarities to Bacon, to the liberal French critics discussed below, and to Samuel Johnson, I have stressed Bacon rather than Jonson as the more widely known and influential of the two. Significant critical references to *Timber* are rare in the neoclassical period. Jonson's stylistic position and his relation to Bacon have been discussed in detail by Trimpi, *Ben Jonson's Poems*, chaps. 1-4.

11. *De Dignitate et Augmentis Scientiarum*, trans. Gilbert Wats (Oxford, 1640), p. 29. For the original passage, see *Bacon*, 1:452.

12. The above remarks on Bacon are indebted to Trimpi, *Ben Jonson's Poems*, pp. 251-52, n.77. See also ibid., pp. 45, 86-89, 144-49.

13. "Reflections upon Philosophy in General," in *The Whole Critical Works of Monsieur Rapin*, trans. Basil Kennett et al. (London, 1706), 2:389. Rapin's essay originally appeared in 1676. For Swift, see *A Tale of a Tub*, ed. A. C. Guthkelch and D. Nichol Smith (Oxford: Oxford University Press, 1920), p. 166.

14. *History of the Royal Society*, ed. Jackson I. Cope and Harold Whitmore Jones (St. Louis, Mo.: Washington University Studies, 1958), p. 119.

15. "The Preface of the Publisher," *Whole Critical Works of Monsieur Rapin*, 1: sig. A8v-a1r. The phrase, *"the first Marriage Articles between the Rational and the Experimental Philosophy,"* alludes to one or more passages in Bacon (*Bacon*, 4:19, 92-93). On the alliance between empiricism and humanistic studies in the eighteenth century, see present study, chap. 2, pp. 36-50; cf. also the title essay of R. S. Crane's *The Idea of the Humanities* (Chicago: University of Chicago Press, 1967), 1:89-121.

16. The standard account of British logic and rhetoric in the seventeenth and eighteenth centuries is that of Wilbur Samuel Howell. On new developments in seventeenth-century logic and rhetoric, see—in addition to his *Eighteenth-Century British Logic and Rhetoric* (cited above, n.2)—*Logic*

and Rhetoric in England, 1500-1700 (Princeton, N.J.: Princeton University Press, 1956), esp. chap. 6, "New Horizons in Logic and Rhetoric." I gratefully acknowledge my broad and deep indebtedness to Howell, whose scholarship on Antoine Arnauld, Bernard Lamy, and Fénelon in particular has proven indispensable to my understanding of these rhetorical sources of the principles of "natural" style.

17. *Bacon*, 3:389-97. In the *Advancement of Learning* Bacon objects to the Ramists' "canker of epitomes" and proceeds to describe not two methods, as Ramus had done, but nine, each adapted to special considerations of subject matter, audience, and the purpose of the discourse (*Bacon*, 3:403-7). In the *De Augmentis* Bacon removes the theory of method from logic and rhetoric, observing that "the placing of it in the train of other arts has led to the passing over of many things relating to it which it is useful to know," and he makes of it a "substantive and principle doctrine" in itself (*Bacon*, 4:448). Here too he describes the Ramist theory of method as "a kind of cloud that overshadowed knowledge for awhile and blew over: a thing no doubt both very weak in itself and very injurious to the sciences" (ibid.). Then he repeats his earlier description of the various methods without substantial alteration.

18. For Bacon's rhetorical theory, see Howell, *Logic and Rhetoric*, pp. 364-75; Karl Wallace, *Francis Bacon on Communication and Rhetoric* (Chapel Hill: University of North Carolina Press, 1943); and George Williamson, *The Senecan Amble: A Study in Prose Form from Bacon to Collier* (Chicago: University of Chicago Press, 1951), chap. 6, "Bacon and Stoic Rhetoric." For Bacon on rhetoric in the *Advancement of Learning*, see *Works*, 3:408-13.

19. The following discussion of Arnauld and Fénelon draws heavily upon the work of Howell. For Arnauld and the Port-Royal Logic, see *Logic and Rhetoric*, pp. 350-63; for the relevance of the Port-Royal rhetorical tradition to Fénelon, see Howell's introduction to *Fénelon's Dialogues on Eloquence*, pp. 1-53. For Fénelon's relation to eighteenth-century British rhetoric, see *Eighteenth-Century British Logic and Rhetoric*, pp. 504-20.

20. On Ramus's utilitarianism, see Howell, *Logic and Rhetoric*, pp. 146-49, 173-85. For a detailed discussion of Ramus's doctrine, see ibid., pp. 146-72. For other accounts of Ramus and Ramism, see Perry Miller, *The New England Mind: The Seventeenth Century* (Cambridge, Mass.: Harvard University Press, 1954), esp. pp. 300-362; Walter J. Ong, *Ramus, Method, and the Decay of Dialogue* (Cambridge, Mass.: Harvard University Press, 1958); and Rosemond Tuve, *Elizabethan and Metaphysical Imagery* (Chicago: University of Chicago Press, 1947), chaps. 11-14.

21. *The Lawier's Logike* (Scolar Press facsimile ed.; London, 1588), sig. B$_{(i)}$v.

22. This view of the implications and consequences of Ramist rhetorical theory is supported by Howell but disputed by Rosemond Tuve; see *Elizabethan and Metaphysical Imagery*, chaps. 12, 14.

23. *The Arcadian Rhetorike* (Scolar Press facsimile ed.; London, 1588), cap. 36.

24. *Logic; or, the Art of Thinking*, trans. by "Several Hands" (London, 1685), 2d pt., pp. 117-42.

25. Porter Gale Perrin concludes that the New England colleges probably relied heavily on Ramist rhetoric until nearly the middle of the eighteenth century (though Farnaby's somewhat more liberal rhetoric was also popular). After about 1743 the study of Cicero, Quintilian, and Longinus seems to have superseded the study of seventeenth-century Ramist texts. In 1744 the American Samuel Johnson recommended that college students study Cicero, Quintilian, Fénelon's *Dialogues*, Rollin's *Belles-lettres*, and Bernard Lamy's Port-Royal-influenced *Art of Speaking*, in addition to the more conservative seventeenth-century rhetorics of Farnaby and Smith (Porter Gale Perrin, *Text and Reference Books in Rhetoric before 1750* [private ed. dist. by University of Chicago Libraries, 1940]). I am indebted to my colleague Charles Gullans for showing me Perrin's pamphlet.

26. Donald J. Greene questions the value of the term "neoclassical" in "Augustinianism and Empiricism," *Eighteenth-Century Studies* 1 (Fall 1967): 33–68. In chapter 5 I sketch in some detail the classical sources of the eighteenth century's approach to the problem of fragmentation in style. Detailed studies are needed exploring the indebtedness of eighteenth-century critics to the classical rhetorical authorities.

27. *Dialogues*, pp. 147–48. Fénelon's view of the sources of corruption in modern style was the usual one of his age; see present study, chap. 5, pp. 157–61.

28. *Dialogues*, "Introduction," pp. 37–38.

29. Howell writes that "Ramus and Talaeus, in confining the theory of rhetorical style to the tropes and figures, had in fact defined effective expression as unusual expression, and had made the quest for good style a quest for every linguistic mode that offers any contrast to ordinary patterns of speech" (ibid., p. 37).

30. For the importance of vivid representation in classical rhetorical doctrine see Cicero, *De Oratore*, III.liii.202, lvi.214–lvii.216; Quintilian, *Institutio Oratoria*, VI.ii.29–34; VIII.iii.61–71, 88–89; IX.ii.40–44; X.vii.15; see also Longinus, *On the Sublime*, trans. W. Hamilton Fyfe, LCL (London, 1965), 15; Demetrius, *On Style*, trans. W. Rhys Roberts, LCL (London, 1965), iv.208–22. Future references to Longinus and Demetrius will be to these editions.

31. On the importance and meaning of "simplicity" in a variety of eighteenth-century cultural contexts, see Raymond D. Havens, "Simplicity, a Changing Concept," *Journal of the History of Ideas* 14, no. 1 (January 1953): 3–32. For the connotations of the term in sixteenth-century England, see R. F. Jones, "The Moral Sense of Simplicity," *Studies in Honor of Frederick W. Shipley* (St. Louis: Washington University Studies, 1942), pp. 265–87.

CHAPTER 2

1. *Eighteenth-Century British Logic and Rhetoric*, chap. 6.

2. Nicolas Malebranche, *De la Recherche de la Vérité* (1674–75; Paris, 1762), 1:366–421; 2:1–7; *An Essay concerning Human Understanding*, ed. Alexander Campbell Fraser, 2 vols. (Oxford: Clarendon Press, 1894), III.x.34 (henceforth cited as *Essay*); see also Locke's remarks on poetry in "Some

Thoughts concerning Education,'' *Works of John Locke* (London, 1824), 8:167–68. For a different view of Locke's attitude toward rhetoric, see Howell, *Eighteenth-Century British Logic and Rhetoric*, pp. 489–502.

3. *Bacon*, 3:284; see also *Novum Organum*, first book, aphorisms CXXVII and CXXVIII (*Works*, 4:112–13).

4. *Novum Organum*, first part, aphorism LXI. For Bacon's view of the general opposition between his method and the traditional method of disputation, see the preface to the *Great Instauration*, in *Bacon* 4:16–18.

5. *Bacon*, 3:343–44, 435, 346; see also the modified discussion of poetry in the *De Augmentis* (*Bacon*, 4:314–35). The best general discussion of Bacon's poetic theory and attitude toward poetry remains that of Murray W. Bundy, ''Bacon's True Opinion of Poetry,'' *Studies in Philology* 27 (1930): 244–64.

6. ''Avertissement,'' *La Manière de Bien Penser dans les ouvrages d'Esprit, Dialogues* (Paris, 1687), sig. a$_{iii}$r.

7. *The Art of Criticism: or, the Method of Making a Right Judgment upon Subjects of Wit and Learning* [anon. trans. of Bouhours's *Manière*] (London, 1705), pt. 1, p. 7.

8. Bouhours's attempts to apply his principle are adequately paraphrased by George Granville in his notes to ''An Essay upon Unnatural Flights in Poetry'' (1701), in J. E. Spingarn, ed., *Critical Essays of the Seventeenth Century* (Oxford: Clarendon Press, 1909), 3:295–98. Johnson commended Granville's poem and the notes (*Lives*, 2:295).

9. ''Preface'' to *Religio Laici*, in *The Works of John Dryden, Vol. II: Poems 1681–1684*, ed. H. T. Swedenberg, Jr. and Vinton Dearing (Berkeley and Los Angeles: University of California Press, 1973), p. 109.

10. On the pragmatic defense of poetry in the seventeenth century, see K. G. Hamilton, *The Two Harmonies: Poetry and Prose in the Seventeenth Century* (Oxford: Oxford University Press, 1963), chap. 2; William H. Youngren, ''Generality, Science, and Poetic Language in the Restoration,'' *ELH* 35 (1968): 158–87. I owe the term *pragmatic* as used here to M. H. Abrams, *The Mirror and the Lamp* (New York: Oxford University Press, 1953), pp. 14–21.

11. *History of the Royal Society*, ed. Cope and Jones, pp. 111–12; *Bacon*, 3:411.

12. See pp. 58–59, 120–24.

13. George Campbell's defense of rhetoric may be taken as typical of its age: ''If the orator would prove successful, it is necessary that he engage in his service all these different powers of the mind, the imagination, the memory, and the passions. These are not the supplanters of reason, or even rivals in her sway; they are her handmaidens, by whose ministry she is enabled to usher truth into the heart, and procure it there a favorable reception'' (*The Philosophy of Rhetoric*, ed. Lloyd F. Bitzer [1776; Carbondale: Southern Illinois University Press, 1963], p. 72). In discussing the poetic value of visual imagery the Abbé Dubos comments:

> The art of moving and persuading mankind, consists principally in knowing how to make a good use of these images. The very severest writer, who professes most seriously, that he intends to employ nothing but plain reason to convince us, soon finds, that to carry his point he must move us;

and that, for this end, he must set before us the pictures of the objects he treats of. Father Mallebranche [*sic*], one of the greatest sticklers for strict reasoning we have had in France, has wrote against the contagious disorder of strong imaginations, whose art of seducing consists in the fecundity of their images, and in the talent they have of giving a lively picture of their objects. But you must not expect dry reasonings in this father's discourse, such as exclude all figures capable of moving and seducing us, and are strictly confined to the sole strength and efficacy of argument. This very discourse is full of images and pictures, with which he speaks to our imagination against the abuse of imagination. [Jean-Baptiste Dubos, *Critical Reflections on Poetry, Painting and Music*, trans. Thomas Nugent (London, 1748), 1:234–35; Nugent translates the fifth French ed. of the *Réflexions critiques sur la poésie et sur la peinture*, originally published in 1719]

In his *Essay on Pope*, Warton remarks in passing that Locke "affected to despise poetry," depreciated the ancients, and had no good taste. He contrasts Locke's attitude with Bacon's view that the poetry of the ancients is a storehouse of knowledge about the nature of the passions and appetites (Joseph Warton, *An Essay on the Genius and Writing of Pope* [London, 1782], 2:278–79). For Bacon's comment, see *Bacon*, 3:435. Johnson remarks of Swift's plain style in prose, "This easy and safe conveyance of meaning it was Swift's desire to attain, and for having attained he deserves praise, though perhaps not the highest praise. For purposes merely didactick, when something is to be told that was not known before, it is the best mode, but against that inattention by which known truths are suffered to lie neglected it makes no provision; it instructs, but does not persuade" (*Lives*, 3:52).

14. *The Idea of the Humanities*, 1:88–123.

15. On the centrality of Arnauld and Fénelon to the development of eighteenth-century British logic and rhetoric, see Howell, *British Logic and Rhetoric*, pp. 328, 343–45, 383–84, 504–24, 531, 612, 656, 666.

16. Howell notes that Fénelon pays some attention to fiction as a principle distinguishing poetry from rhetoric: "In the last analysis, poetry is nothing but a lively fiction which portrays nature" (*Dialogues*, p. 94); see Howell, "Oratory and Poetry in Fénelon's Literary Theory," *Quarterly Journal of Speech* 37, no. 1 (1951): 1–10.

17. Cf., in addition to Campbell's *Philosophy of Rhetoric*, Hugh Blair, *Lectures on Rhetoric and Belles Lettres*, ed. Harold F. Harding, 2 vols. (1783; reprint ed., Carbondale: Southern Illinois University Press, 1965); Henry Home, Lord Kames, *Elements of Criticism* (1762), 4th ed., 2 vols. (Edinburgh, 1769); Joseph Priestley, *A Course of Lectures on Oratory and Criticism*, ed. Vincent M. Bevilacqua and Richard Murphy (1777; reprint ed., Carbondale: Southern Illinois University Press, 1965); Adam Smith, *Lectures on Rhetoric and Belles Lettres Delivered in the University of Glasgow . . . , Reported by a Student in 1762–63*, ed., John M. Lothian (London: Thomas Nelson & Sons, 1963).

18. See n.2 , chap. 1.

19. Campbell, *Philosophy*, p. 1; Blair, *Lectures,* 2:312–13; Johnson, *Lives,* 3:251.

20. In his "Life of Boerhaave" (1739), Johnson commends the great Dutch physician, scientist, and philosopher for being not

"unacquainted with the art of recommending truth by elegance, and embellishing the philosopher with polite literature: he knew that but a small part of mankind will sacrifice their pleasure to their improvement, and those authors who would find many readers, must endeavour to please while they instruct.

He knew the importance of his own writings to mankind, and lest he might by a roughness and barbarity of style, too frequent among men of great learning, disappoint his own intentions, and make his labours less useful, he did not neglect the politer arts of eloquence and poetry. Thus was his learning at once various and exact, profound and agreeable"

(*The Works of Samuel Johnson, LL.D.*, ed. Arthur Murphy[London, 1801], 12:36). All subsequent references to this edition will be cited hereafter as *Works*. In the *Lectures* Blair remarks:

Aristotle is the thorough example of [the] Dry Style. Never, perhaps, was there any author who adhered so rigidly to the strictness of a didactic manner, throughout all his writings, and conveyed so much instruction without the least approach to ornament. With the most profound genius, and extensive views, he writes like a pure intelligence, who addresses himself solely to the understanding, without making any use of the channel of the imagination. But this is a manner which deserves not to be imitated. For, although the goodness of the matter may compensate the dryness or harshness of the Style, yet is that dryness a considerable defect; as it fatigues attention, and conveys our sentiments, with disadvantage, to the reader or hearer. [*Lectures*, 1:380]

21. *The Two Harmonies*, p. 138.

22. See *Essay*, IV.vii, viii, xvii, passim. Johnson remarks in his preface to Dodsley's *Preceptor* that "the *logick* which for so many ages kept possession of the schools, has at last been condemned as a mere art of wrangling, of very little use in the pursuit of truth" (*Works*, 2:248). In the *Essay*, IV.vii.11, Locke speaks of the "Peripatetic Philosophy" as having become established in the schools, "where it continued many ages, without teaching the world anything but the art of wrangling."

23. *Essay*, esp. III.ix–xi, and IV.vii, viii, and xvii.

24. "Thus we see, that killing a man with a sword or a hatchet are looked on as no distinct species of action; but if the point of the sword first enter the body, it passes for a distinct species, where it has a distinct name, as in England, in whose language it is called *stabbing*: but in another country, where it has not happened to be specified under a peculiar name, it passes not for a distinct species" (*Essay*, III.v.11).

25. *Essay*, IV.iii.18; cf. the model of moral reasoning exhibited in IV.xvii.4 (vol. 2, pp. 393–94).

26. See esp. *Essay*, III.ix.5–9 and III.v.10. In making a "mixed mode" the understanding may "with great liberty unite often into one abstract idea things that, in their nature, have no coherence; and so under one term bundle together a great variety of compounded and decompounded ideas. Thus the name of *procession*: what a great mixture of independent ideas of persons, habits, tapers, orders, motions, sounds, does it contain in that complex one,

which the mind of man has arbitrarily put together, to express by that one name?'' (ibid., III.v.13).

27. Francis Hutcheson, who followed Locke and Shaftesbury, attempted to supply a mathematical basis for moral choice—to invent an ethical calculus—in *An Inquiry concerning the Original of our Ideas of Virtue or Moral Good* (1725). For this work, as well as major documents in the history of eighteenth-century sentimentalist ethical theory, see L. A. Selby-Bigge, *British Moralists*, 2 vols. (1897; reprint ed., New York: Bobbs-Merrill, 1964); see Selby-Bigge's introduction, esp. pp. xxxiii–xcii.

28. *Gulliver's Travels*, ed. Herbert Davis (Oxford: Basil Blackwell, 1959), p. 267.

29. ''*Sensus Communis*: An Essay on the Freedom of Wit and Humor'' (1709), treatise II of *Characteristics*, ed. John M. Robertson (1711, reprint ed., New York: Bobbs-Merrill, 1964), 1:88; *The Twickenham Edition of the Poems of Alexander Pope, Vol. III-i: An Essay on Man*, ed. Maynard Mack (New Haven, Conn.: Yale University Press, 1951), epistle iv, lines 29–30.

30. ''Epistle to Cobham,'' Twickenham ed., vol. III-ii: *Epistles to Several Persons*, ed. F. W. Bateson (New Haven, Conn.: Yale University Press, 1951), lines 29–40.

31. *Pensées*, ed. Brunschvicg (Paris: Garnier Frères, 1964), pp. 73–74. For Pascal in relation to subsequent views of the epistemological status of fiction, see Trimpi, *AHF*, appendix C, pp. 72f.

32. ''On Hurd's Commentary,'' *The Miscellaneous Works of Edward Gibbon* (London, 1814), 4:134–35. The distinction between ideas of substance and modes of thinking, or moral combinations, is of course Locke's.

33. *Works*, 12:26; 7:93–94; cf. *Rambler* 41 (*Works*, 4:265). For other aspects of Johnson's relation to Locke, see W. K. Wimsatt, *Philosophic Words* (New Haven, Conn.: Yale University Press, 1948), pp. 94–104; Robert Voitle, *Samuel Johnson the Moralist* (Cambridge, Mass.: Harvard University Press, 1961), chap. 1, ''Reason and Empiricism''; and for Locke and Bacon, respectively, Paul Kent Alkon, *Samuel Johnson and the Moral Discipline* (Evanston, Ill.: Northwestern University Press, 1967), chaps. 3 and 6. On Locke and Johnson's concept of method, see John W. Wright, ''Samuel Johnson and Traditional Methodology,'' *PMLA* 86, no. 1 (January 1971): 40–50.

34. *Reflections on the Revolution in France*, ed. Thomas H. D. Maloney (1790: reprint ed., New York: Bobbs-Merril, 1955), pp. 8, 70–71.

35. Ibid., pp. 69, 37, 39. For Burke's understanding of empirical method and an attack on definition, see the ''Introduction on Taste'' which precedes the *Philosophical Enquiry into the Origin of our Ideas of the Sublime and Beautiful*, ed. J. T. Boulton, 2d ed. (1759; London: Routledge & Kegan Paul, 1958), pp. 12–13. The first edition of Burke's *Enquiry* appeared in 1757.

36. The premises, here being described, of an empiricist approach to the cognitive and moral value of fictional particulars eventually make possible Shelley's sharp distinction, in ''A Defense of Poetry'' (1821), between didactic fiction, governed by the conceptual intellect, and genuine mimesis. ''A man,'' he writes, ''to be greatly good, must imagine intensely and comprehensively; he must put himself in the place of another and of many others; the pains and pleasures of his species must become his own. The great

instrument of moral good is the imagination; and poetry administers to the effect by acting upon the cause. . . . Poetry strengthens the faculty which is the organ of the moral nature of man, in the same manner as exercise strengthens a limb. A poet therefore would do ill to embody his own conceptions of right and wrong, which are usually those of his place and time, in his poetical creations, which participate in neither.'' Later Shelley remarks, apropos of the intrusive didacticism of Calderón, that ''more is lost than gained by the substitution of the rigidly defined and ever-repeated idealisms of a distorted superstition for the living impersonations of the truth of human passion.'' See also Shelley's remarks on Dante and Milton's *Paradise Lost* (''A Defense of Poetry,'' in *Critical Theory since Plato*, ed. Hazard Adams [New York: Harcourt, Brace, Jovanovich, 1971], pp. 503–6, 508).

37. ''Of the Different Species of Philosophy,'' section I of *An Inquiry concerning Human Understanding* (1748), in *Philosophical Works of David Hume* (Edinburgh, 1826), 4:2–8; cited hereafter as *Philosophical Works*.

38. The phrase in quotation marks is from William K. Wimsatt, Jr. and Cleanth Brooks, *Literary Criticism: A Short History* (New York: Alfred A. Knopf, 1957), chap. 15, ''The Neo-Classical Universal: Samuel Johnson,'' p. 331.

39. The following discussion of neo-Platonic esthetics is indebted to R. D. Stock, *Samuel Johnson and Neoclassical Dramatic Theory* (Lincoln: University of Nebraska Press, 1973), chap. 2, ''The Poet of Nature.''

40. *Defense of Poesy*, ed. Dorothy M. Macardle (1919; reprint ed., New York: St. Martin's Press, 1966), pp. 7, 9. On Renaissance neo-Platonist esthetics, see Erwin Panofsky, *Idea: A Concept in Art Theory*, trans. Joseph J. S. Peake (1924; Columbia: University of South Carolina Press, 1968), esp. pp. 56–57, 93–99, 129–53.

41. Quoted in Stock, *Samuel Johnson and Dramatic Theory*, pp. 33–34.

42. Sir Joshua Reynolds, *Discourses on Art*, ed. Stephen O. Mitchell (1797; reprint ed., New York: Bobbs-Merrill, 1965), pp. 29–32. For Bellori, see Panofsky, *Idea*, pp. 103–11, 155–75; cf. Reynolds's *Idler* essay no. 82, in Johnson, *Works*, 7:330–31.

43. *Discourses*, p. 30; emphasis mine except for *divine*.

44. Jean Hagstrum argues, in accordance with the view presented here, that Johnson's conception of ''general nature'' must be ''sharply distinguished'' from the neo-Platonic principles described by Louis I. Bredvold (''The Tendency toward Platonism in Neoclassical Esthetics,'' *ELH* 1 [September 1934]: 91–119) and describes Dryden's diffidence in treating the neo-Platonic ideas of Bellori in his commentary on DuFresnoy in *Samuel Johnson's Literary Criticism* (1952; reprint ed., Chicago: University of Chicago Press, 1967), pp. 190–91, n.18.

45. Sir William Davenant, ''Preface to *Gondibert*,'' in Spingarn, *Critical Essays*, 2:48; John Dennis, ''Epistle Dedicatory'' to the *Advancement and Reformation of Poetry*, in *Critical Works of John Dennis*, ed. Edward Niles Hooker (Baltimore: Johns Hopkins Press, 1939–43), 1:202; Charles Gildon, *The Complete Art of Poetry* (1718), in Willard Higley Durham, *Critical Essays of the Eighteenth Century* (1915; reprint ed., New York: Russell & Russell, 1961), pp. 23, 61–62.

46. *The Works of Richard Hurd* (London, 1811), 2:184.

47. *Q. Horatii Flacci Epistolae ad Pisones et Augustum: With an English Commentary and Notes . . . by the Reverend Mr. Hurd* (1757; 5th ed., London, 1776), 1:253-54.

48. Hurd's *Horace*, 1:59; *Works*, 2:127, cf. Hume's remarks on particularity cited in present study, p. 72.

49. For Hume's psychological approach to *la belle nature*, see "Of Simplicity and Refinement in Writing," *Philosophical Works*, 3:218-19. R. D. Stock comments on the general willingness of eighteenth-century critics to blur the distinction between *la vraie* and *la belle nature* in *Samuel Johnson and Dramatic Theory*, chap. 2, p. 56, n.48.

50. Dennis, *Critical Works*, ed. Hooker, 2:5; Rymer, "A Short View of Tragedy," in *Critical Essays*, ed. Spingarn, 2:224. The most general rule for painting manners, says Rapin, "is to exhibit every person in his proper character: a slave, with base thoughts and servile incilinations; a prince, with a liberal heart and air of majesty; a soldier, fierce, insolent, surly, inconstant; an old man, covetous, wary, jealous." Rapin's conceptualist approach to characterization seems to rest on a basis of skepticism. A few sentences after the remarks just quoted he goes on, "The sovereign rule for treating of manners is to copy them after nature, and above all to study well the heart of man to know how to distinguish all its motions. It is this which none are acquainted with. The heart of man is an abyss, where none can sound the bottom; it is a mystery which the most quick-sighted cannot pierce into, and in which the most cunning are mistaken. At the worst the poet is obliged to speak of manners according to the common opinion. Ajax must be represented grim, as Sophocles; Polyxena and Iphigenia generous, as Euripides has represented them" ("Reflections on Aristotle's Treatise of Poesy" [1674], trans. Thomas Rymer, in *The Continental Model: Selected French Critical Essays of the Seventeenth Century, in English Translation*, ed. Scott Elledge and Donald Schier [Ithaca, N.Y.: Cornell University Press, 1970], pp. 289-90).

51. Elledge and Schier, eds., *The Continental Model*, p. 282.

52. Gildon is quoted by Stock, *Samuel Johnson and Dramatic Theory*, p. 33. Sir Richard Blackmore equates *"Fables"* with *"Apologues"* in discussing the didactic function of epic poetry in his "Preface to *Prince Arthur*" (1695), in Spingarn, *Critical Essays*, 3:235-36. Le Bossu says that "l'Epopée est un discours inventé avec art, pour former les moeurs par des instructions déguisées sous les allégories d'une action importante, qui est racontée en Vers d'une manière vraisemblable, divertissante, & merveilleuse" (Spingarn, ed., *Critical Essays*, n. to p. 235, line 9, 3:334). For Dennis's pragmatic view of epic, see *Critical Works*, ed. Hooker, 2:110.

53. See Hobbes's "Answer to Davenant" (1650), in Spingarn, ed. *Critical Essays*, 2:62-65, and Blackmore, in Spingarn, ed., *Critical Essays*, 3:238-39.

54. *Bacon*, 3:453.

55. *Bacon*, 3:453-54.

56. *A Letter from the Archbishop of Cambray to the French Academy; concerning Rhetoric, Poetry, History*, trans. anon. (Glasgow, 1750), p. 43. We are reminded here of Arnauld's "internal sophism of self-love," as well as of Pascal's rule concerning the effaced author.

57. *Dialogues*, pp. 118, 96; cf. Fénelon's remarks in the *Letter*: "I prefer

what is amiable, to what is surprizing and wonderful. I would have a man that makes me forget he is an author; and seems to converse with me upon the level. I would have him set before my eyes, a labourer who is concerned for his crop; a shepherd that knows nothing beyond his flock and his village; a nurse tenderly anxious for her infant. I would have him turn my attention, not on himself, but on the shepherds whom he makes to speak'' (pp. 44–45). Fénelon alludes here to Virgil's *Bucolics* and *Georgics*.

58. The following discussion is indebted to R. D. Stock's distinction between ''reflective'' and ''sentimental'' approaches to the moral value of the drama in eighteenth-century criticism; see his *Samuel Johnson and Neoclassical Dramatic Theory*, chap. 3, ''Aut Prodesse aut Delectare,'' esp. p. 84. See also the indispensable essay by W. R. Keast, ''The Theoretical Foundations of Johnson's Criticism,'' in *Critics and Criticism, Ancient and Modern*, ed. R. S. Crane (1952; reprint ed., Chicago: University of Chicago Press, 1968), pp. 389–407.

59. *An Essay on Taste* (1759), ed. Walter J. Hipple, Jr., 3d ed. (1780; reprint ed., Gainesville: Scholars' Facsimiles and Reprints, 1963), p. 132. For a full statement of Gerard's critical program, see ibid., pp. 246–74.

60. *Spectator* 411, *The Works of Joseph Addison*, ed. G. W. Green (Philadelphia: J. B. Lippincott, 1883), 6:324.

61. Dubos considers didactic verse a legitimate kind, but only because it is capable of giving pleasure: ''Poems are not read for instruction, but amusement; and when they have no charms capable of engaging us, they are generally laid aside'' (*Critical Reflections*, 1:63).

62. Ibid., 1:239–40; cf. 2:237.

63. Ibid., 1:240; 2:237–45. Johnson's empirical test of poetic excellence— ''length of duration, and continuance of esteem''—had in Dubos its most influential eighteenth-century defender.

64. 1:166–69, 104–6, 173–75.

65. Ibid., 1:228–33, 235–37 (emphasis mine).

66. *Lectures on Oratory and Criticism*, ed. Bevilacqua and Murphy, p. 84; cf. Kames, *Elements of Criticism*, 1:235–36; 2:329, 350–51; Blair, *Lectures*, ed. Harding, 2:371–72; Campbell, *Philosophy of Rhetoric*, ed. Bitzer, pp. 256–65, 287–93.

67. *An Essay on Poetry and Music, as They Affect the Mind* (1762; Edinburgh, 1778), p. 11.

68. Warton, *Essay on Pope*, 1:v; Gerard, *Essay on Genius* (London, 1774), p. 392; Hurd, *Works*, 2:6; *Aristotle's Treatise on Poetry*, trans. Thomas Twining (1789; 2d ed., London, 1812), 1:xxvii–xxviii.

69. On Castelvetro and Renaissance hedonistic theories of poetry, see Bernard Weinberg, ''Castelvetro's Theory of Poetics,'' in *Critics and Criticism*, ed. Crane, pp. 349–71.

70. *Philosophical Works*, 2:367; 1:162–63; 4:28.

71. Of course the ''sugar'd pill'' theory of the Renaissance, in its simplest form, was a theory of unconscious edification, but it is doubtful that this aspect of it was ever taken very seriously.

72. For a clear statement of the principles of sentimentalism, see Hume, *Treatise of Human Nature*, bk. 3, pt. 1: ''Of Virtue and Vice in General''

(*Philosophical Works*, 2:219-43), and *An Inquiry concerning the Principles of Morals*, section 1 and appendix 1 (*Philosophical Works*, 4:237-44, 366-77).

73. Shelley's *Defence of Poetry* (1821) is a famous example; see Bate's excellent *From Classic to Romantic: Premises of Taste in Eighteenth-Century England* (1946; reprint ed., New York: Harper & Bros., 1961), chaps. 4, 5, and 6.

74. *Essay on Taste*, ed. Hipple, pp. 69-72.

75. *Elements of Criticism*, 1:93-95, 61-66, 103-4.

76. Cf. Burke, *Enquiry*, pp. 22-27; Gerard, *Essay on Taste*, pp. 88-90; Blair, *Lectures*, 1:21-22.

77. *Preface*, pp. 77, 78; that Johnson conceived of the pathetic in oratory in generally Fénelonian terms is suggested by a conversation recorded in Boswell's *Journal of a Tour to the Hebrides*. Boswell suggested that the preacher Whitefield " 'had great effect on the passions.'—*Johnson*. 'Why, sir, I don't think so. *He could not represent a succession of pathetic images.* He vociferated, and made an impression' " (James Boswell, *The Journal of a Tour to the Hebrides with Samuel Johnson*, ed. L. F. Powell [1909; rev. and reprint. ed., London: J. M. Dent & Sons, 1968], p. 16); emphasis mine.

78. Cf. R. D. Stock's parallel distinction between "reflective" and "sentimental" critics, *Samuel Johnson and Dramatic Theory*, chap. 3, pp. 84-85, 89-95, and passim.

79. Johnson's epistemological position can be distinguished from Aristotelian realism, but only with difficulty. Whether Johnson consciously adhered to the moderate conceptualism of Locke, or whether he accepted the extreme nominalism of Berkeley, Burke, Hume, and some of the Scottish "common sense" school—or whether, indeed, he was aware of the possibility of choosing between these positions—it seems impossible to say. His concept of "general nature" asks to be understood along either realist or conceptualist lines, as I try to show in the next chapter. But Johnson was not a systematic philosopher, and his carelessness in describing his own epistemological assumptions has made his concept of "general nature" difficult to interpret. For the sense in which I understand "realism" and "conceptualism" for present purposes, see Frederick Copleston, S.J., *A History of Philosophy, Vol. II, Part II: Medieval Philosophy: Albert the Great to Duns Scotus* (1950; reprint ed., Garden City, N.J.: Doubleday & Co., 1962), chap. 38, pp. 108-17, and ibid., *Vol. III, Part I: Late Medieval and Renaissance Philosophy: Ockham to the Speculative Mystics* (1952; reprint ed., Garden City, N.J.: Doubleday & Co., 1963), chap. 4, esp. pp. 65-72. For Aristotelian realism, see Copleston's *History, Vol. I, Part II: Greece and Rome* (1944; reprint ed., Garden City, N.J.: Doubleday & Co., 1962), chaps. 28, 29. (On the similarity, however, between Johnson and Aristotle see present study, pp. 86-90.) For a concise exposition and critique of the nominalism of Berkeley and Hume, see Hilary Staniland, *Universals* (Garden City, N.J.: Doubleday & Co., 1972), chap. 2. For Burke's nominalism see *Enquiry*, ed. Boulton, pp. 163-66.

CHAPTER 3

1. *Lives*, 3:235, 437-38; for similar *loci* in Johnson, see René Wellek, *A*

History of Modern Criticism: 1750–1950, Vol. I: The Later Eighteenth Century (New Haven, Conn.: Yale University Press, 1955), 1:79–85.

2. *A History of Modern Criticism*, 1:79, 85. Like Wimsatt, Wellek identifies Johnson with the neo-Platonic tradition of Bellori, DuFresnoy, and Reynolds (p. 87).

3. "The art of poetry will be best learned from *Bossu* and *Bohours* [*sic*] in *French*, together with *Dryden*'s Essays and Prefaces, the critical Papers of *Addison*, *Spence* on *Pope*'s *Odyssey*, and *Trapp*'s *Praelectiones Poeticae*" (*Works*, 2:247).

4. See p. 34.

5. See *La Manière de Bien Penser* (Paris, 1687), pp. 10–13; and Granville's paraphrase in Spingarn, ed., *Critical Essays*, 3:295.

6. Trapp, *Lectures on Poetry* (trans. of *Praelectiones*), p. 112.

7. *Lives*, 2:315, 16; 1:163. "Of the ancient poets every reader feels the mythology tedious and oppressive" (*Lives*, 1:213).

8. *Lives*, 2:129. Scott is quoted by Hill in n.5 to p. 129.

9. Johnson gives this as a definition of *nature* in the *Life of Pope* (*Lives*, 3:255).

10. My emphasis; *Preface*, pp. 89, 63–64, 89–90, 63.

11. *Lives*, 1:213–15; *Preface*, pp. 61–62, 78.

12. Johnson's distinction between characters of nature and characters of manners is made quite clear in his discussion of Polonius. In a note to his edition of Shakespeare, Warburton describes Polonius's character as "that of a weak, pedant, minister of state," and makes much of his "declamation" to Claudius and Gertrude for being "a fine satire on the impertinent oratory then in vogue, which placed reason in the formality of method, and wit in the gingle and play of words." Johnson replies, after quoting from Warburton's remarks, that

> the commentator makes the character of Polonius, a character only of manners, discriminated by properties superficial, accidental, and acquired. The poet intended a nobler delineation of a mixed character of manners and of nature. Polonius is a man bred in courts, exercised in business, stored with observation, confident of his knowledge, proud of his eloquence, and declining into dotage. His mode of oratory is truly represented as designed to ridicule the practice of those times, of prefaces that made no introduction, and of method that embarrassed rather than explained. This part of his character is accidental, the rest is natural. Such a man is positive and confident, because he knows that his mind was once strong, and knows not that it is become weak. Such a man excels in general principles, but fails in the particular application. He is knowing in retrospect, and ignorant in foresight. While he depends upon his memory, and can draw from his repositories of knowledge, he utters weighty sentences, and gives useful counsel; but as the mind in its enfeebled state cannot be kept long busy and intent, the old man is subject to sudden dereliction of his faculties, he loses the order of his ideas, and entangles himself in his own thoughts, till he recovers the leading principle, and falls again into his former train. This idea of dotage encroaching upon wisdom, will solve all the phaenomena of the character of Polonius. [*Works*, Yale ed., 8:973–74].

13. *Aristotle* (New York: Columbia University Press, 1960), p. 43. I am arguing that Johnson's conception of literary character is much like W. K. Wimsatt's as explained in his well-known essay "The Concrete Universal" (*The Verbal Icon: Studies in the Meaning of Poetry* [Lexington: University of Kentucky Press, 1954], pp. 69-83). Having described Johnson as a neo-Platonic theorist, Wimsatt would presumably deny this similarity.

It is worth noting that Imlac's phrasing in *Rasselas* is compatible with the principles of realism advanced in *Adventurer* 95. Imlac asserts that the poet "must divest himself of the prejudices of his age or country; he must consider right and wrong in their abstracted and invariable state; he must disregard present laws and opinions, and rise to general and transcendental truths, which will always be the same." These remarks have been interpreted as expressing a neo-Platonic point of view. But they are immediately preceded by Imlac's requirement that the poet "observe the power of all the passions in all their combinations, and trace the changes of the human mind *as they are modified by various institutions, and accidental influences, of climate or custom*, from the sprightliness of infancy to the despondence of decrepitude." Neither Johnson nor Imlac is an esthetic neo-Platonist (*Works*, 3:329-30, emphasis mine). See Howard Weinbrot, "The Reader, the General, and the Particular," *Eighteenth-Century Studies* 5 (Fall 1971): 80-96.

14. In the *Life of Dryden* Johnson remarks that "the mind can be captivated only by recollection or by curiosity; by reviving natural sentiments or impressing new appearances of things: sentences were readier at [Dryden's] call than images; he could more easily fill the ear with some splendid novelty than awaken those ideas that slumber in the heart" (*Lives*, 1:458-59).

15. *The Journal of John Cardan* (Denver: Alan Swallow, 1964), p. 6.

16. Cf. Arthur Schopenhauer's belief that "the life of the individual when described with truth, in a narrow sphere, shows the conduct of men in all its forms and subtleties. . . ." This remark, from Book III of *The World as Will and Idea* occurs in a discussion of biography and autobiography apparently indebted to Johnson's *Rambler* and *Idler* essays on those subjects; see *Critical Theory since Plato*, ed. Adams, p. 485. On the relation between the general and the particular in fiction, and especially the principle that the more specific a mimetic representation is the more general it is, see Trimpi, *AHF*, pp. 51-55 and *QF*, pp. 12, 27-28, n.65 on p. 55, 101-13, including n.127 on p. 110.

17. For the empiricist rejection of "abstract ideas" or concepts in the sense of the word used here, see George Berkeley, "Introduction" to *A Treatise Concerning the Principles of Human Knowledge* (1710), ed. Colin Murray Turbayne (New York: Bobbs-Merrill Co., 1965), sections 6-25; Hume, *A Treatise of Human Nature*, bk. 1, pt. 1, section 7 (*Philosophical Works*, 1:34-45); Edmund Burke, *Enquiry*, ed. Boulton, pp. 163-73; Kames, *Elements*, 4th ed., 2:515 n.

18. Consider the phrasing of Johnson's praise of Addison's periodical fiction: "His figures neither divert by distortion, nor amaze by aggravation. He copies life with so much fidelity that he can be hardly said to invent; yet his exhibitions have an air so much original that it is difficult to suppose them not merely the product of imagination" (*Lives*, 2: 148).

19. I follow the Yale editor in supposing these remarks to refer to Caliban,

of whose language Johnson says in part: "let any other being entertain the same thoughts, and he will find them easily issue in the same expressions" (*Preface*, p. 64, n.2; p. 123).

20. The fallacy implicit in the *Preface to Shakespeare* is touched upon by Coleridge in *Table Talk*, 21 September 1830: "[Mr.______] . . . told me that facts gave birth to, and were, the absolute ground of principles; to which I said, that unless he had a principle of selection, he would not have taken notice of those facts upon which he grounded his principle. You must have a lantern in your hand to give light, otherwise all the materials in the world are useless, for you can not find them, and if you could, you could not arrange them. 'But then,' said Mr.______, '*that* principle of selection came from facts: '—'To be sure!' I replied: 'but there must have been again an antecedent light to see those antecedent facts. The relapse may be carried in imagination backwards forever,—but go back as you may, you cannot come to a man without a previous aim or principle' " (*Complete Works of Samuel Taylor Coleridge*, ed. Shedd [New York: Harper & Bros., 1854], 6:345). According to Boswell, Johnson

> was particularly indignant against the almost universal use of the word *idea* in the sense of *notion* or *opinion*, when it is clear that *idea* can only signify something of which an image can be formed in the mind. We may have an *idea* or *image* of a mountain, a tree, a building; but we cannot surely have an *idea* or *image* of an *argument* or *proposition*. Yet we hear the sages of the law 'delivering their ideas upon the question under considera-tion;' and the first speakers in parliament 'entirely coinciding in the *idea* which has been ably stated by an honourable member;' . . . Johnson called this 'modern cant.' " [*Life*, 3:196–97]

The passage portrays Johnson as a stickler for the terminology of Lockean tradition, but unfortunately Boswell's phrasing does not allow us to determine whether Johnson was, like Locke, a conceptualist who believed in the existence of abstract ideas, or a nominalist like most of his philosophical contemporaries: *idea* is not made expressly synonymous with *image*; to say that "*idea* can only signify something of which an image can be formed in the mind" leaves open both possibilities. In any event, it is enough to say that Johnson writes in the *Preface to Shakespeare* as though he were a nominalist; he has the difficulties of a nominalist in accounting for the fictional process. The function of concepts in focusing and limiting our apprehension of individuals was sensitively treated by Aristotle and Aquinas and is indispensable to their realist epistemology. It was rediscovered by Kant, who refuted the empiricist equation of idea and image. For a remarkable discussion of the whole issue in its application to the visual arts, see E. H. Gombrich, *Art and Illusion* (1960; rev. and reprint, Princeton, N.J.: Princeton University Press, 1972), esp. chaps. 2, 3, and 5.

21. See Walter Jackson Bate's perceptive treatment of some of the con-sequences of this individualism for eighteenth- and nineteenth-century poetic theory and practice in *The Burden of the Past and the English Poet* (London: Chatto & Windus, 1971). For another view of Johnson on generality and particularity, see Arieh Sachs, *Passionate Intelligence* (Baltimore, Md.: Johns Hopkins Press, 1967), chap. 5.

22. *Bacon*, 4:61.

23. "That which has most contributed to hinder the due teaching of our ideas, and finding out their relations, and agreements or disagreements, one with another, has been, I suppose, the ill use of words. It is impossible that men should ever truly seek or certainly discover the agreement or disagreement of ideas themselves, whilst their thoughts flutter about, or stick only in sounds of doubtful and uncertain significations. . . . For whilst they stick in words of undetermined and uncertain signification, they are unable to distinguish true from false, certain from probable, consistent from inconsistent, in their own opinions. This having been the fate or misfortune of a great part of men of letters, the increase brought into the stock of real knowledge has been very little, in proportion to the schools disputes, and writings, the world has been filled with; whilst students, being lost in the great wood of words, knew not whereabouts they were, how far their discoveries were advanced, or what was wanting in their own, or the general stock of knowledge. Had men, in the discoveries of the material, done as they have in those of the intellectual world, involved all in the obscurity of uncertain and doubtful ways of talking, volumes writ of navigation and voyages, theories and stories of zones and tides, multiplied and disputed; nay, ships built, and fleets sent out, would never have taught us the way beyond the line; and the Antipodes would be still as much unknown, as when it was declared heresy to hold there were any." [*Essay*, IV.iii.30]

24. I should like to refer the reader at this point to appendix A, where I try to reconcile Imlac's warning against numbering the streaks of the tulip with the empiricist principles described above.

CHAPTER 4

1. "An Essay of Dramatic Poesy" (1668), in *Essays of John Dryden*, ed. W. P. Ker (Oxford: Clarendon Press, 1926), 1:36; "Preface to *Valentinian*" (1685), in Spingarn, ed., *Critical Essays*, 3:16–23; "Of Poetry" (1690), in Spingarn, 3:85.

2. In Ker, 1:100–101. In seventeenth-century France *le vraisemblable* was commonly opposed to *la vraie nature* as a principle of idealization. *"La seule nature que l'art doive imiter,"* says Pierre Clarac in summarizing the common view, *"est celle des caractères et des sentiments, la nature morale, et encore à la condition qu'elle ait été épurée et ordonnée par notre esprit, qu'il l'ait rendue à la fois intelligible et édifiante, conforme aux exigences de la morale comme à celles de la raison"* (*Littérature Française: L'Age Classique II, 1660–1680* (Paris: Arthaud, 1969), p. 77; see also Antoine Adam, *Histoire de la Littérature Française* (Paris: Editions Mondiales, 1962), 2:361–63.

3. In *Idea*, Panofsky describes the empirically oriented idealism of Bellori and other spokesmen for seventeenth-century "classicism" in the theory of the visual arts as attempting to steer a middle course between two extremes. On the one hand, the classicists reacted against the Mannerists for relying "on mere phantasy instead of concrete observation"; but they also condemned the naturalism of Caravaggio and his school for preferring truth to individual

nature before beauty, which inheres in the general idea. In English literary theory of the later seventeenth century the demand for "truth to nature," especially in the character drawing and dialogue of the drama, parallels Bellori's response to Mannerism, whose literary equivalent is to be found in metaphysical poetry and the extremer styles of Baroque prose. But there seems to be little in the English literary theory of the time corresponding to Bellori's distrust of naturalism; see *Idea*, chap. 6, passim.

4. *Essays*, ed. Ker, 1:71, 68; see the full discussion, pp. 67–80.

5. Ibid., 1:86, 79–80; cf. the Earl of Mulgrave's long attack on excessive wit in comic and excessive ornament in tragic dialogue, beginning, "Think not so much where shining thoughts to place,/As what a man would say in such a case," in "An Essay upon Poetry" (1682), Spingarn, ed., *Critical Essays*, 2:293–95; also see Granville's "Essay upon Unnatural Flights in Poetry," in Spingarn, 3:292–95, passim. We should remember too that during the later seventeenth century the term *image* was acquiring the specifically empiricist associations which it was to carry into eighteenth-century esthetics. The commonplace that words are the images of things is prominent in Bacon; Hobbes said that *"to know well"* is "to have images of nature in the memory distinct and clear" ("Answer to Davenant" [1650], in Spingarn, ed., *Critical Essays*, 2:63); Sprat speaks of true eloquence as "onely employ'd to describe *Goodness, Honesty, Obedience*; in larger, fairer, and more moving Images: to represent *Truth* cloth'd with Bodies; and to bring *Knowledg* back again to our very senses, from whence it was at first deriv'd to our understandings" (*History of the Royal Society*, ed. Cope and Jones, p. 112); and Joseph Glanvill defines true wit in preaching as "a perfection in our faculties, chiefly in the understanding, and imagination; Wit in the understanding is a sagacity to find out the nature, relations, and consequences of things; Wit in the imagination, is a quickness in the phancy to give things proper Images" (*An Essay concerning Preaching* [London, 1678], pp. 71–72). For the general significance of images in neoclassical literary theory, see the article by William H. Youngren cited above, n.11 to chap. 1; and George Williamson, *The Proper Wit of Poetry* (Chicago: University of Chicago Press, 1961), chap. 5.

6. *Essays*, ed. Ker, 1:14–15. Williamson comments on this passage in *The Proper Wit of Poetry*, pp. 85–87.

7. *Satires, Epistles, and Ars Poetica*, trans. H. Rushton Fairclough, LCL (1926; rev. and reprint, London: Heinemann, 1947), p. 452, lines 32–37. In describing "simplicity" in style, the neoclassical critics often quote or allude to Horace's defense of the plain style: "My aim shall be poetry so moulded from the familiar that anybody may hope for the same success, may sweat much and yet toil in vain when attempting the same: such is the power of order and connection, such the beauty that may crown the commonplace" (ibid., lines 240–43). Two of the most often cited passages on simplicity in Quintilian deserve to be quoted. The first is from the preface to Book VIII of the *Institutes*, a long attack on the decadence of Silver Latin oratory the whole of which may be taken as a relevant commentary on Johnson's objections to metaphysical style. "As a rule," says Quintilian,

the best words are essentially suggested by the subject matter and are discovered by their own intrinsic light. But to-day we hunt for these words as though they were always hiding themselves and striving to elude our grasp. And thus we fail to realize that they are to be found in the subject of our speech, and seek them elsewhere, and, when we have found them, force them to suit their context. It is with a more virile spirit that we should pursue eloquence, who, if only her whole body be sound, will never think it her duty to polish her nails and tire her hair.

The usual result of over-attention to the niceties of style is the deterioration of our eloquence. The main reason for this is that those words are best which are least far-fetched and give the impression of simplicity and reality [*ab ipsa veritate profectis similia*]. For those words which are obviously the result of careful search and even seem to parade their self-conscious art, fail to attain the grace at which they aim and lose all appearance of sincerity because they darken the sense and choke the good seed by their own luxuriant overgrowth. For in our passion for words we paraphrase what might be said in plain language, repeat what we have already said at sufficient length, pile up a number of words where one would suffice, and regard allusion as better than directness of speech. So, too, all directness of speech is at a discount, and we think no phrase eloquent that another could conceivably have used. We borrow figures and metaphors from the most decadent poets, and regard it as a real sign of genius that it should require a genius to understand our meaning. And yet Cicero long since laid down this rule in the clearest of language, that the worst fault in speaking is to adopt a style inconsistent with the idiom of ordinary speech and contrary to the common feeling of mankind. [VIII. Pr.21–25]

In the second passage, Quintilian is discussing the style appropriate to the statement of facts, the second part of a standard classical oration. It is "specially important in this part of our speech to avoid anything suggestive of artful design, for the judge is never more on his guard than at this stage. Nothing must seem fictitious (*fictum*), nought betray anxiety; everything must seem to spring from the case itself rather than the art of the orator. But our modern orators cannot endure this and imagine that their art is wasted unless it obtrudes itself, whereas as a matter of fact the moment it is detected it ceases to be art. We are the slaves of applause and think it the goal of all our effort" (IV.ii.126–27). On these and other classical statements of plain style ideals see Trimpi, *Ben Jonson's Poems*, chap. 1.

Addison provided a popular formula for simplicity in style in praising incidents in *Paradise Lost* that "seem to rise of themselves from the subject of which [Milton] treats. In a word, though they are natural they are not obvious, which is the true character of all fine writing" (*Spectator* 345). See Hume's use of the formula "natural but not obvious" in his essay "Of Simplicity and Refinement in Writing," *Philosophical Works*, 3:218–23. For other classical statements of the value of simplicity and unobtrusive ornament see Quintilian, II.v.11–12, xi.6–xii.8; XI.i.52–56; Demetrius, *On Style*, 21–28, 221; Longinus, 17; Cicero, *De Oratore*, III.xxiv.94–xxvii.104, xli.165; *Orator*, 78–79, 81–85.

8. "A Letter to a Young Clergyman Lately Entered into Holy Orders," *Works of Jonathan Swift*, ed. J. Hawkesworth (London, 1781), 10:9.

9. See, for example, Blair, *Lectures*, 1:387-407; Bouhours, *Art of Criticism*, dialogue 4, passim; Richard Flecknoe, "A Short Discourse of the English Stage" (1664); Spingarn, ed., *Critical Essays,* 2:94; La Bruyère, *Characters,* p. 9; Rapin, *Whole Critical Works,* 2:132; Spence, *Essay on Pope's Odyssey,* dialogue 1, pp. 18-25, 35; dialogue 5, pp. 176-77.

10. "Of Poetry" (1690), Spingarn, ed., *Critical Essays,* 3:83-84; Temple's poetic bee is modeled on Seneca's humanist bee, a figure used by Bouhours and others; see *Letter* 84 in *Select Letters of Seneca,* ed. Walter C. Summers (1910; reprint ed., London: Macmillian & Co., 1968), pp. 97-100.

11. *The Works of Mr. de St. Evremont* [*sic*] . . . *Translated from the French* (London, 1700), 1:483; 2:388-89.

12. *Entretiens d'Ariste et d'Eugène* (1671; Paris, 1748), p. 260.

13. Ibid., p. 257.

14. *Works of St. Evremont,* 1:483, 428-30; 2:64-65. Croll discusses the change in the doctrine of literary imitation between the sixteenth and the eighteenth centuries in "Juste Lipse et le Mouvement Anticicéronien," in *Style, Rhetoric, and Rhythm,* pp. 34-40.

15. Thus Bouhours, for example, at once considers the moderns at least potentially equal if not superior to the ancients, insists upon the necessity of imitating the best ancient models of style, and warns against the vice of "subtlety" or "refinement" which in his view often stems from the attempt to improve upon the particular beauties of one's model; on the latter point, see *The Art of Criticism,* dialogue 3, p. 60.

16. *Whole Critical Works,* 2:146; 2:viii, 6-7; 2:62-63, 14; 1:55-79; 2:25, 53, 80-81; 2:19; 1:55.

17. Ibid., 2:382-83; *The Comparison of Plato and Aristotle, with the Opinions of the Fathers on their Doctrine, and Some Christian Reflections. Translated from the French of René Rapin by John Dancer* (London, 1673), pp. 189-91.

18. *Whole Critical Works,* 2:395. For Seneca's objections to false refinement in philosophy, see *Lucius Annaeus Seneca, Ad Lucilium Epistulae Morales,* trans. Richard H. Gummere, LCL (Cambridge, Mass.: Harvard University Press, 1953), vol. 1, *Letter* 45; vol. 2, *Letter* 89; vol. 3, *Letter* 117.

19. *Whole Critical Works,* 1:237. Note however that Rapin admires Livy perhaps as much as Thucydides, though the former "speaks more to the Understanding, than to the Eye or Ear" (1:294). Rapin's praise of Thucydides echoes Plutarch's. See *Plutarch's Moralia,* trans. Frank Cole Babbitt, LCL (London: Heinemann, 1936), 4:347-347C.

20. *Whole Critical Works,* 1:221; 2:259, 273, 280, 293, 307-8, 340-41.

21. *Works,* 1:103. Rapin and St.-Evremond echo the views of Strada and Boccalini. But Tacitus had many admirers in the neoclassical period, including Dryden, Gray, and Adam Smith, who defends him in his *Lectures on Rhetoric,* pp. 90, 107-10.

22. See the OED, s.v. *aesthetic.*

23. *Lectures on Oratory and Criticism,* p. 136.

24. *Essays on the Nature and Principles of Taste* (Edinburgh, 1790), pp. 120-21. By "ideas of emotion" Alison means ideas (images) accompanied by or productive of "some simple Emotion or other. Thus the ideas suggested by

the scenery of Spring, are ideas productive of emotions of Cheerfulness, of Gladness, and of Tenderness'' (p.53).

25. Ibid., pp. 29–30, 41–42 (emphasis mine).

26. Locke, *Essay*, III.ix.9; cf. Berkeley, *Principles of Human Knowledge*, ''Introduction,'' secs. 19–20.

27. ''Hence we may observe that poetry, taken in its most general sense, cannot with strict propriety be called an art of imitation. It is indeed an imitation so far as it describes the manners and passions of men which their words can express; where *animi motus effert interprete lingua*. There it is strictly imitation; and all merely *dramatic* poetry is of this sort. But *descriptive* poetry operates chiefly by *substitution*; by the means of sounds, which by custom have the effect of realities. Nothing is an imitation further than as it resembles some other thing; and words undoubtedly have no sort of resemblance to the ideas for which they stand'' (*Enquiry*, pp. 172–73).

28. It may be said that Burke and Alison were both extremists in eighteenth-century criticism. And it is true that few critics went as far as Alison toward a poetics of revery, and few if any accepted the whole of Burke's attack on *ut pictura poesis*. But both critics are valuable for revealing the logic of tendencies which declared themselves more obscurely in the thought of many of their contemporaries. In their very different ways, both help us to understand why, by the end of the century, Wordsworth and Coleridge found the subject-object distinction not merely important but fundamental to critical theory.

29. *Rhetoric*, 1410^{b}5–20; cf. 1412^{a}10, 1405^a–1405^{b}15.

30. *De Oratore*, III.xxxviii.155–68; *Institutio Oratoria*, VIII.vi.5–6, 14–18.

31. As with the tropes, Cicero and Quintilian discuss the figures of thought in pragmatic terms, only occasionally linking them with the representation of emotion, as in *Institutio Oratoria*, IX.ii.26–27.

32. Dryden, ''Preface to *Troilus and Cressida*,'' *Essays*, ed. Ker, 1:224–27; Dennis, *Critical Works*, 1:2–3.

33. Cf. *Spectator* 160; Trapp, *Lectures on Poetry*, p. 139; Edward Manwaring, *Institutes of Learning* (London, 1737), p. 8; John Husbands, ''Preface'' to *A Miscellany of Poems by Several Hands* (1731), in Elledge, ed., *Eighteenth-Century Critical Essays*, 1:416–31, passim, esp. p. 421; Kames, *Elements*, 4th ed., 1:501–15; Blair, *Lectures*, lecture 14, passim, 1:272–94; Beattie, *Essay on Poetry and Music*, pp. 264–88; Gerard, *Essay on Genius*, in Elledge, ed., *Critical Essays*, 2:895–913; for Adam Smith, see present study, p. 124. Johnson's acceptance of the mimetic standard appears in scattered remarks on the pathetic in poetry, and is implicit in his premise that poetry is to represent ''the operations of intellect'' (*Lives*, 1:19) (see present study, p. 135). Gibbon calls attention to the novelty of the mimetic theory of ornament in his remarks on Hurd's commentary on Horace. ''The herd of critics,'' he says ''allow [''poetical expressions,'' that is, ornaments] to the [tragic] hero in his calmer moments, and forbid them in his more passionate ones. On the contrary, (says Mr. Hurd, and I think with reason,) it is that very passion that calls them forth, by rouzing every faculty, and exciting images suitable to the grandeur of his situation. Anger indeed, which exhalts the mind, inspires more bold and daring images; those of grief are more weak,

humble, and broken: but when passion sleeps, it is fancy alone that can create figures, and fancy is a very improper guide for the severe genius of dramatic poetry.'' Gibbon goes on to give a lengthy analysis of the figurative character of passionate speech (*Miscellaneous Works*, 4:115–18). It may be noted that the eighteenth century's approach to the figurative language of ''Hebrew poetry'' probably reflects the influence of Fénelon, who praises Old Testament style in the *Dialogues* (Howell ed., pp. 130–31). Husbands cites Fénelon in his early discussion of Hebrew style.

34. *The Mirror and the Lamp*, chap. 4, pp. 71–99. K. G. Hamilton also discusses the rise of eighteenth-century expressive theory; see *The Two Harmonies*, pp. 182–92.

35. *A Critical Dissertation on the Poems of Ossian, Son of Fingal* (1763), in Elledge, ed., *Critical Essays*, 2:849.

36. ''On the Arts Commonly Called Imitative,'' in Elledge, ed., *Critical Essays*, 2:872–81. In this essay Jones repeats Burke's argument against considering poetry an imitative art, and even borrows his terminology.

37. *Elements*, 4th ed., 1:450–51; cf. Cicero's view, more representative of seventeenth-century thinking: ''There can be no doubt that reality beats imitation in everything; and if reality unaided were sufficiently effective in presentation, we should have no need at all for art. But because emotion ... is often so confused as to be obscured and almost smothered out of sight, we have to dispel the things that obscure it and take up its prominent and striking points'' (*De Oratore*, III.lvii.215).

38. So William Duff questions whether ''an Author can be said to invent sentiments which rise to the imagination, in a manner by a simple volition, without any labour, and almost without any effort. Such a person being endued with a vivacity and vigour of Imagination, as well as an exquisite sensibility of every emotion, whether pleasant or painful, which can affect the human heart, has nothing else to do, in order to move the passions of others, but to represent his own feelings in a strong and lively manner; and to exhibit the object, event or action he proposes to describe, in that particular attitude or view, which has most powerfully interested his own affections'' (*An Essay on Original Genius* [London, 1767], pp. 153–54).

39. ''Preface to the Second Edition of ... *Lyrical Ballads*,'' in *The Poetical Works of William Wordsworth*, ed. E. de Selincourt (Oxford: Clarendon Press, 1944), 2:387–88, 386, 388 n., 390, 387, 394.

40. This point of view has been especially emphasized in modern criticism by Cleanth Brooks; see *The Well Wrought Urn* (New York: Harcourt, Brace & World, 1947), chaps. 1, 4, and 11, and ''Irony as a Principle of Structure'' (1949), reprint. in *Critical Theory since Plato*, ed. Adams, pp.1041–48

41. Arnauld himself reveals no indebtedness to Longinus.

42. See W. K. Wimsatt's objection to the current sense of *denotation* and *connotation* in literary criticism, *The Verbal Icon*, pp. 145–48. There is much to be gained by returning to J. S. Mill's use of these terms, which Wimsatt prefers.

43. Thus we can understand why, despite his Cartesian love of a ''plain'' and ''barren'' precision in oratory and all discourse, Arnauld condemns those who treat important moral and religious truths in a ''flat and meager Stile,

like that of the Scholastics." Arnauld is consistent with the principles described above in his refusal to consider the expression of moral truth as incompatible with affecting or "emotive" utterance.

44. See pp. 46-47, 48-50.

45. *Dialogues*, pp. 96-97. Speaker A here is following Longinus, 18-20.

46. Catullus 85:

>   I hate and love her. If you ask me why
>   I don't know. But I feel it and am torn.

(Trans. J. V. Cunningham, *Collected Poems and Epigrams* [London: Faber & Faber, 1971], p. 132.)

47. Smith, *Lectures*, pp. 22-23; Blair takes much the same view in his chapter on figurative language in the *Lectures on Rhetoric* (begun about 1760), and so does Priestley in his *Lectures on Oratory and Criticism*, composed in 1762. The terminology of both these authors is strongly reminiscent of Arnauld. Incidentally, in the *Lectures* Blair praises Fénelon's *Dialogues on Eloquence* and "reflections on oratory and poetry" (presumably the *Letter to the French Academy* is meant) "as containing, I think, the justest ideas on the subject [of eloquence], that are to be met with in any modern critical writer" (2:33-34). Howell discusses Smith's views on ornament in *Eighteenth-Century British Logic and Rhetoric*, pp. 548-53.

48. *De Oratore*, III.xvi.61; the rivalry between dialectic and rhetoric had to all intents and purposes ceased earlier, as was noted in chapter 2; the theory justifying the cessation does not become clear, however, until the 1760s.

49. Cf. Johnson's comments on Hamlet's soliloquy, *Works*, Yale ed., 8:981. On the differences between genuinely mimetic and merely "descriptive" styles in the drama see Kames's *Elements*, chaps. 16 and 17 passim.

50. *Essay on Genius*, in Elledge, ed., *Critical Essays*, 2:906-7. For the growth of Shakespeare's reputation as the "poet of nature" and master of a "natural" style, see vol. 1, pt. 1 of Capell's *The Plays of Shakespeare* (Dublin, 1771), which collects the prefaces of Shakespeare's eighteenth-century editors up to that time.

51. *Poetical Works*, 2:390, 397, 406, 394, 392-93.

52. *Literary Criticism of William Wordsworth*, ed. Paul M. Zall (Lincoln: University of Nebraska Press, 1966), pp. 117-18 (emphasis mine).

53. Ibid., pp. 125-26. Cf. the individualistic standard of poetic diction implicit in the following remarks of Coleridge: "In poetry, in which every line, every phrase, may pass the ordeal of deliberation and deliberate choice, it is possible, and barely possible, to attain that ultimatum which I have ventured to propose as the infallible test of a blameless style; its *untranslatableness* in words of the same language without injury to the meaning. Be it observed, however, that I include in the *meaning* of a word not only its correspondent object, but likewise all the associations which it recalls. For language is framed to convey not the object alone, but likewise the character, mood and intentions of the person who is representing it. In poetry it *is* practicable to preserve the diction uncorrupted by the affectations and misappropriations, which promiscuous authorship, and reading not promiscuous only because it is disproportionally most conversant with the compositions of the day, have rendered general. Yet even to the poet,

composing in his own province, it is an arduous work: and as the result and pledge of a watchful good sense, of fine and luminous distinction, and of complete self-possession, may justly claim all the honor which belongs to an attainment equally difficult and valuable, and the more valuable for being rare. It is at *all* times the proper food of the understanding; but in an age of corrupt eloquence it is both food and antidote'' (*Biographia Literaria*, ed. John Shawcross [1907; reprint ed., Oxford: Oxford University Press, 1962], 2:115–16).

54. *Biographia Literaria*, 2:83–84.

55. Ibid., 2:56. For other statements on the nature of poetical imitation, see ibid., 2:32–34, 101–4, 255–63.

56. *Poetical Works*, 2:436–39; also see appendix B.

57. James A. W. Heffernan documents Wordsworth's concern for accuracy of observation in *Wordsworth's Theory of Poetry: The Transforming Imagination* (Ithaca, N.Y.: Cornell University Press, 1969), chap. 1, pp. 6–29.

58. *The Necessary Angel* (New York: Random House, 1951), p. 96.

CHAPTER 5

1. *Lives*, 1:20. For ''natural and new'' in Bouhours, see *The Art of Criticism*, Dialogue 1, 51–52.

2. For Pope's conception of ''Descriptions or Images'' as including ''Descriptions of the Internal Passions,'' see Hagstrum, *Samuel Johnson's Literary Criticism*, pp. 114–15; see also Adam Smith's detailed discussion of description, including the description of ''compound invisible objects, as of a character,'' in his *Lectures on Rhetoric and Belles Lettres*, ed. Lothian, pp. 58–71.

3. See appendix A, pp. 204–5; cf. Adam Smith's distinction between ''direct description''—''describing the thing itself by its parts''—and ''indirect'' description, which displays ''the effect [an object] has on those who behold it'' (*Lectures on Rhetoric and Belles Lettres*, p. 60).

4. Johnson remarks of Dryden's *Religio Laici* that ''unhappily the subject is rather argumentative than poetical: [Dryden] intended only a specimen of metrical disputation. . . . This however is a composition of great excellence in its kind'' (*Lives*, 1:442). ''Though Davies has reasoned in rhyme before him, it may be perhaps maintained that [Dryden] was the first who joined argument with poetry'' (*Lives*, 1:469). In *Timber, or Discoveries* Ben Jonson writes: ''*Some*, that turne over all bookes, and are equally searching in all papers; that write out of what they presently find or meet, without choice; by which meanes it happens that what they have discredited and impugned in one worke, they have before or after extolled the same in another. Such are all the *Essayists*, even their Master *Mountaigne*. These in all they write confesse still what bookes they have read last, and therein their owne folly so much that they bring it to the *Stake* raw and undigested; not that the place did need it neither, but that they thought themselves furnished and would vent it'' (Spingarn, ed., *Critical Essays*, 1:21). On this passage see Trimpi, *Ben Jonson's Poems*, pp. 33–38.

5. *Poetical Works* (London, 1741), 2:18.

6. See Blair, *Lectures*, 2:355–59; Dennis, *Critical Works*, 1:6, 44–45; Gildon, *The Complete Art of Poetry* (London, 1718), 1:179; Rapin, *Reflections on Aristotle's Treatise of Poesy*, trans. Rymer (London, 1694), pp. 26–30; Trapp, *Lectures on Poetry*, pp. 202–17.

7. *The Complete Art of Poetry*, 1:158.

8. For a detailed account of the theory and practice of English pulpit oratory in the seventeenth century, and in particular of the development of neo-classical standards for the genre, see W. Fraser Mitchell, *English Pulpit Oratory from Andrewes to Tillotson: A Study of Its Literary Aspects* (London, 1932). Mitchell describes the effect on style of the "metaphysical" practice of "crumbling" a text as "the total break up of anything approaching a connected prose style and the multiplying of endless divisions, due not to the careful working out of a rhetorical plan, but to the caprice and ingenuity of the preachers" (p. 362). Puritan sermon method during the first half of the seventeenth century, though opposed to the "metaphysical" style in its dialectical severity, could also be extremely elaborate and mechanical; see ibid., pp. 112–15.

Mitchell quotes Gilbert Burnet's summary of the reforms achieved in pulpit eloquence by 1713:

> The impertinent Way of dividing Texts is laid aside, the needless setting
> out of the Originals, and the vulgar Version, is worn out. The trifling Shews
> of Learning in many Quotations of Passages, that very few could understand,
> do no more flat the Auditory. *Pert Wit* and *luscious Eloquence* have lost
> their Relish. So that Sermons are reduced to the plain opening the meaning
> of the Text, in a few short illustrations of its Coherence with what goes
> before and after, and of the Parts of which it is composed; to that is joined
> the clear Stating of such Propositions as arise out of it, in their Nature,
> Truth, and Reasonableness; by which, the Hearers may form clear Notions
> of the several Parts of Religion, such as are best suited to their Capacities
> and Apprehensions: In all which Applications are added, tending to the
> Reproving, Directing, Encouraging, or Comforting the Hearers....
>
> This is indeed all that can truly be intended in Preaching, to make some
> Portions of Scripture to be rightly understood; to make those Truths
> contained in them to be more fully apprehended; and then to lay the
> Matter home to the Consciences of the Hearers, so directing all to some
> good and practical End. [P. 129]

9. *A Dissertation on Reading the Classics and Forming a Just Style* (1709; London, 1715), p. 118.

10. "Miscellaneous Reflections," in *Characteristics*, ed. John M. Robertson, 2:168–69; cf. "Advice to an Author," 1:166–69.

11. For a perceptive account of the differences between implicit, or classical, and explicit, or medieval, poetic form, see J. V. Cunningham, "Classical and Medieval: Statius, on Sleep," in *Tradition and Poetic Structure* (Denver: Alan Swallow, 1960), pp. 25–39.

12. This description of form applies best to the short poem, the sermon, and the essay, not to longer works of complicated plot such as drama and epic, where for the seventeenth and much of the eighteenth centuries the neo-Aristotelian rules obtained. For a sensitive description of implicit form,

compatible with that of Cunningham but based upon Aristotelian meta-physical principles, see R. S. Crane, *The Languages of Criticism and the Structure of Poetry* (Toronto: University of Toronto Press, 1953), pp. 140-43. William Bowman Piper says of the structure of Pope's epistolary poems: "This discursiveness, which is the rule in all of Pope's essays and epistles, this lack of an iron-bound structure, suggests the ease, the graceful associative quality of polite talk. Such an unforced, such a flexible, notion of topics and arguments and evidence is naturally capable of being interrupted or amended, extended or cut off short without loss of order and coherence. It is, of course, the couplet, with its persistent impression of intelligence and control, that allows the poet to organize in so easy and polite a way without giving the impression of mental weakness or confusion. Thus the closed couplet, with its close grained system of pauses, allows the poet to suggest a persistent responsiveness to his society, a persistent readiness to change course in order to accommodate his interlocutors' questions and doubts. And, with its impression of con-tinuous order and control, it allows him a freedom in the larger ranges of his utterance by which this impression of his social responsiveness is augmented" (*The Heroic Couplet* [Cleveland: Case Western Reserve University Press, 1969], p. 141).

13. *Poetics*, 1450ᵃ35-1451ᵃ; *Phaedrus*, 264b-264e; *On the Sublime*, 10, 40. Mixing his metaphors, the Earl of Roscommon writes, in "An Essay on Translated Verse" (1684):

> On *sure Foundations* let your *Fabrick Rise*,
> And with attractive *Majesty*, surprise,
> Not by affected, *meritricious Arts*,
> But strict *harmonious Symetry* of *Parts*,
> Which through the *Whole* insensibly must pass,
> With vital Heat to animate the Mass,
> A *pure*, an *Active*, an Auspicious flame.

[Spingarn, ed., *Critical Essays*, 2:301]

And Pope writes in the *Essay on Criticism* (Twickenham ed., vol. 1: *Pastoral Poetry and an Essay on Criticism*, ed. E. Audra and Aubrey Williams [New Haven, Conn.: Yale University Press, 1961]):

> *Art* from that Fund [that is, from "Nature"] each
>   *just Supply* provides,
> Works *without Show*, and *without Pomp* presides:
> In some fair Body thus th' informing Soul
> With Spirits feeds, with Vigour fills the whole,
> Each motion guides, and ev'ry Nerve sustains;
> *It self unseen*, but in th' *Effects*, remains.

[Lines 74-79]

14. Cf. *De Oratore*, III.xlv.177-xlvii.182, lii.199; Demetrius, *On Style*, 12-14; Tacitus, "A Dialogue on Oratory," 21-23; Dionysius of Halicarnussus, *On Literary Composition*, trans. W. Rhys Roberts, LCL (London: Heinemann, 1910), pp. 73. 75, 105-7.

15. *Satires, Epistles and Ars Poetica*, LCL, p. 452, lines 32-37.

16. *An Essay on Criticism*, lines 244-52.

17. "Of Simplicity and Refinement in Writing," *Philosophical Works*,

3:219. Addison's Gothic metaphor has its chief English source in Temple's "Of Poetry," Spingarn, ed., *Critical Essays*, 3:91-101.

18. Aristotle maintains that "the first essential, the life and soul, so to speak, of Tragedy is the Plot; and that the Characters come second—compare the parallel in painting, where the most beautiful colours laid on without order will not give one the same pleasure as a simple black-and-white sketch of a portrait" (*Poetics*, 1450^{a}35-1450^b); "Isaeus," section 4, in *The Critical Essays of Dionysius of Halicarnassus*, trans. Stephen Usher, LCL (London: Heinemann, 1974), 1:179-81. Cf. Dryden, "Preface to *Fables*" (1700): "Words, indeed, like glaring colours, are the first beauties that arise and strike the sight; but, if the draught be false or lame, the figures ill disposed, the manners obscure or inconsistent, or the thoughts unnatural, then the finest colours are but daubing, and the piece is a beautiful monster at the best" (*Essays*, ed. Ker, 2:253).

19. "Answer to Davenant," Spingarn, ed., *Critical Essays*, 2:61.

20. Ibid., p. 44; but see Pope's *Essay on Criticism*, lines 301-2, 485-93.

21. The following survey of classical criticism is indebted to Wesley Trimpi, who was studying the *ut pictura* tradition in Greek and Roman criticism in connection with Horace at about the same time that I was studying it in connection with Johnson. See his remarkable essay, "The Meaning of Horace's *Ut Pictura Poesis*," *Journal of the Warburg and Courtauld Institutes* 36 (1973): 1-34.

22. *De Oratore*, III.lvi.213-lviii.219; Demetrius, *On Style*, 193-94. Quintilian insists (XII.x.49-57) that there is no difference between spoken and written style, but nevertheless consistently emphasizes the dramatic character of the *genus grande*. For Fénelon, see present study, pp.122-23.

23. Trimpi suggests that a skiagraphic painting "might correspond today to large figures sprayed, somewhat diffusely, on a wall or formed by highlights being shaded in with broad strokes of a length of charcoal held flat against the surface. In each case the viewer must stand back to recognize the figures" ("The Meaning of Horace's *Ut Pictura*," p. 5, n.7; see Trimpi's bibliography on skiagraphic painting, p. 5, n.7). Trimpi associates Johnson with the skiagraphic tradition, ibid., p. 33.

24. Cf. Pope's *Essay on Criticism*:
> I know there are, to whose presumptuous Thoughts
> Those *Freer Beauties*, ev'n in *Them* [the ancients]
>   seem Faults:
> Some Figures *monstruous* and *mis-shap'd* appear,
> Consider'd *singly*, or beheld too *near*,
> Which, but *proportion'd* to their *Light*, or *Place*,
> Due distance *reconciles* to Form and Grace.
>
> [Lines 169-74]

25. *Orator*, 77-79.

26. *Brutus*, trans. G. L. Hendrickson (LCL, 1939; reprint ed., London: Heinemann, 1962), pp. 289-90; *Orator*, 19-26, 97-101.

27. *Brutus*, 188; *De Oratore*, II.xxxviii.159; I.iii.12; the last passage quoted is cited by Quintilian, VIII. Pr.25; see n.7 to chap. 4 above.

28. *Brutus*, 284-85, 291, 283; cf. ibid., 63-68; *Orator*, 22-32, 168-70. By

Attici and "Atticists" I mean those who, in Cicero's opinion, held much too narrow a view of Attic eloquence.

29. *Orator*, 37–42; for Fénelon, see present study, pp. 23, 27. Cicero's estimate of Isocrates was much higher than Fénelon's. See *Orator*, 40–42.

30. See pp. 7–8.

31. I.xxxiv.157.

32. *Orator*, 42; *Brutus*, 32.

33. *Brutus*, 37; *Orator*, 63–64.

34. *Institutio Oratoria*, XII.x.13–15. Speaking of the excessive pursuit of ornament in contemporary eloquence, Quintilian remarks: "Such passages shine only in the absence of the sunlight, just as certain tiny insects seem transformed in the darkness to little flames of fire" (XII.x.76).

35. Trans. Trimpi; see *Controverses et Suasoires*, ed. Bornecque, 2:123–24.

36. E.g., in the Preface to *The Preceptor*," where Johnson remarks that the laws of morality have "no coercive power; and, however they may by conviction of their fitness please the reasoner in the shade, when the passions stagnate without impulse, and the appetites are secluded from their objects, they will be of little force against the ardour of desire, or the vehemence of rage, amidst the pleasure and tumults of the world" (*Works*, 2:251). Cf. the following comment from *Rambler* 180: "The most frequent reproach of the scholastick race is the want of fortitude, not martial but philosophick. Men bred in shades and silence, taught to immure themselves at sunset, and accustomed to no other weapon than syllogism, may be allowed to feel terror at personal danger, and to be disconcerted by tumult and alarm." Cf. also Johnson's fine poem, "To Miss ______ On her Playing upon the Harpsicord . . . ," in *Works, Yale ed., Vol. VI: Poems*, ed. E. L. McAdam, Jr. (New Haven, Conn.: Yale University Press, 1964), p. 78, lines 25–28.

37. *On the Sublime*, 1, 8–10, 12, 15–27, 30–34.

38. Ibid., 36, 2, 33, 35. In the *Life of Prior* Johnson associates correctness with faintness and lack of originality; "judgment in the operations of intellect can hinder faults, but not produce excellence" (*Lives*, 2:208).

39. See p. 72.

40. *Spectator* 160; cf. Pope's similar comparison in his preface to *The Works of Shakespeare* (1725): "I will conclude by saying of Shakespeare that with all his faults, and with all the irregularity of his drama, one may look upon his works, in comparison of those that are more finished and regular, as upon an ancient majestic piece of Gothic architecture compared with a neat modern building: the latter is more elegant and glaring, but the former is more strong and more solemn. It must be allowed that in one of these there are materials enough to make many of the other. It has much the greater variety, and much the nobler apartments, though we are often conducted to them by dark, odd, and uncouth passages. Nor does the whole fail to strike us with greater reverence, though many of the parts are childish, ill-placed, and unequal to its grandeur" (Elledge, ed., *Critical Essays*, 1:290).

41. *Preface*, p. 84; cf. Johnson's remark to Mrs. Thrale: "Corneille is to Shakespeare as a clipped hedge is to a forest" (cited by Sherbo, n.4).

42. Johnson's criticisms of *Cato* correspond closely to Longinus's objections to the cold Atticism of Hypereides, while his criticisms of metaphysical style, as noted earlier, bring to mind Longinus's remarks about the puerile style.

43. See sect. 35, which concludes with the remark that "what is useful and indeed necessary is cheap enough; it is always the unusual which wins our wonder."

44. Tacitus's "bright Sallies of Wit may be compared to Flashes of Lightning, which rather dazzle than illuminate" (*Whole Critical Works*, 2:273); in the "Dedication" to his *Père Dominique Bouhours, The Arts of Logick and Rhetorick, adapted into English with parallel examples from English authors* (London, 1728), John Oldmixon remarks: "How many great Genius's have miscarry'd, by not thinking rightly on Subjects they were otherwise well able to handle and adorn, and for Want of considering that Truth, in all the Productions of the Mind, is what only renders them agreeable and useful, and that the false Brillant of Thoughts is like the Glare of Lightning, which dazles and hurts the Sight, as that does the Understanding" (p. vi).

45. Ibid., p. 10. "What gives supreme merit to [Sappho's] art" is "the skill with which she chooses the most striking [details] and combines them into a single whole."

46. Cf. Pope's *Essay on Criticism*, which however turns the chiaroscuro figure to a somewhat different use:

> True *Wit* is *Nature* to Advantage drest,
> What oft was *Thought*, but ne'er so well *Exprest*,
> *Something*, whose Truth Convinc'd at Sight we find,
> That gives us back the Image of our Mind:
> As Shades more sweetly recommend the Light,
> So modest Plainness sets off sprightly Wit.
>
> [Lines 297–302]

47. And in poetry as well as prose; see *Satyricon*, 118 and Quintilian, I.viii.8-9.

48. Twickenham ed., lines 309-17. Compare the Earl of Mulgrave's use of the sun figure:

> 'Tis not a Flash of Fancy which sometimes
> Dasling our Minds, sets off the slightest Rimes,
> Bright as a blaze, but in a moment done;
> True Wit is everlasting, like the Sun,
> Which though sometimes beneath a cloud retir'd,
> Breaks out again, and is by all admir'd.
>
> ["An Essay upon Poetry," Spingarn, ed.,
> *Critical Essays*, 2:286, lines 8-13]

49. "How to Write History," *Works*, 6:63; cf. Bacon's belief that "the truth of being and the truth of knowing are one, differing no more than the direct beam and the beam reflected."

50. Twickenham ed., Epistle III, lines 231-32.

51. See Warburton's gloss on the "prismatic glass" passage, *The Works of Alexander Pope* (London, 1757), 1:124.

52. The phrases "Golden Age" and "Silver Age," common in nineteenth- and twentieth-century literary histories of Rome, are rare in seventeenth- and eighteenth-century criticism, but the adjectival use of "golden" and "silver" is common. At the end of Bouhours's *Manière*, Philanthus, cured of his modern taste for "what is florid and glittering," promises never again to

"prefer *Seneca*'s Points to *Cicero*'s good Sense, nor *Tasso*'s Tinsel to *Virgil*'s Gold." Dryden writes in his verse epistle to Roscommon that "Dante's polished page/Restor'd a silver, not a golden Age."

53. Johnson comments that Cowley "unhappily adopted that [style] which was predominant. He saw a certain way to present praise; and not sufficiently enquiring by what means the ancients have continued to delight through all the changes of human manners he contented himself with a deciduous laurel, of which the verdure in its spring was bright and gay, but which time has been continually stealing from his brows" (*Lives*, 1:56).

54. Neoclassical discussions of these principles are numberless; cf. James Arbuckle, *Hibernicus's Letters*, letter 58 (2:25-32); Dryden's verse epistle "To the Earl of *Roscomon*, on his Excellent *Essay* on *Translated Verse*," (*Poems 1681-1684*, ed. Swedenberg, pp. 172-74); Dubos, *Critical Reflections*, 2:99-138, 314-18; Rapin, *Whole Critical Works*, 1: sig. blv-b2r; St.-Evremond, "A Discourse upon the Word VAST" (*Works*, 1:365-67); Temple, "An Essay upon the Ancient and Modern Learning" (1690), and "Of Poetry." Hume gives a concise account of the neoclassical cyclical theory in his *History of England* (London, 1789), 6:189-94.

55. Temple traces the modern vogue of conceit to "the decays of the *Roman* Learning and Wit as well as Language, [when] *Martial, Ausonius*, and others fell into this Vein, and applied it indifferently to all Subjects" ("Of Poetry," in *Critical Essays*, ed. Spingarn, 3:100; cf. Rapin, *Whole Critical Works*, 1:167).

56. *Institutio Oratoria*, X.i.130. The usual neoclassical distinction between "fancy" and "judgment" corresponds to Quintilian's distinction here between *ingenium* and *judicium*. For other criticisms of Silver Latin sententiousness, cf. I.viii.9; II.xi.6-xii.8; VII.i.44; VIII.v.13-14. For Quintilian's criticism of Seneca in relation to Ben Jonson's stylistic position, see Trimpi, *Ben Jonson's Poems*, pp. 19-27, n.27 on p. 242, and n.77 on pp. 251-52.

57. For South, see Mitchell, *English Pulpit Oratory*, p. 215; St.-Evremond, *Works*, 1:214-15; Dryden, "Life of Plutarch," *Works of John Dryden*, ed. Walter Scott (London, 1808), 17:72, 74; Sprat, *History of the Royal Society*, p. 332; Bouhours, *Entretiens*, p. 271; *Art of Criticism*, dialogue 3, pp. 44-45. In the eighteenth century Quintilian's judgment of Seneca is repeated by John Constable, Hume, Gerard, Campbell, and Charles Rollin among others. For what is probably the century's most detailed appropriation of Quintilian's stylistic criticism for contemporary uses, see Constable, *Reflections upon Accuracy of Style* (London, 1734). Seneca is defended by Diderot, in terms surprisingly similar to Croll's; see his "Essai sur les Regnes de Claude et de Néron," *Oeuvres Complètes*, ed. J. Assézat (Paris, 1875), 3:223-37, 266-70, 367-74.

58. On the theory and practice of Restoration prose, see, in addition to the essays of Croll and R. F. Jones, Williamson's *Senecan Amble*; Robert Adolph, *The Rise of Modern Prose Style* (Cambridge, Mass.: M.I.T. Press, 1968); and Ian Gordon, *The Movement of English Prose* (London: Longmans, 1966), esp. pts. 4 and 5.

59. *The Arts of Logick and Rhetorick*, pp. 290-91. For the allusion to Seneca rhetor, see Bornecque, 2:187. Dryden says of Cowley: "One of our late

great poets is sunk in his reputation, because he could never forgive any conceit which came in his way; but swept like a drag-net, great and small. There was plenty enough, but the dishes were ill sorted; whole pyramids of sweatmeats for boys and women, but little of solid meat for men. All this proceeded not from any want of knowledge, but of judgment'' (''Preface to the *Fables*,'' in *Essays*, Ker, ed., 2:258).

60. ''The Baroque Style in Prose,'' *Style, Rhetoric, and Rhythm*, p. 212.

61. I give for convenience the middle stanza from Marvell:

> But at my back I alwaies hear
> Times winged Charriot hurrying near:
> And Yonder all before us lye
> Desarts of vast Eternity.
> Thy Beauty shall no more be found;
> Nor, in thy marble Vault, shall sound
> My ecchoing Song: then Worms shall try
> That long preserv'd Virginity:
> And your quaint Honour turn to dust;
> And into ashes all my Lust.
> The Grave's a fine and private place,
> But none I think do there embrace.

62. *Essay on Criticism*, Twickenham ed., lines 289–92. Pope's ''Thoughts'' literally translates the Latin *sententiae*.

63. On the continuity of seventeenth-century prose style, see Croll, '' 'Attic Prose' in the Seventeenth Century,'' in *Style, Rhetoric, and Rhythm*, pp. 51–101; Williamson, ''Senecan Style in the Seventeenth Century,'' in *Milton and Others* (London: Faber & Faber, 1965), pp. 192–223, and *The Senecan Amble*, chaps. 10 and 11. Croll's oversimplifications and distortions have been partially corrected by R. F. Jones. Robert Adolph reexamines the Croll-Jones controversy, probably from too Jonesian a point of view, in *The Rise of Modern Prose Style*, chap. 1 and passim.

64. ''Epistle to Arbuthnot,'' Twickenham ed., *Vol. IV: Imitations of Horace*, ed. John Butt (London: Methuen & Co., 1939), pp. 109–11, lines 193–214.

65. On the achievement of Dryden and Pope in bringing order and connection to couplet verse, and on the couplet generally, see Piper's distinguished study, *The Heroic Couplet*, esp. chaps. 2, 7, 8, and 9.

66. Johnson's ''exility,'' which, as Hill notes, is not in his *Dictionary*, domesticates the Latin *exilitas*, a critical term which Cicero applies to the coterie style of the Stoics (*De Oratore*, II.xxxviii.159 and present study, p. 146). For *exilitas* Lewis and Short give ''thinness, meagerness, weakness, poorness.'' On Johnson's criticism of fragmentation in Metaphysical style, see Trimpi, *Ben Jonson's Poems* pp. 251–52, n.77.

67. See Joseph A. Mazzeo, ''A Seventeenth-Century Theory of Metaphysical Poetry'' and ''Metaphysical Poetry and the Poetics of Correspondence'' in *Renaissance and Seventeenth-Century Studies* (London: Routledge & Kegan Paul, 1964), pp. 29–59.

68. ''Discourse on the Original and Progress of Satire'' (1693), *Prose Works*, ed. Malone, 3:79.

69. *Letters and Poems, Amorous and Gallant* (London, 1692), sig. A3r–A4v.

70. *Lives*, 2:314–15, 202; "[Dryden] is therefore, with all his variety of excellence, not often pathetick; and had so little sensibility of the power of effusions purely natural that he did not esteem them in others. Simplicity gave him no pleasure; and for the first part of his life he looked on Otway with contempt, though at last, indeed very late, he confessed that in his play 'there was Nature, which is the chief beauty' " (*Lives*, 1:458).

71. The original headnote to the poem reads: "In this Monody the Author bewails a learned Friend, unfortunately drown'd in his Passage from *Chester* on the *Irish* Seas, 1637. And by occasion foretells the ruin of our corrupted Clergy then in their height."

72. *Lives*, 1:163; Hagstrum comments on the limitations of Johnson's ear in *Samuel Johnson's Literary Criticism*, p. 106.

73. Thus the subject of *Religio Laici* is, as we have seen, "rather argumentative than poetical," and the subject of Pope's *Essay on Man* is "perhaps not very proper for poetry" (*Lives*, 1:442; 3:242). As Donald Greene has pointed out, Johnson looked for images in poetry and was invariably disappointed when he found none. Of *Absolom and Achitophel* he remarks: "The subject had likewise another inconvenience [besides the defectiveness of the allegory]: it admitted little imagery or description, and a long poem of mere sentiments easily becomes tedious; though all the parts are forcible and every line kindles new rapture, the reader, if not relieved by the interposition of something that sooths the fancy, grows weary of admiration, and defers the rest" (*Lives*, 1:437); see Donald Greene, " 'Pictures to the Mind': Johnson and Imagery," in *Johnson, Boswell, and Their Circle: Essays Presented to Lawrence Fitzroy Powell* (Oxford: Clarendon Press, 1965), pp. 137–58. On Johnson's standards for poetic imagery and their relation to his criticism of metaphysical conceit, see William Edinger, "Johnson on Conceit: The Limits of Particularity," *ELH* 39, no. 4 (1972): 597–619.

74. See Patricia Ingham, "Dr. Johnson's 'Elegance,' " *Review of English Studies* 19 (1968): 271–78.

Chapter 6

1. Wordsworth, *Poetical Works*, 2:418–20; *Biographia Literaria*, 1:11–15. Coleridge remarks that "the matter and diction" of the imitators of Pope "seemed to me characterized not so much by poetic thoughts, as by thoughts *translated* into the language of poetry."

2. In discussing Milton's epic style in *Spectator* 285 Addison cites Aristotle as his authority for the theory of epic elevation. In the *Poetics*, chap. 22, Aristotle discusses verbal ornament simply as language which "deviates from the ordinary modes of speech." Distinction in style arises from the use of strange words, metaphors, ornamental equivalents, and in particular of "lengthened, curtailed, and altered forms of words." Addison mentions with approval Milton's use of (1) metaphor, (2) idioms borrowed from other tongues (that is, as Virgil and Horace used Greekisms, so Milton latinizes his English), (3) lengthened words (that is, eremite for hermit) and periphrasis, (4) archaisms and coinages. By these devices, says Addison, Milton has "carried our language to a greater height than any of the English poets have

ever done before or after him" though his style is occasionally "too much stiffened and obscured by the frequent use of those methods, which Aristotle has prescribed for the raising of it."

3. "Pope wrote for his own age and his own nation: he knew that it was necessary to colour the images and point the sentiments of his author; he therefore made him graceful, but lost him some of his sublimity" (*Lives*, 3:240).

4. *Preface*, p. 70. Cf. Johnson's praise of Cowley's *Anacreontiques*: "The diction shews nothing of the mould of time, and the sentiments are at no great distance from our present habitudes of thought.... Levity of thought naturally produced familiarity of language, and the familiar part of language continues long the same: the dialogue of comedy, when it is transcribed from popular manners and real life, is read from age to age with equal pleasure. The artifice of inversion, by which the established order of words is changed, or of innovation, by which new words or new meanings of words are introduced, is practiced, not by those who talk to be understood, but by those who write to be admired" (*Lives*, 1:39–40).

5. Unlike Blair, who condemns the eighteenth-century kenning: "there are many epithets, which, though they appear to raise the signification of the word to which they are joined, yet leave it so undetermined, and are now become so trite and beaten in poetical language, as to be perfectly insipid. Of this kind are 'barbarous discord–hateful envy–mighty chiefs–bloody war–gloomy shades–direful scenes' and a thousand more of the same kind which we meet with occasionally in good poets; but with which poets of inferior genius abound every where, as the great props of their affected sublimity. They give a sort of swell to the language, and raise it above the tone of prose; but they serve not in the least to illustrate the object described; on the contrary, they load the style with a languid verbosity" (*Lectures*, 2:381–82).

6. "[Milton's religious truths] are too important to be new: they have been taught to our infancy; they have mingled with out solitary thoughts and familiar conversation, and are habitually interwoven with the whole texture of life. Being therefore not new they raise no unaccustomed emotion in the mind; what we know before we cannot learn; what is not unexpected, cannot surprise" (*Lives*, 1:182).

7. One may compare Wordsworth's remarks on the poetic treatment of moral commonplaces in the *Essay on Epitaphs* (*Literary Criticism*, ed. Zall, pp. 114–26) to see the advantage of a mimetically oriented criticism over Johnson's on this subject.

8. *Johnson on Shakespeare, Works*, Yale ed., 8:1032–33; *Samuel Johnson's Literary Criticism*, pp. 72–73. For other examples of Johnson's didactic interest see *Works*, Yale ed., 7:265; 8:704, 1011.

9. On the whole subject of neoclassical attitudes toward poetic justice see Stock, *Samuel Johnson and Dramatic Theory*, pp. 103–26. Though I disagree in part with the account of Johnson given in these pages, I am nevertheless indebted to it.

10. See Stock, p. 120.

11. I do not mean here only comic expectations, such as the happy ending we wish for the sympathetic heroine. It can be said too (as Aristotle seems to imply) that a tragic plot arouses expectations of events productive of pity, fear,

and wonder and that in a deep sense the undeserved misfortunes of the tragic hero gratify a wish on our part, not for the misfortunes themselves, but for the "catharsis" of emotion which they produce. This sort of tragic gratification no doubt goes beyond anything Coleridge could be expected to mean by the satisfaction of the moral sense.

12. Stock's view of Johnson on *King Lear* is similar to the one expressed here; see *Samuel Johnson and Dramatic Theory*, pp. 121-22.

13. But not Johnson's understanding. There are remarkably few echoes of Bacon's poetic theory in Johnson, the clearest being, perhaps, the remark that "poetry pleases by exhibiting an idea more grateful to the mind than things themselves afford" (*Lives*, 1:292). Significantly, however, Johnson's characteristic view of poetry is expressed at one point in language which echoes Bacon's *rhetorical* theory: "Poetry is the art of uniting pleasure with truth, by calling imagination to the help of reason" (*Lives*, 1:170). In the *Advancement* Bacon says that "the duty and office of Rhetoric is *to apply Reason to Imagination* for the better moving of the will" (Bacon, 3:409). Johnson naturally wished to avoid the opposition between truth and poetry inherent in Bacon's poetics.

14. *Bacon*, 4:314-17. While most eighteenth-century critics take little or no notice of Bacon's opposition of poetry to truth, Richard Hurd makes it the basis of his defense of the "Gothic" and "Romantic" in poetry; see "On the Idea of Universal Poetry," *Works*, 2:3-9.

15. *Rasselas* (*Works*, 3:420-21); *Rambler* 4; also see present study pp. 79-81.

16. See pp. 109-11.

17. *Rambler* 124; *Adventurer* 95; *Lives*, 3:298-99.

18. *Rambler* 169; *Idler* 3; cf. *Rambler* 86, *Idlers* 66, 85.

19. *Rambler* 36; cf. *Rambler* 143: "Many subjects fall under the consideration of an author, which being limited by nature can admit only of slight and accidental diversities. All definitions of the same thing must be nearly the same; and descriptions, which are definitions of a more lax and fanciful kind, must always have in some degree the resemblance to each other which they all have to their object."

20. Perhaps I should note that this conflict has no direct bearing on the central issue of chap. 3, which is the consistency of Johnson's taste for literary realism with his notion of "general nature." The empirical approach to the representation of general nature presented in *Adventurer* 95 is toherent, and the *Preface to Shakespeare* and much else in Johnson's criticism can be read in terms of it. The conflict just described concerns natural description in poetry more crucially than the imitation or expression of "sentiments." Where it does concern the latter, it is at moments when Johnson seems to back away from the premises of his literary realism, as in the passage quoted above from *Rambler* 36.

It may be noted that Blair, Smith, and Hurd all deal more successfully than Johnson with the problem of reconciling the natural and new in poetic description by avoiding Johnson's emphasis on the selection of properties "alike obvious to vigilance and carelessness." See Blair, *Lectures*, 2:371-72; Smith, *Lectures*, pp. 66-68; and Hurd, "A Discourse on Poetical Imitation," *Works*, 2:121-27.

21. "In poems, equally as in philosophic disquisitions, genius produces the strongest impressions of novelty, while it rescues the most admitted truths from the impotence caused by the very circumstance of their universal admission" (*Biographia Literaria*, 1:60).

22. See p. 129.

Appendix A

1. The phrase "genuinely neo-Platonic" should be understood with the qualifications expressed in chap. 2; see present study, pp. 54, 56.

2. See *Discourses*, ed. Mitchell, pp. 33, 35. Johnson returned the compliment by echoing Reynolds in the *Life of Cowley*. In the sixth Discourse (1774) Reynolds says: "The works of Albert Durer, Lucas Van Leyden, the numerous inventions of Tobias Stimer, and Jost Ammon, afford a rich mass of genuine materials, which wrought up and polished to elegance, will add copiousness to what, perhaps, without such aid, could have aspired only to justness and propriety" (ibid., pp. 86–87). Johnson says of the metaphysical poets: "If their greatness seldom elevates, their acuteness often surprises; if the imagination is not always gratified, at least the powers of reflection and comparison are employed; and in the mass of materials, which ingenious absurdity has thrown together, genuine wit and useful knowledge may be sometimes found, buried perhaps in grossness of expression, but useful to those who know their value, and such as, when they are expanded to perspicuity and polished to elegance, may give lustre to works which have more propriety though less copiousness of sentiment" (*Lives*, 1:22).

3. *Samuel Johnson's Literary Criticism*, p. 88. For neo-Platonic readings of the tulip passage, see David Daiches, *Critical Approaches to Literature* (Englewood Cliffs, N.J.: Prentice-Hall, 1956), p. 258; Martin Kallich, "Samuel Johnson's Principles of Criticism and Imlac's Dissertation upon Poetry," *Journal of Aesthetics and Art Criticism* 25 (Fall 1966): 71–82; René Wellek, *A History of Modern Criticism*, 1:85–87; W. K. Wimsatt, *The Verbal Icon*, pp. 71–74. For the more recent emphasis upon empiricist elements in Johnson and Reynolds, see Lionel Basney, " 'Lucidus Ordo': Johnson and Generality," *Eighteenth-Century Studies* 5, no. 1 (Fall 1971): 39–57; Donald Greene, " 'Pictures to the Mind': Johnson and Imagery" (cited above, n. 73 to chap. 5) and the same author's *Samuel Johnson* (New York: Twayne Publishers, Inc., 1970), pp. 200–205; Harvey D. Goldstein, "*Ut Poesis Pictura*: Reynolds on Imitation and Imagination," *Eighteenth-Century Studies* 1, no. 3 (Spring 1968): 213–35; Howard Weinbrot, "The Reader, the General, and the Particular" (cited above, n.13 to chap. 3).

4. *Lives*, 1:53; emphasis mine. I have given the Cowley passage as Johnson quoted it from memory; Hill notes Johnson's verbal substitutions.

5. For the difficulties inherent in this theory see pp. 188–92.

6. See esp. *Essay*, III.ii.2–3 and III.vi.29–31.

7. *Three Treatises* (London, 1744), p. 77, n.(a).

8. *The Works of Joseph Addison*, ed., Greene (Philadelphia, 1868), 2:382.

9. See *Spectators* 417 and 418.

10. *Lectures*, 2:359; cf. ibid., 2:371–76. For similar statements see Priestley, *Lectures on Oratory and Criticism*, pp. 84–85, 101–2; and Adam Smith,

Lectures on Rhetoric, p. 68. The Addisonian tradition of descriptive theory and Johnson's relation to it have been described in detail by Scott Elledge, "The Background and Development in English Criticism of the Theories of Generality and Particularity," *PMLA* 62 (March 1947): 147–82. Elledge's distinguished essay should have put a stop to the controversy over Johnson's tulip years ago.

11. *Discourses*, p. 48; *Lectures*, 2:377; cf. Joseph Spence, *An Essay on Pope's Odyssey* (London, 1726), Dialogue 5, pp. 125–26; and Warburton's notes on Pope's imagery, in *The Works of Alexander Pope*, ed. W. L. Bowles (London, 1806), 1: 109 n., 110 n.

12. *Works*, Bowles ed., 6:213–14.

13. *Enquiry*, p. 172. See the discussion of Burke in present study, pp. 114–15.

14. But plastic representations must nevertheless be distinct, and in this they differ from poetic: "A great part of the beauty of the celebrated description of Eve in Milton's *Paradise Lost*, consists in using only general indistinct expressions, every reader making out the detail according to his own particular imagination,—his own idea of beauty, grace, expression, dignity, or loveliness: but a painter, when he represents Eve on a canvas, is obliged to give a determined form, and his own idea of beauty distinctly expressed" (*Discourse* no. 8 [1778], p. 138). For the principle that poetry imitates the perceptual process rather than the reality of things, see James Arbuckle, *Hibernicus's Letters: or, a Philosophical Miscellany* (London, 1734), 2:79–80; James Beattie, *Dissertations Moral and Critical* (London, 1783), pp. 639–42; Kames, *Elements*, 4th ed., 2:327–28; Twining, *Aristotle's Treatise on Poetry*, 1:42, n.(m). Twining's view is expressly neo-Platonic, however.

15. *Johnson on Shakespeare*, 8:695; *Life*, 2:87. Cf. Johnson's comment that "in the description of night in Macbeth, the beetle and the bat detract from the general idea of darkness,—inspissated gloom" (*Life*, 2:90). See Geoffrey Tillotson, "Imlac and the Business of a Poet," in *Studies in Criticism and Aesthetics, 1660–1800: Essays in Honor of Samuel Holt Monk*, ed. Howard Anderson and John S. Shea (Minneapolis: University of Minnesota Press, 1967), pp. 296–314. Johnson's standards for poetic description are also discussed by Lionel Basney in " 'Lucidus Ordo': Johnson and Generality," (cited above, appendix A, n.3). Basney provides an excellent brief description of the principles governing Johnson's approach to style and form.

16. *On the Sublime*, 10, 43, 3: *Satyricon*, 2.

17. *Lucian*, trans. K Kilburn, LCL (London, 1959), 6:secs. 19, 57, 27–28.

18. Dryden, *The Critical and Miscellaneous Prose Works of John Dryden*, ed. Edmund Malone (London, 1800), 3:327; Rapin, *Whole Critical Works*, 2:172.

19. Bouhours, *Entretiens D'Ariste et D'Eugène* (Paris, 1748), Dialogue 4, pp. 264–65; *The Works of Monsieur Boileau, Made English . . . by Several Hands* (London, 1711–12), 2:108; La Bruyère, *The Characters, or The Manners of the Age . . . Made English by several hands* (London, 1700), p. 16; Dennis, *Critical Works*, ed. Hooker, 1:45, 142–43. For a touchstone on this matter one may take Le Bossu's advice (*Treatise of the Epick Poem . . . Done into English . . . by W. J.* [London, 1695], pp. 239–45) and compare

Seneca's description of the sacred grove in his *Oedipus* to the absence of any such description in the corresponding portion of Sophocles' original. Seneca's description is full of sensational detail and runs on for about 128 lines; it establishes the relationship between particularity and the decadent pursuit of novelty if anything does (*Seneca's Tragedies*, trans. Frank Justus Miller, LCL [London, 1917], 1:472–82). Cf. also Racine's version of the death of Hippolyte in *Phèdre*, with its description of the *monstre* (*Indomptable taureau, dragon impétueux* . . .), with its Senecan original: Seneca's description takes 115 lines, Racine's about 75; the difference involves not merely length but the texture and purpose of the details. Racine's shortened imitation was censured in its day as an instance of decadent particularity.

Appendix B

1. Johnson of course made no distinction between imagination and fancy, and would have described all the activities which Taylor mentions by either term.

2. *Biographia Literaria*, 2:101–2. "From my very childhood," says Wordsworth, "I have felt the falsehood that pervades the volumes imposed upon the world under the name of Ossian. From what I saw with my own eyes, I knew that the imagery was spurious. In nature everything is distinct, yet nothing defined into absolute independent singleness. In Macpherson's work, it is exactly the reverse; everything (that is not stolen) is in this manner defined, insulated, dislocated, deadened,—yet nothing distinct. It will always be so when words are substituted for things" (*Poetical Works*, 2:423–24).

3. Cited in Shawcross, 2:316, n.13.

4. Cited in Shawcross, 1:227, n.17.

5. *The Collected Works of Samuel Taylor Coleridge, Vol. 6: Lay Sermons*, ed. J. R. White (London: Routledge & Kegan Paul, 1972), pp. 30–31.

6. *Coleridge's Essays and Lectures on Shakespeare*, ed. Ernest Rhys (1907; reprint ed., London: Dent & Sons, 1919), pp. 39–40.

7. On Wordsworth's view of the value of poetry see Heffernan, *Wordsworth's Theory of Poetry*, and M. H. Abrams, *Natural Supernaturalism: Tradition and Revolution in Romantic Literature* (New York: Norton & Co., 1971), esp. chaps. 1 and 2.

Index

254